Complex Words in English

ENGLISH LANGUAGE SERIES

General Editor: Randolph Quirk

Complex Words in English

Valerie Adams

Longman

An imprint of **Pearson Education**

Harlow, England · London · New York · Reading, Massachusetts · San Francisco · Toronto · Don Mills, Ontario · Sydney
Tokyo · Singapore · Hong Kong · Seoul · Taipei · Cape Town · Madrid · Mexico City · Amsterdam · Munich · Paris · Milan

Pearson Education Limited
Edinburgh Gate
Harlow
Essex CM20 2JE
England

and Associated Companies throughout the world

Visit us on the World Wide Web at:
www.pearsoneduc.com

First published 2001

ISBN 0-582-23964-8 PPR

British Library Cataloguing-in-Publication Data
A catalogue record for this book is available from the British Library

Library of Congress Cataloging-in-Publication Data
A catalog record for this book is available from the Library of
Congress

Set by 35 in 10/12pt Janson Text
Produced by
Printed in Malaysia,

Contents

Preface

This book was first planned as a second edition of *An Introduction to Modern English Word-formation* (1973). In the event, nothing of that work has remained, aside from a handful of examples which I was unwilling to relinquish. The earlier book coalesced rather fortuitously, it now seems to me, around an initial interest in some of the more eccentric kinds of word creation, specifically blends. My aim in this one has been to give a much more inclusive account of word formation in English.

In the intervening period, morphology has made considerable advances in status and scope, and there have been some varied and innovative approaches to the description of complex words. In investigating the different kinds of word-making, more and less systematic, I have gained much from the descriptive studies which have appeared in the last twenty-five years or so.

An appreciable number of examples in my first book were elucidated and vouched for by the phrases and sentences in which I found them. Such illustrations in context are a more prominent feature of this book, thanks largely to the new edition of the *Oxford English Dictionary* and its Compact Disc version. Its resources have been an essential counterbalance to my intuitions about likely, unlikely and impossible complex words.

I am very grateful to Bas Aarts and Jill House for their advice on parts of the book, and to Randolph Quirk for helpful comments on all of it.

Valerie Adams

Picture an overzealous gardener who broadcasts onion seed at the rate of a dozen per square inch, lets the plants grow to a tangled mass, and extracts one to describe. Its central stalk is more or less intact but its roots are torn and the resulting description, while grossly true, will forever stand in need of repair because of those missing tendrils.

Dwight Bolinger (1985)

1

Preliminaries

1.1 Word formation

The term *word formation* can be understood in several ways. *Word* can mean 'word-form', a unit defined in writing by preceding and following spaces, and in speech – sometimes – by phonological clues. In this sense, *wolf* and *wolves*, *ride*, *rides* and *rode* are five different words. *Word* can mean 'grammatical word': just as singular *wolf* and plural *wolves* or past tense *rode* and past participle *ridden* are different grammatical words, so are singular and plural *sheep*, and past tense *walked* and past participle *walked*. And thirdly, word can mean 'lexeme', the unit of vocabulary which subsumes grammatical variants and is their representative in dictionaries – the nouns *wolf* and *sheep*, the verbs *ride* and *walk*. When its first element has all three of these senses, *word formation* is a synonym of *morphology*, the study of the structure of words.

In this book, *word formation* will be less inclusive: it will mean **lexeme formation**: we shall be interested, not in series of forms like those just mentioned, which exhibit inflectional distinctions, but rather, for example, in the possibility of a verb *to wolf*, related in some sense to the noun, or a noun *rider*, related to the verb. But here we encounter another uncertainty of meaning. *Formation*, like many nominalized words – nouns based on a lexeme of another class (in this case the verb *to form*) – can mean 'the act of giving or assuming form', as in *the formation of new words was easy for James Joyce*: we can understand *word formation* as 'how people form new words'. In another context, a *formation* can be a fait accompli, the result of an act of forming. Both these senses are relevant here, since our expectations about new words are necessarily founded on those we have already encountered. Word (lexeme) formation in this book is necessarily as much concerned with the relationships of form and meaning which connect known lexemes to one another as with the ways in which speakers make new lexemes out of old ones. We begin with a closer look at the word as lexeme.

1.2   Lexemes

1.2.1   Complex words

Words like *derail, preshrink, post-war, jumpy, censorable, sexist* are all complex:
more than one component is recognizable in them. Each word contains an
affix, a 'bound' element which as a rule never occurs on its own. Initial bound
elements like *de-, pre-, post-* are **prefixes**, attached to the bases *rail, shrink,
war*. The bound elements *-y, -able, -ist*, following their bases *jump, censor, sex*
are suffixes. **Suffixes** are generally not semantically autonomous, having
no meanings of their own which are independent of the meanings of the
bases they attach to and those of the words in which they appear. The few
exceptions to this include suffixes like adjective-forming *-ful*, *-like* and *-less*,
which retain some resemblance to the free elements from which they have
developed. Prefixes on the other hand, many of which are related to adverbs
or prepositions, typically do have distinct meanings.

Affixes attach to **bases**, which are identifiable with members of the major
word classes, noun, adjective and verb. Bases may be free elements, able to
occur on their own, or they may be bound forms with no independent
existence, as in words like *dental, holism, amorphous*, whose bases have meanings like those of English words – 'tooth', 'whole', 'form'. Bound bases will
be referred to as **stems**. Bases, both words and stems, may combine to form
compounds: *credit card, oviraptor, pesticide*. **Particles**, free elements with spatial
meanings like *over, out, up*, also figure in compounds: *overhang, outcrop, upshift*.
Unlike other words, and unlike affixes, particles never combine with stems.

Derivation comprises prefixation, suffixation and the processes by which
verbs like *to wolf* and *to tense* and nouns like *guide* are formed. These words
are based on – derived from – their noun, adjective and verb bases respectively, and we can extend the description 'complex word' to them too. Derivation and compounding account for the great majority of word-formational
patterns. This brief naming of parts, however, does not exhaust the possibilities: in later chapters we encounter formative elements which cannot be
identified as words, stems or affixes, and even words which it makes sense to
see as derived from more complex ones.

1.2.2   Lexemes and phrases

Complex words, it is generally agreed, are unlike phrases in that their constituents cannot be interrupted or rearranged, though in fact prefixes and
compound elements can sometimes be coordinated, as in '*pro-* and *anti-
hunting* factions', 'clusters of *water-, rodent-* and *mosquito-borne* infections'.
Some types of phrasal collocation exhibit degrees of word-like fixedness.
'Binomials', for example – sequences of two words, usually nouns or adjectives,

linked usually by a conjunction – may be more or less fixed. *Fun and games, wild and woolly*, are not reversible; *gold and silver, knife and fork* are, though this order is the preferred one; *tables and chairs* is as likely to occur as *chairs and tables*. Complex prepositions like *by dint of, in process of, at the request of*, exhibit different degrees of fixedness. *Dint* appears only in this idiom, *process* has lost its determiner, but *the request* can be augmented by a premodifier like any other noun phrase: *at the urgent request of*, and an alternative wording *at someone's request* is possible. Sequences of verb + noun + preposition like *give rise to, take advantage of*, vary in their fixity: *rise* cannot be premodified but *advantage* can, as in **rise was given to . . .* , *advantage was taken of . . .* . Though phrases like these may in time come to be seen as words – nouns, prepositions and verbs – the difference between them and complex words as defined in the previous section is clear.

Any phrase, retaining its phrasal character, can function as a modifier within a larger phrase, as in 'a *ground-to-air* missile', '*easy-to-read* stories', 'an *I-knew-it-all-along* expression'. Some suffixes, like *-ism, -ish, -ness, -y*, can readily attach to phrases, e.g. *not-in-my-backyardism, morning-afterish, what-have-we-got-to-loseness, milk-and-watery*. We might say that these hyphenated strings behave like words in these contexts, but not that they are complex words. According to the **no-phrase constraint** (see e.g. Carstairs-McCarthy 1992, 99f), complex words are not formed from phrases.

The distinction between phrase and complex word, however, is not always so clear. The **head** in syntax is the central constituent of a phrase which comes closest to characterizing the phrase as a whole. Criteria of different kinds may conflict in particular cases and the head status of items may be debatable (see especially Hudson 1987). In general, though, the head of a construction is normally obligatory, other elements assume forms which match it, it is the element on which any inflections appear, and it refers to the same kind of entity as the whole construction. If the notion of head is extended to words it has to be modified, since some kinds of element only occur in words. However, it is useful to invoke it when we inspect the borderland inhabited by word-like phrases and phrase-like words. According to the **right-hand head rule** (Williams 1981), we should expect the head of a word to be on the right. Any expression which we can see as not right-headed will be distinctive or untypical in some way, or will have the character of a phrase. In coordinative expressions for example, such as *shed-cum-greenhouse, poacher-turned-gamekeeper*, '*doctor–patient* relationship', '*public–private* partnership', '*sweet-and-sour* pork', neither element is dominant: these are phrases, not complex words.

With the phrasal verb *to change over*, the criteria for syntactic head are decisive: 'changing over' is a kind of 'changing', and the left-hand element, the verb, is the head. In the related nominal expression *change-over*, the particle has one claim to headhood in that, being on the right, it necessarily carries any inflection: we can treat such nouns as complex words, though of an untypical kind. Similar expressions whose first elements are suffixed nouns, like *runner up* and *telling off*, are more obviously intermediate between phrase and word: phrase-like in that plural *s* can regularly intervene between the two elements, attaching to the verbal head, but word-like in that nothing else can. Occasional coinages like those illustrated in 'Nancy was . . . an habitual tidier-upper' (OED: 1976), 'But Dunham was more than a washer-upper' (OED: 1961) are evidence of attempts to make such hybrids more word-like. Participial adjectives like '*boarded-up* shops', '*wired-in* connections' are similarly both word- and phrase-like. Nominal examples like those in 'With a *dart up* and a *scurry off*, the rabbit disappeared in the brush' (example from Bolinger 1961, 309) denote an instance of the verb's action: the accentuation on the particle, usual in verb + particle collocations, underlines their partly phrase-like character.

Crystallize, squeaky, supportive have suffixes which indicate their word-class membership. The base of *balloonist* is an inanimate noun, but its suffix shows that the referent of the complex word is the name of an individual. The suffix of *hermithood* identifies the word as a non-count noun with a 'state' meaning. Suffixes, then, characterizing the words in which they occur, are plausible heads.[1] By contrast, in prefixed verbs like *disconnect, recirculate* or adjectives like *non-catholic* the nature of the word is indicated by the base, which thus qualifies as the head. But prefixes sometimes have an effect on their bases. *Outswim*, for example, illustrates the prefixing of an intransitive verb to make it transitive, though *swim* retains its characteristic way of forming the past tense (*Mary outswam John on sports day*), and we can still see the base as the head. Prefixing the noun *night* has a greater effect, making it into a verb: 'I would outnight you did nobody come' (*Merchant of Venice*, V. i). In this case we might say that prefixation and noun-to-verb derivation apply in tandem. Similarly, in *decaffeinate* and *anti-bacterial*, prefix and suffix operate together to derive a verb and an adjective from the nouns *caffeine* and *bacteria*. Cases like these are often referred to as **parasynthetic** formations.

We can take prepositional phrases to be left-headed: the preposition is the head. The attributive expressions in '*on-line* editing' and '*off-screen* voice' are phrases, but those in '*inter-city* train' and '*trans-world* airline', containing preposition-like prefixes meaning 'between' and 'across' respectively, are complex words. Like *anti-bacterial, inter-city* and *trans-world* are parasynthetic rather than left-headed, since the prefixing and attributive function of *city* and *world* go together. There is good reason to see determiners as heads of noun phrases (Hudson 1987, Abney 1987); the italicized parts of '*no-phrase* constraint' '*no-claim* bonus', '*no-win* situation' are phrases, but the comparable prefixed expressions in '*non-slip* surface', '*anti-freeze* liquid', are complex words. Again, prefixation and attributive function combine in these examples to make parasynthetic formations.

In **endocentric** expressions, a central element is functionally equivalent to the whole. The phrase *to change over* is endocentric, as are most compound words, in which the element on the right, the head, is of the same kind as the word as a whole. A *dustbin* is a kind of bin, and *energy-efficient* specifies a way of being efficient. The term **exocentric** describes expressions in which no part seems to be of the same kind as the whole or to be central to it. The noun *change-over* is exocentric, and so are 'verb–complement' noun compounds like *stop-gap*, along with adjective + noun and noun + noun compounds like *air-head, paperback, lowlife*. These compounds, a rather small group in modern English, do not denote the same kind of entity as their final elements and are thus not clearly right-headed. The fact that the plural form of a compound like *lowlife* is *lowlifes*, not *lowlives* can be taken to indicate that *life* is not the head. Either *lowlife* is perceived as a simple word, or it is a 'headless' compound. Alternatively, *life* in this compound is simply a homonym of the independent noun *life*, and forms its plural differently.

Finally, adjective + noun collocations like *wild animal*, which are clearly endocentric and right-headed, pose problems of delimitation between phrase and compound word. The modifier in *busy road* is a phrase in its own right and can be expanded: *extremely busy road*. *Wild animal* can be interrupted in limited ways: *wild and tame animals*, unlike *hardwood*. The usual sense of *cold* is not discernible in *cold war*. We may want to call all but the first of these 'compounds', and reflect that some compounds at least result from the same process of idiomatization that we see in collocations like *in (the) process of*.

1.2.3   Lexemes and word-forms

The various forms which lexemes assume in different syntactic surroundings – *boat* and *boats*, *big* and *bigger*, *look*, *looks*, *looking* and *looked* – are marked by inflectional affixes. Inflections are dependable in their effects and specifiable by syntactic rule. Derivational affixes by contrast can be unpredictable in form and have unpredictable effects on bases. *Unstable* contrasts with *instability*, and *inflatable* with *convertible*. Pigs are kept in a *piggery* but a *robbery* is an event or the result of an event. We may choose to use an affix as in *replay*, or not, as in *play again*.

There are many expressions which make the distinction between derivation and inflection, lexeme and word-form, look hazy. Derivational suffixes sometimes do little more than signal the syntactic role of their bases. In *Shakespearean imitators usually fail to capture his style* (example from Kastovsky 1982, 184), a derived word stands in for an inflected one (*Shakespeare's*). Forms usually thought of as inflectional can add meaning: *airs*, *damages*, *works* differ idiosyncratically from the corresponding singular forms, and there is no singular form corresponding to *amends*, *belongings* or *odds* (Plank 1994). More than just plurality is implied in 'Coco's *attentions*' or 'Melissa's *charms*' (Carroll and Tanenhaus 1975). The difference in form between singular *wheat*, *rice*, *furniture* and plural *oats*, *beans*, *leftovers* correlates with a difference in conceptualization (Wierzbicka 1988).

The dual character, inflectional and derivational, of *-ed* and *-ing* is more troublesome. Any transitive verb, along with its subject and object, can occur in a gerundive construction like '*my/John('s) announcing the news* took people by surprise'. *Announcing* is un-verb-like only in that its subject, when marked as genitive, has the appearance of a determiner. It is more noun-like in *my/ John's/the announcing of the news*: the definite article is allowed, and *the news* is not a direct object but the complement in a postmodifying prepositional phrase. Yet is *announcing* in this second example any more a new lexeme than it is in the first? Yes, since its syntax is more nominal than verbal, but no, in that it is part of the grammar of transitive verbs that they can appear in this construction. However, we can substitute an exactly synonymous form: *the announcement of the news*. The suffix *-ment* is undoubtedly derivational: it functions only to form nouns with verbal bases, and moreover *announcement*, unlike *announcing*, which denotes a process, can have more concrete senses, as in '*the announcement* was received with cheers' or even '*the announcement* was plastered on every bus-stop'.

Participles are so called because they share the characteristics of two different classes of lexeme, verbs and adjectives (cf. Latin *participium* 'a sharing'). The present participles of intransitive verbs can premodify nouns, as in *a cooking egg, escaping gas*, which elsewhere head phrases which serve as the subjects of these verbs: *the egg is cooking*. Can we say that the premodifying *-ing* formations are adjectives, distinct from the verbs *cook* and *escape*? They have no further adjective-like characteristics: they can be preceded by verbal modifiers like *rapidly* or *slowly*, and in *the egg is cooking, gas is escaping*, the participle is not a complement but part of a present progressive phrase. As attributive expressions, *cooking* and *escaping* retain their progressive meaning, and we can reasonably say that they still represent verbal lexemes. (Cf. Huddleston 1984, 318–20).

But what about *a flowering plant* or *flying ants*, 'plants that flower', 'ants that can fly'? The *-ing* forms in these phrases are likely not to be progressive in meaning, but descriptive, like adjectives, and in this case they have a greater claim to be considered lexemes distinct from the verbs *to flower* and *to fly*. Some verbs denoting emotional events, like *depress, encourage, frighten, shock*, have subjects whose referents are non-agentive causers of the emotion, and objects whose referents experience it (*the storm frightened John*). When the *-ing* participles of such verbs modify nouns, they cannot have progressive meaning. They are gradable: *a very frightening storm*, and they can easily be predicative: *the sign seemed quite encouraging* (Borer 1990). It is part of the grammar of all such verbs that their present participles behave in this way – but these participles in attributive and predicative function have all the appearance of adjectives. We may or may not regard them as different lexemes from the verbs *to frighten, to encourage*.

The past participles of many transitive verbs can also be verbal or adjectival. Participles of verbs which take 'affected' objects, like *bite*, can denote a resultant state, and hence have the character of adjectives (Huddleston 1984, 323–4). *Bitten* is verbal in *the keeper was bitten by a lion*, which corresponds to an active sentence: *a lion bit the keeper*, but it is adjectival in *the keeper's hand was severely bitten*. Verbs whose objects are not perceived as affected, like *operate*, have participles which remain verbal in nature: *a carelessly operated machine, the machine was carelessly operated (by the supervisor)*. Verbs like *depress* have only adjectival past participles, and, like their present participles, these have all the characteristics of typical adjectives: *John was/seemed quite depressed by his failure, a very shocked spectator*.

   -ing and *-ed* have some claim to be lexeme-forming suffixes in words with apparently nominal bases. Compare *alarmed* in *the building was alarmed* ('provided with alarms') with the participial adjective in *John was alarmed*. There are two ways of looking at this situation. We can assume either that there are two suffixes of the form *-ed*, one each for verb and noun bases (2.5.1 and 2.5.2 below), or that there is only one, for verb bases, and that *alarmed* in the first example implies the existence of a verb meaning 'to equip with an alarm' derived from the noun. There is a similar indeterminacy in *cricketing* or *lawyering*, as in *I prefer boating to cricketing; a cricketing nation,* 'He trained as a lawyer but . . . he was no great shakes at lawyering' (Guardian: 1997). We might assume the existence of *to cricket* and *to lawyer*, or recognize two *-ings*, one attaching to verbs and the other to nouns. Bases with concrete referents like *scaffolding, shirting, tubing* of course cannot easily be related to possible verbs.

1.3   Motivation

Complex words are motivated by their parts, or understandable in terms of them, to varying degrees. Some patterns of derivation or compounding seem to be as freely available as the patterns of phrases or sentences for the formation of new words in any appropriate context, for example the suffixation of adjectives to form adverbs in *-ly* (*obliteratingly, muscle-achingly*), or of adjectives to form nouns in *-ness* (*plasticness, watertightness*), or the compounding of nouns and *-ing* participles ('*job-seeking* graduates'). Words like these are assumed to be semantically 'compositional' – regular, transparent and instantly understandable, and even if they are unfamiliar they do not seem especially unusual. The processes which enable them to be formed are described as productive. **Productivity** is an essential concept in any discussion of word formation, though it is also complex, elusive and difficult to discuss with any precision. The productivity of a particular pattern, for example verbs in *-ify* like *purify*, obviously cannot simply be estimated in relation to how many verbs of this form there are in current use. (*Purify* itself is the kind of word which speakers learn and remember. It has been current since the fifteenth century and was not formed in English but taken over from

French or Latin.) But users of language do have intuitions about the productivity of different processes – that is, about how likely these are to give rise to new words. *Productive* and *productivity* are often employed rather loosely to reflect such intuitions, and I have tried to use these useful but slippery words as sparingly as possible in the chapters that follow.

In recent years work has been done (by Baayen and his collaborators) on ways of being more objective about productivity, with the aid of large quantities of text accessible by computer. Items with particular affixes which occur only once are the focus of interest, since these are most likely to have been formed by a speaker or writer 'on line', and least likely to have been previously learned and memorized as wholes. The number of such once-only words in, for example, *-ness*, divided by the total number of occurrences of *-ness* words in a sufficiently large corpus gives a figure which can be taken to indicate the probability of coming across new words in *-ness*, and hence to be a measure of the productivity of *-ness*. However, for a variety of different reasons (see 12.2), some patterns are much less often resorted to than others, even though they may remain available for new formations. Some available patterns in fact are comparatively rarely used, like the one illustrated by *rabbithood* in 'There are predictable consequences of rabbithood that cut across whether it is scurrying, eating or sleeping' (Steven Pinker, *The Language Instinct*, 1994, 155). For the productivity of *-hood* to be discussed in the same terms as that of *-ness*, the difference in the extent of the use of these suffixes and their contribution to the vocabulary would have to be taken into account (see Baayen 1993).

Aronoff (1976) proposes that the study of 'healthy specimens' of word formation (34) such as nouns in *-ness* with adjective bases, should be the main focus in studies of word formation. Similarly, in their quantitative study of 1996, Baayen and Renouf are primarily concerned with 'the spontaneous, unintentional and ephemeral use of productive word formation' (78), such as the formation from adjectives of nouns in *-ness* and *-ity* and adverbs in *-ly*, and they liken such processes to the ways in which syntactic structures are formed. They observe: 'If a word-formation pattern is unproductive, no rule is available for the perception and production of novel forms' (74).

But what is a 'rule', in this context? The idea of a rule is very often used in connection with phenomena which can be described as reasonably regular (Marcus *et al.* 1995), such as 'English words have their heads on the right', or 'English nouns form their plurals in *-s*', or '*-ness* attaches to adjective bases to form nouns'. In a different definition however, a rule is a mental operation in which variable symbols (such as 'noun' and 'regular plural suffix') are combined. A rule in this sense creates regular forms 'when they are needed, and then they can be thrown away, because the rule is always around to create them again the next time' (Pinker 1999, 280).

Much recent discussion of regular and irregular verb inflection has focused on the contrast between rule in this sense and analogy, the comparing of forms newly encountered with forms retrieved from memory. Pinker (1999) brings together a body of evidence to support the view that regular verbs are inflected by combinatory rule, in contrast with irregular inflection, which depends on generalizations made on the basis of known similar words. The regular rule operates by default, failing to apply only when pre-empted, or **blocked**, by an irregular form. It may be that there is a similar distinction to be made among derivational processes. The formation of -*ly* adverbs from adjectives is certainly rule-like. New nouns in -*ness* from gradable adjectives may not seem any more novel than new phrases – though by no means all gradable adjectives are suitable bases (2.4.2). *Out*- can be attached to any base to form a verb meaning 'surpass in VERBing' – though the scarcity of established examples suggests that this does not happen very often (5.3.1). By contrast, it is obvious that *glitterati* (11.4) and *fasherati*: 'Black suedette one-bar shoes were a hit with the fasherati' (Guardian: 1999) are based specifically on *literati*.

Other writers, for example Bybee (1988, 1995), assume that there is no such qualitative distinction: regular and irregular word-forms alike 'emerge from the connections made among related stored items' (Bybee 1995, 452). In this book, 'rule' will mean no more than 'regularity', and we shall assume that productive (regular) patterns of lexeme-formation are not essentially different from unproductive (irregular) patterns. Rather, some are perceivable on the basis of very large numbers of lexical items, as in the case of -*ness* nouns and -*ly* adverbs; others, like that of particle + base verbs such as *backcomb*, *download*, *upgrade* (5.2.1) depend on much smaller numbers, down to individual items in the case of *glitterati*.

Noun compounds may be understandable in terms of other noun compounds: *nuclear* in *nuclear winter* and 'a *nuclear-free* zone' is referable to *nuclear energy*, energy released by the fusion of nuclei and used in *nuclear weapons* and *nuclear power*. Words suffixed by -*ship* often denote 'states' or 'activities' (*tycoonship*, *sponsorship*), but in a minority of cases they denote 'collectivities', as in *a membership of thirty, the readership of a magazine* (see 4.4). The formation of words like *viewership*, *listenership* and even *butlership* in 'No doubt the broad swath of butlership was circumspect, sober, and alert to every small solecism' (Guardian: 1999) may owe more to a few familiar words of similar make-up than to a general pattern of -*ship* noun formation. Where one word is evoked by a series of others, and is a possible model for them, the term **leader-word**, coined by Malkiel (see Malkiel 1966, 333) is useful. *Beatnik* has been a leader-word for other -*nik* nouns denoting individuals (4.2); *kingdom* has a 'following' of occasional formations like *Babeldom*, *citydom*, *czardom*, *shahdom* (4.4).

'Compositional' complex words are in principle fully analysable, but in practice they need not be analysed. *Childhood* is as regularly formed as *rabbithood*, but as a familiar word it is much more likely to have been learned by a user and remembered as a whole. By contrast, part of *wiseacre* is obscure, but the word can still be understood as complex – adjective modifier + noun, or perhaps adjective base and suffix. A great many words with stem bases, like *citrous, viroid, vorticism*, may be more analysable for some speakers than for others. Words may be perceived in more than one way, like *alarmed* and *cricketing* in the previous section. Compositionality, a property of structures, does not always equate with analysability, a matter of perception (cf. Langacker 1987, 457). With a conception of rules as patterns which emerge from our encounters with words we can accommodate in our description of complex words 'all degrees of standardized efficiency and junkyard irregularity' (Bolinger and Sears 1981, 59).

Lexicalization in one sense is the expression of a concept or concepts in one lexeme. Thus the condition of 'being a rabbit' is lexicalized in *rabbithood*. But the term has a number of other common uses. It can refer to various ways in which complex words may in time become less analysable in terms of their parts. When words are no longer representative of the patterns on which they were formed, they must obviously be learned as wholes. *Cupboard* (kʌbəd) is lexicalized phonologically, and since its meaning is not 'board for cups', semantically as well. The base of *width* differs in form as well as pronunciation from *wide*; *gospel* (Old English *god spel* 'good tidings') is lexicalized in terms of pronunciation, form and meaning. A more modern example of lexicalization involving meaning alone would be a verb like *to badger*, related to the noun in a way that is no longer clear (OED defines it as 'to bait like a badger'), or a compound like *hedgehog*, which does not denote a hog, or even an animal obviously associated with hedges.

An alternative term for 'lexicalization' such as 'idiomatization' would be appropriate for these examples. The term 'fossilization' is sometimes used as an alternative to 'lexicalization' in connection with patterns which are not obscured but seem unlikely to give rise to new formations, for example denominal adjectives in *-en* like *wooden*. In a variety of other cases sometimes described as lexicalized, the descriptions 'conventionalized', 'established' or 'institutionalized' would be suitable, for example *eatable* in the sense 'good to eat' as well as 'can be eaten', or nouns based on verbs which denote concrete entities ('office *equipment*') as well as processes ('the *equipment* of offices'). Another pattern that we might see as 'conventionalized' is that of countable words in *-ism* meaning 'peculiarity of speech' (*a colloquialism, an American-ism*), in contrast to the more commonly encountered senses of 'activity' or 'belief' (*diversionism, Marxism*) (4.4). Nouns in *-dom* have a spectrum of meanings (4.4) but *officialdom* is only ever used to mean 'officials collect-ively'. *To deaden* exemplifies a regular way of forming verbs from adjectives, as in *fatten, sharpen, tauten*, but it cannot mean 'to render dead', i.e. 'to kill'. The collocation *to take away* can be used of a wide range of activities, but the related noun *take-away* conventionally denotes only a shop which sells food to take away, or the food itself.

1.4   Present and past

At many points in the following chapters, there will be occasion to refer to developments which have taken place in the past. The scarcity of modern particle + base verbs and nouns (*to offload, an out-take*) beside base + particle expressions (*to plant out, the kick-off*) (Chapter 5) is connected with changes in word order since Old English times. Change of course is constant: some ways in which affixes arise or are reshaped (11.2) can be usefully illustrated by examples from more than one period. The existence of different patterns with similar functions is often relatable to historical circumstance, for instance de-adjectival verbs in 'zero' and *-en* (*black* and *blacken*) (2.3.2), negatively prefixed adjectives in *in-*, *un-* and *non-* (3.3), or nouns suffixed by *-er* and *-ist* (4.2). Some affixes, like *-eer* and *-ster* (4.2), only rarely appear in new forms, but older examples show that they have been doing so for centuries.

Most importantly, no account of English word formation can ignore the mixed nature of the English vocabulary and the circumstances in which this situation came about. English is a Germanic language: its most frequently occurring words, such as articles, pronouns, auxiliary verbs, prepositions, are Germanic, but a large proportion of its nouns, adjectives and verbs – around 70 per cent according to some estimates – are from Latin and Greek, which belong to two other branches of the Indo-European 'tree', Italic and Hellenic. Latin and Greek words have reached English by various routes. French is a development of Latin, and large numbers of French words were borrowed into English in the thirteenth and fourteenth centuries. With the revival of learning in the early modern period and the subsequent development of modern science, many more Latin words were borrowed directly into English, and new words on their patterns were formed by English writers. The Latin vocabulary includes many Greek words: some English words of Greek origin arrived by way of Latin, and others were taken over directly from Greek. In what follows, the short-hand label 'foreign' will often be used in referring to French, Latin and Greek elements or words. 'Native' will always mean 'Germanic'.

The dual route to English taken by Latin words accounts for many variations in form among related words. The verb *to determine* for example, is from French *determiner*, corresponding to a Latin infinitive form *determinare*, whereas the closely related verb *terminate*, a later arrival in English, is based on the Latin past participial form of *terminare* (*terminat-us*). It replaced fourteenth-century *termine*, from the French infinitive form. Consequently the suffix of the related nouns *termination* and *determination*, from either French or Latin, has variant forms: *-ion* and *-ation*. *Coagulant* does not have an English base; the word may have been borrowed from French, or its base may be a Middle English verb *coagule*, corresponding to a French infinitive form *coaguler*, which was superseded by *coagulate*, reflecting a Latin participial form. *Isolable* and *isolatable* both represent productive patterns in modern English, the first modelled on adjectives whose bases correspond to French infinitives, the second on those with Latin past participle bases.

Foreign words used in the formation of new English words naturally have to fit into the English system, so we find that nearly all native affixes combine easily with foreign bases. Some foreign affixes by contrast, as a consequence of the way they came into English, do not usually attach to native bases. An affix is first borrowed as part of a word and then, if it occurs in a series of similar loans, becomes recognizable as an affix in the new language (11.2). New words formed with it are likely to resemble the loan-word models, and so foreign affixes may continue to combine only or chiefly with foreign bases.

Users of English of course cannot be expected to distinguish native from foreign, except perhaps where the contrast has been deliberately exploited, within words in obviously 'hybrid' combinations of native base and foreign affix like *speechify*, *gossipaceous*, *twitteration*, or between words by using 'learned' items in non-learned contexts, cf. 'A must for the diehard mycophage' (Guardian: 1996, reviewing a book entitled *The Mushroom Feast*). But the native–foreign distinction does correlate to some extent with differences in the shapes of words. Native words are often monosyllabic, or have two syllables with the accent on the first. Foreign words often have three or more syllables and are typically not accented on the initial syllable. Stems are always foreign: in Greek and Latin, nouns, verbs and adjectives usually do not appear without a suffix, or, in compounds, a 'combining vowel' (9.4.3).[2] As elements of English complex words, consequently, they have no independent counterparts. Though stems may occasionally be compounded with native words (*biofeedback*, *weedicide*), the affixes they combine with are always foreign. Suffixes attaching to bases which differ in accent and in other ways from the independent forms to which they correspond are foreign (9.1, 9.2): compare *grammar* and *grammarian*, *medicine* and *medicinal*, *diary* and *diarist*. Since words serve as models for other words, the bases of complex words with an affix in common often bear some formal resemblance to one another. Thus the terms 'native' and 'foreign' will turn out to be convenient in many cases in pointing to such family likenesses.

1.5   Examples and the OED

Many of the illustrative examples in the following chapters take the form of quotations from a variety of sources which show complex words in context. Quotations have many uses. Unfamiliar words are an important focus of attention in the study of word formation: as Clark (1993, 126) points out, 'it is in coinages [i.e. new complex words] that speakers' preferences appear'. But coinages in isolation, even regular, fully motivated ones, can sometimes look unacceptable or at best unlikely. One might for instance rule out a verb *to kangaroo* before encountering it in a passage like 'She's hit the kerb. She's kangarooing up the road. It's nerves you know' (Guardian: 1994). One might assume that *difficultness* was invariably pre-empted, or blocked, by the more conventional *difficulty*. Blocking is often said to account for cases where a word seems not to exist because of a more familiar synonym, but in some circumstances, such as the need to express a slightly different meaning, it can be seen not to operate, as in 'everybody he knew delighted in him, in his spirit, his talent, his wilfulness and – let it be said – his difficultness' (Guardian: 1996).

Affixes often signal more than one sense, and it may not be enough simply to show them in combination with particular bases. *Piggery*, 'a place where pigs are kept and reared' can have a collective meaning: 'That sackful of rebellious piggery heaving and struggling' (OED: 1888), and it can be a name for an attitude or an activity: 'A black citadel of male-chauvinist piggery' (OED: 1977). *Victimhood* in 'the contemporary cult of victimhood' (Guardian: 1997) denotes a state, but *womanhood* in 'swarthy molesters of British womanhood' (Guardian: 1998) has a collective referent. Words which seem securely established in a particular sense can quite easily be used 'for the nonce' in another way, as this illustration of *forked* in a sense parallel with *starred* demonstrates: 'a French touring guide that listed many splendid restaurants, forked and starred' (V. Nabokov, *Transparent Things*, 1972, ch. 19). On the strength of some familiar examples, complex words denoting people or their activities are often said to be regularly associated with 'pejorative' shades of meaning. Quotations can support or cast doubt on this: contrast *featurette* and *lecturette* in the following: 'Disney's man in Space – a featurette which was an excellent piece of documentary fiction' (OED: 1959); 'My second telephone call produced a lecturette on the regulations governing the use of Elastoplast in hotels' (Guardian: 1995).

A great many examples and illustrative quotations have been taken from the second edition of the Oxford English Dictionary. The great value of the OED for the student of word formation lies in the quantity and range of its source texts and the copiousness of its illustrative quotations for every kind of word. For example, the increased emphasis on scientific and technical vocabulary in the Supplements of the 1970s and 1980s makes it an excellent resource for demonstrating the present-day vitality of stem formations (Chapter 9). OED also furnishes much detailed information on words like *whoomph*, *swipe* and *twitter* which must be seen in use for their versatility to be appreciated (Chapter 10). It is invaluable in helping to establish the domains of affixes – the range of bases to which they can attach. Suffixes like *-dom*, *-hood* and *-ship* have complex domains which overlap to varying extents, and they represent productive processes which are not extensively resorted to. Too few items would be gathered by relying on everyday reading, or even by using a large corpus of texts. OED's plentiful illustrated examples make it possible to study the polysemy and synonymy of words with these suffixes (4.4).

At the same time there are various notes of caution to be registered. Dictionaries of course, as the repositories of words at every stage on the path towards unanalysability, are likely to foster a misleading view of the present state of word formation. They are likely to give preference to words with something obscure or remarkable about their make-up and to omit regular and transparent items that users will probably not need to look up. They are of limited use as indicators of what future developments might be like.

The 'common' English at the 'well-defined centre' of the 1932 *New English Dictionary on Historical Principles*[3] has a closer relationship with 'literary' English than a present-day conception of 'common' would allow. The consequent tension between the ordinariness of everyday language and the creativity of writers' language is neatly indicated in the editor's complaint (quoted in Murray 1979, 235): 'Browning constantly used words without regard to their proper meaning. He has added greatly to the difficulties of the Dictionary'. The nineteenth century figures more prominently in the Dictionary than any other, and the complex words favoured by lexically inventive writers like Carlyle, Thackeray, Dickens and Hardy are generously represented.

As the Preface to the fourth Supplement (1985) points out, it would have been impractical for the Second Edition to augment every still-current entry with more recent examples. I have often found it convenient to cite a nineteenth-century use where I felt I could assume that a process of word formation has not essentially changed during the last two centuries. But as a guide to estimates of present-day productivity, the Dictionary's nineteenth-century records can be misleading. As a consequence of the fuller documentation, many affixes appear to be at their most productive in the nineteenth century. Diminutive *-let* and denominal *-ish* are notable examples: there are around 230 nouns in *-let* with first uses between 1800 and 1899 and under 20 after 1900, and over 230 nineteenth-century denominal *-ish* adjectives as against 90 for the twentieth; 121 nouns in *-ee* have a first use in the nineteenth century and 46 in the twentieth.[4] It seems unlikely however that *-let*, *-ish* and *-ee* have become less productive. The wholly unproductive pattern of *wooden* is illustrated in eight nineteenth-century adjectives, all of them strange to a twentieth-century reader, and probably to most nineteenth-century readers as well: *bricken, bronzen, crapen, larchen, mudden, peachen, tapen, wolfen*. Post-1800 words suffixed by *-dom* and *-hood* make up about 82 per cent and 64 per cent respectively of the Dictionary's totals for these suffixes, which may well indicate a substantial nineteenth-century rise in productivity, but if there has since been any decline, it is probably far less pronounced than the scarce twentieth-century records (about 11 per cent and 4 per cent respectively) suggest.

Where a process may be productive in spoken language, or produces words which are generally transparent in meaning and not in need of definition, the numbers in OED cannot be expected to reflect its productivity. There are just four illustrations of 'point-of-view' adverbial -*wise*, for example, as in 'Work-wise, your future is clear'.[5] However, derived complex words are on the whole more characteristic of written registers (Plag, Dalton-Puffer and Baayen 1999), and many other processes seem to be more adequately represented in OED. In a study of the British National Corpus of about 100 million words, Plag *et al.* (1999) claim that partitive -*ful* (*suitcaseful, nibful*) is productive, and this receives some support from OED's 21 twentieth-century examples – though their finding that adjectival -*ful* is unproductive is challenged by OED's fourteen twentieth-century words on the pattern of *characterful*. Baayen and Renouf's (1996) study of *The Times* 1989–92 yielded only ten new reversative verbs in *un*- like *unbunch*, and OED records only ten such verbs since 1900. Plag (1999, ch. 5) in a study of verbs derived from nouns and adjectives (2.3 below) found the productivity of various processes as indicated in OED comparable with what could be learned from about 20 million words of the Cobuild Corpus. OED's deverbal noun + particle combinations on the patterns of *hold-up, run-off, kick-back, push-down, take-over* and *give-away* may reflect a genuine increase in the extent of their use: numbers are consistently somewhat greater in the twentieth century than in the nineteenth. The records are not plentiful – ranging from around ten twentieth-century words for NOUN + *away* to over 50 for NOUN + *up* – and this is in line with Berg's (1998, 257) conclusion on the evidence of dictionaries, including a frequency diction-ary relying on occurrences in the London–Oslo–Bergen corpus, that this pattern is not very productive. The OED's twentieth-century records can it seems be useful to some extent in estimating productivity.

1.6   Varieties of complex word

Section 1.2.1 introduced two major headings under which the patterns of complex words can be placed: derivation and compounding. Derivation is the topic of three of the following chapters, Transposition (2), Prefixes (3) and Suffixes (4). **Transposition** includes all cases in which the base of a complex word belongs to one word class and the derived word to another.[6] The prefixed words of Chapter 3 and the suffixed words of Chapter 4 in general belong to the same word classes as their bases, but the distinction between transpositional and nontranspositional is not a precise one. The prefixes *de-*, *dis-* and *un-*, for example, form verbs with both noun bases (2.3.1) and verb bases (3.2). Adjectival -*able* (2.5.1) and nominal -*ee* (2.4.1) have nominal as well as verbal bases. The noun-forming suffixes of Chapter 4 occasionally have adjectival or verbal bases.

On the whole, though, a division into 'class-changing' and 'class-maintaining' derivation is convenient and makes good descriptive sense. In Chapter 3 we consider the kinds of meaning that prefixes can have, and how this affects the nature of the verbs, adjectives and nouns that can be formed with them. The suffixes of Chapter 4, with a couple of insignificant exceptions, form nouns, and these fall into three broad semantic groups within which we can compare the effects of different suffixes. These groups consist of names for individuals (4.2), 'diminutives' (4.3) – a label which includes various patterns of words with meanings related to a central notion 'small' – and a group of overlapping patterns of words with predominantly abstract meanings like 'state' or 'activity' (4.4).

The boundary between derivation and compounding is crossed at many points. Particles, as we noted in 1.2.1, can be parts of compound words. Chapter 5 assembles all the patterns which feature particles, and shows that in some of them certain particles look more like prefixes than constituents of compounds. Some elements treated as suffixes, e.g. -like (2.5.2), can also be seen as compound elements and vice versa, e.g. free, proof (7.4.1). Many examples in the chapters on noun compounds (6) and adjective compounds (7) illustrate transposition as well as compounding in that their head elements are nominalized verbs and participial adjectives. Some adjective compounds would be more accurately described as suffixed formations with complex bases, e.g. 'a space-suited alien' (7.3.2). Some verb compounds (Chapter 8) are properly cases of transposition without change of form: to machine-gun, illustrates a pattern described in 2.3.1. In Chapter 9, in which we see that complex words with stem bases can represent productive patterns, prefixed, suffixed and compounded stem formations are looked at together.

Chapter 10 introduces another kind of formative element, the **phonaestheme**, exemplified in the initial clusters of squirl and squiggle and the final portions of bump and dump. We look at ways of defining the phonaestheme, at various patterns in which it can be seen to play a part and at how far we can see these patterns as similar to those of other chapters. The differences between this area of word formation, which we can label 'expressive'[7] and most of the processes described elsewhere in the book are considerable, but there are connections to be made, with some of the 'diminutives' of Chapter 4, and with some formations in Chapter 11.

A number of patterns are discussed under the heading of **reanalysis** in Chapter 11. They include **blends**, e.g. breathalyser and **shortened forms**, e.g. decaff. Words of these kinds often show the effects of splitting up words at unexpected points. Another manifestation of reanalysis is **backformation**, a term descriptive of a situation in which a complex form is felt to be more basic than a related shorter one – for example, the noun commentator as compared with the verb to commentate. Unlike blending and shortening, backformation typically does not involve the division of words in arbitrary ways. We encounter examples of it in most of the preceding chapters: many of the complex verbs of Chapter 8, for example, such as *to telephone-tap* are backformations. In Chapter 11 we look more closely at the nature of the phenomenon.

Some writers make a sharp distinction between 'productivity' and 'creativity' in word formation, the latter term including blends, shortened forms and usually also cases of backformation. The ways in which such words come to be formed are assumed on reasonable grounds to be different from the processes of 'genuine' word formation (cf. Spencer 1991, 461–2). However, this is another distinction which is not watertight. Both compounds and affixed formations are subject to reanalysis, and they may even have something of the character of blends. Reanalysis in fact is pervasive in word formation and Chapter 11 touches on all of the patterns described earlier in the book.

The final chapter draws together material from all the other chapters. Patterns described in various parts of the book are reviewed and compared (12.1). I have attached more importance to grasping the significance and scope of the term 'productivity' than to the task – a more formidable one, for a different kind of book – of establishing and comparing the productivity of particular processes. The final section (12.2) looks at the diverse factors which can have a bearing on productivity, and the various impulses behind the formation of complex words.

Notes

1. I assume here that this applies only to derivational suffixes, but Williams (1981) defines the head of a word as the right-*most* constituent. For him, that is, inflectional suffixes can also be heads.

   For some writers, derivational suffixes have no independent existence: they appear in complex words as the result of a rule operating on a base. This, as Aronoff (1976, 70f) points out, avoids the need to imagine a 'zero' suffix for derived verbs like *to wolf*. If suffixes are conceived of in this way however, they cannot easily be seen as heads.

2. 'Root' and 'stem' are usually distinguished. A root is usually defined as a form stripped of all inflectional, derivational or combining elements. A stem is a member of a word class without its inflectional ending. 'Stem' in the following chapters, however, will simply mean a bound lexical element from Latin or Greek.

3. These are Sir James Murray's words accompanying the diagram in the first volume, A–B (1888): 'the circle of the English language has a well-defined centre but no discernible circumference'. In a footnote, 'common' words are those 'in which literary and colloquial usage meet' (xvii).

4. Approximate figures are given, here and elsewhere in the book, because the OED software cannot be depended on to turn up all relevant examples. I have tried to make any figures derived from the OED as accurate as possible.

5. Plag, Dalton-Puffer and Baayen (1999) find -wise to be 'at least as productive in spoken as in written language' but they do not say whether this applies to adjectives and manner adverbs like cross-wise, or point-of-view adverbials, or both.

6. The term 'transposition' has been variously used. Marchand's definition is broader: he includes cases like hermithood, an abstract noun with a person-denoting base noun. I discuss examples like these in Chapter 4. Beard (1995, 1998) defines the term more narrowly. For him 'transposition' involves simply a change of category, as with bad and badness, herb and herbal, whereas 'functional derivation' adds some element of meaning to the base: mixer, based on the verb mix, denotes an instrument. I have not made this distinction in Chapter 2.

7. The term 'expressive' (see, e.g., Beard 1995, 1998) is often used to characterize processes, usually of suffixation, in which a derived word differs in connotation but not in reference from the word that forms its base, e.g. doggie and dog, cheapo and cheap (see 4.3). An alternative term is 'evaluative' (cf. Scalise 1986, 131ff).

2

Transposition

2.1 Scope

In this chapter we shall look at the various patterns in which a member of one word class can serve as base for a member of another. Verbs are formed from nouns and adjectives, nouns from verbs and adjectives, and adjectives from verbs and nouns. Adverbs are derived from nouns and adjectives, but do not themselves serve as bases for words of other classes. A range of patterns covered by the term 'transposition' is set out below.

	Verb base	*Noun base*	*Adjective base*
Derived verbs (2.3)	–	vandal**ize**	tender**ize**
		acid**ify**	pur**ify**
		carbon**ate**	blunt
		parrot	rough**en**
		uncork	
		derail	
		displace	
Derived nouns (2.4)	driv**er**	–	changeable**ness**
	claim**ant**		creativ**ity**
	grant**ee**		
	spy		
	observ**ance**		
	computeriz**ation**		
	annul**ment**		
	travers**al**		
	flavour**ing**		

	Verb base	*Noun base*	*Adjective base*
Derived adjectives	amaz**ing**	pivot**al**	–
(2.5)	express**ive**	aller**gic**	
	cling**y**	diet**ary**	
	accept**able**	migrain**ous**	
	paint**ed**	gangster**ish**	
		act**ory**	
		painter**ly**	
		Turner**esque**	
		henna**ed**	
		insight**ful**	
		victim**less**	
		vice-**like**	
Derived adverbs (2.6)	–	percentage**wise**	technical**ly**

2.2 'Zero'

Changes of word-class without change of form, exemplified by examples like *parrot* and *blunt* among the derived verbs, and *spy* in the deverbal noun column, are often referred to as cases of **conversion**. Transposition without affix, however, is not essentially different from other transpositional patterns, and we need not give it a special label. Alternatively, words like these are sometimes said to have a 'zero' suffix, though if the analogy with affixed examples is pursued, we might compare *peel* (a potato) with *unpeel* (a banana) and say that *peel* has a 'zero' prefix. However, 'zero' is a convenient shorthand term for 'without affix', and as such I have sometimes used it, though always inside quotation marks.

The table above might have included, under 'adjective base', adjectives which function as heads of noun phrases, like *the innocent* or *the wealthy* – traditionally described as 'partial conversion', since such expressions can have both adverbial and adjectival modifiers (*the completely innocent, the ostentatious rich*). These are not treated here as cases of word formation, since any adjective can function like a noun in a definite noun phrase denoting a class of people, or a quality (*the sublime*). There are a few fully nominalized and countable nouns based on adjectives, like *an alien, an innocent, a juvenile, an empty* (bottle), *a submersible* (vessel). These, though, hardly count as a pattern. Attributively used nouns have not been treated as denominal adjectives, since any noun can be used in this way. Despite the fact that *coast road* is synonymous with *coastal road* and *herb tea* with *herbal tea*, it would be difficult to make a case for assuming *coast* and *herb* to be transposed. There are a few adjective-like nouns with senses peculiar to their attributive function, as in *dwarf* (azalea), *fringe* (theatre), but again, these are not evidence of a pattern.

Both nouns and verbs can be 'zero' formations, based on verbs and nouns respectively, and it is worth looking at how denominal and deverbal derived words can be distinguished from one another in the absence of an affix. Historical evidence, such as it is – lexicographical records cannot always tell us all we want to know – may not be helpful, and we should not expect it to be, since we are not usually aware of the history of words when we use them. *To crowd* is Old English and its corresponding noun is dated in the sixteenth century by the OED, but we may still judge the noun to be basic and the verb derived. There are three kinds of criteria, not always conclusive and not always in harmony with one another. They concern form, meaning and frequency.

Kiparsky (1997, 489–90) points out that the regular past tense form, *ringed*, of *to ring* (pigeons) and the accentuation of *to áffix* shows these verbs to be based on the identical nouns. By contrast, *to sting* (with a needle) (past tense *stung*) and *to affíx* are not derived. Verbs like *to sandpaper* and *to jack-knife* are obviously derived, since compound verbs are never formed independently of compound nouns or adjectives related in form (see Chapter 8). In words prefixed by *re-*, accent on the prefix is a reliable sign that a noun is derived: *réfund*, *réhash*, *réplay*, *réprint*, provided the base is independently current (Raffelsiefen 1992, 141). In other two-syllable words with foreign prefixes, accent may not reliably support our intuitions about the direction of derivation. The nouns *cónstruct*, *éxport*, *ínvite*, *pérmit*, *próduce* and the verbs *constrúct*, *expórt*, *invíte*, *permít*, *prodúce* are like the *affix* pair above, but both members of some noun and verb pairs may be accented on the prefix (*combat*, *contact*, *process*) or on the base (*concern*, *rebuke*, *return*).

Meaning affects our intuitions about which member of a pair is derived. Verbs generally refer to dynamic situations, hence the noun *spy*, denoting someone with a characteristic activity, can be seen as based on the verb. Nouns refer prototypically to discrete entities: the verbs *to bicycle* and *to handcuff* are obviously derived from the nouns. *To bicycle* can only mean 'to travel by bicycle' and reasonable definitions of *to handcuff* are 'to restrain someone with handcuffs' or 'put handcuffs on someone'. Marchand (1964) assumes that a verb must be derived if its definition is dependent on the related noun. In some verbs, though, the meaning of the base noun is less prominent than it is in *to bicycle* or *to handcuff*. 'To *handcuff* someone with a piece of rope' sounds strange, but '*to drum* on the table with one's fingers' or '*to saw* (something) with a nail-file' are acceptable. For Marchand, the derived verb *saw* is most naturally defined as 'to use a saw', but since sawing can be done with various instruments, a definition of the (derived) noun might make use of the verb: 'instrument with which one saws'. Sense extension may also complicate matters, as with the verb *to cushion*, 'to protect', which we can see as derived from the noun meaning 'bag filled with feathers', and also as the base of the noun in the figurative sense illustrated in *a cushion against threats of redundancy*.

To the extent that the nouns *campaign, duel, experiment, gesture*, denoting actions or activities, are comparable with nominalizations, we can see them as derived from the verbs (cf. Karius 1985, 111–13). Marchand (1969, 370–1) however assumes that the verbs are derived (as historically they are, in English). In these cases, the comparative unfamiliarity of the verbs makes it easier to perceive them as derived, and as definable in terms of the nouns: 'to conduct, serve in, or go on a campaign' (Collins), 'to fight in a duel', etc. The verbs *cover, queue, stitch* and *wound*, by contrast, seem no less familiar than the related nouns, and in these cases it would be hard to say which is derived.

2.3   Verbs

2.3.1   Noun to verb

Denominal verbs are formed most often without affix; there are many formations in Greek-derived *-ize*, and rather fewer in Latin-derived *-ify* and *-ate*. There are also prefixed formations in foreign *de-* and *dis-*, and native *un-*.

Bases of verbs in *-ate* and *-ize* are usually of more than one syllable and have an unstressed syllable next to the suffix: *Balkanize, parasitize, fluoridate*. Bases of *-ize* verbs may lose their final syllable, as in *feminize* (avoiding adjacent syllables beginning with the same consonant: see Raffelsiefen 1998, 243–4). Bases of more than two syllables usually lose a final vowel, as in *economize, diarize*. A stressed syllable next to the suffix is generally avoided, so *-ize* rarely attaches to monosyllabic bases, as in *dockize* 'to form docks in a river'. *-ify*, by contrast, requires the adjacent syllable to have main stress: *humidify*, and often attaches to monosyllabic bases: *gasify*.[1] Verbs are not usually derived from suffixed nouns (Marchand 1969, 372–3), but they may be derived without affix from compound noun bases: *to snowball, to sandpaper*.

As comprehensively demonstrated by Clark and Clark (1979) in their study of verbs derived without affix from nouns with concrete referents, many denominal verbs fall readily into broad categories which reflect how people perceive the referents of those nouns, or what they know about them. Such categories as 'result', 'instrument', 'location' have been proposed in many descriptions of derivational patterns involving nouns – denominal adjectives and noun compounds as well as denominal verbs. Clark and Clark (1979) show that groups of denominal verbs can be distinguished on the basis of paraphrases in which 'the parent noun denotes one role in the situation, and the remaining surface arguments of the denominal verb denote other roles in the situation' (1979, 787).[2] The groups set out below are similar to those adopted by other writers on this topic, though there are differences of detail.

Verbs we can label 'ornative'[3] – a word related to Latin *ornare* 'to fit, equip, adorn' – are always transitive, and mean generally 'to cause someone or something to have, in some sense, the referent of the base noun'. Examples are

arm, blanket, commission, dust (e.g. with sugar), *fence, leaflet, man, oil, ornament, seed* (a vegetable patch), *staff, tar, varnish*

accessorize, circularize, computerize: 'We are currently computerizing the Inland Revenue' (Cobuild), *dieselize* 'equip with a diesel engine', *incentivize, moisturize, parasitize*: 'The worms that parasitize these snails invade their eyestalks' (Guardian: 1993), *rubberize, transistorize*

nitrify, yuppify: 'developers who want to "yuppify" the Charing Cross area' (OED: 1987), *zincify*

carbonate, chlorinate, fluoridate, hyphenate, nitrogenate, oxygenate.

In a 'locative' group it is the referent of the base, a location, which has, or contains, or receives another entity:

bank, bottle, cage, can, cloister, coast, corner, floor, garage, ground, house, stage, table; *dock and land* can be intransitive; *coast* and *surface* are only intransitive;

anthologize, containerize, diarize, ghettoize, hospitalize, palletize: 'Goods being palletized in advance' (OED: 1964).

'Privative' verbs, in some cases the counterparts of ornatives, can be glossed as 'to remove the base noun's referent from something', and 'ablative' verbs meaning 'to remove an entity from the base noun's referent' may reverse the kinds of action implied in locatives. *Unsaddle* is privative in 'unsaddle a horse', and ablative in 'unsaddle a rider'.[4] There are no suffixed privative and ablative verbs. A small group of 'zero' formations are verbs which mean 'to remove something from a situation in which it occurs naturally' (Buck 1997), e.g. privative *core, dust, fleece, hull, milk, peel, skin, stone, weed, worm*, and ablative *mine, quarry, shell* (peas). A few such verbs have synonyms in *de-*: *bark* and *debark* (a tree), *flea* and *deflea*, *gut* and *degut*: 'Open him at any page: and there lies the English language degutted and desouled' (OED: 1933), *husk* and *dehusk*, *scale* and *descale*. Contrast however ablative *mine* (silver, etc.) and privative *demine* 'remove mines from': 'The time that it will take to "demine" France is incalculable' (OED: 1945).

Privative *de-* verbs most often denote a technical or semi-technical process, as in:

debeak, debug, defat, deflea, defrost, defuzz, de-ice, de-index, delouse, demist.

Compare 'A process for dekinking the hair' (OED: 1957) with 'Gradually my soul began to unkink' (OED: 1972). Further privative *un-* verbs include *unburden, uncork, unmask, unmuzzle*. There are a few long-established verbs prefixed by *dis-*, such as *disarm, disbar, disburden, disforest, displace*, but post-1800 formations are rare: *discompanion*: 'A youth, fresh from college and suddenly discompanioned at home' (OED: 1883), *disillusion, dismarket*: 'The Court proposed to dismarket the two existing Leadenhall markets' (OED: 1878). Ablative formations in *de-* and *un-* include *deplane, derail, dethrone*; *unbosom, uncage, unearth, unhinge, unhorse, unspool*.

'Instrumental' examples mean 'to put the referent of the base noun to use' – a use usually but not always typical for the noun's referent:

axe, bicycle, cart, drum, elbow (someone out of the way), *handcuff, harp, knife, mirror, sandpaper, subpoena, tandem*: 'I *tandemed* one of my boys to school' (New Cyclist: 1993), *toboggan, trumpet.*

Suffixed verbs which are clearly instrumental are scarce or non-existent (cf. Farrell 1998, 40); *blenderize* 'process by means of a blender' can also be seen as locative, and *pressurize* 'persuade by pressure': 'U.S. officials are pressurising the Saudis to increase production' (OED: 1978) as ornative. Two other examples interpretable as either instrumental or ornative are illustrated in 'The Party . . . propagandised Marxist–Leninist theory' (OED: 1974); 'has he been unconsciously psychologized by the lawyer who has the biggest fee in his pocket?' (OED: 1886).

In 'resultative' examples, the base may indicate a change of nature or form which can be brought about by the action of the verb, or something that is brought into existence, assembled, gathered, caught, by means of the action:

apprentice, beggar, bundle, cake, caricature, cash, cripple, fool, honeycomb, outlaw, orphan, parcel, powder, prostitute

Arabize, Balkanize, bastardize, carbonize, itemize, miniaturize, pelletize, robotize, sloganize: 'a provincial régime that sloganized the Rights of Man' (OED: 1941), *synthesize, weaponize*: 'Chemical warfare agents were weaponized with Soviet assistance' (OED: 1982)

massify: 'We shall further massify and denature our people' (OED: 1954), *pulpify, trustify* (industry), 'to make into a trust'.

Resultative examples can be intransitively used if they denote actions of which the agent need not be made explicit: *caramelize, crystallize, fossilize, hybridize, polymerize, gasify*: 'Liquid ammonia gasifies under considerable pressure' (OED: 1881). Some examples, like *blackberry, bloom, bud, fish* and *lamb* can only be intransitively used; *neologize*, and *sloganize* in the sense 'compose slogans': 'The conspirators met in a pub and sloganised about tyrants' (OED: 1975) are also intransitive.

'Performative' examples,[5] transitive and intransitive, are generally paraphrasable as 'perform, practice, be what the base denotes':

boss, captain, chauffeur, engineer, guest, host, jack-knife, pilot

burglarize, parasitize, symbolize, symptomize, taxidermize, ventriloquize.

The following can be glossed as 'behave like what the base denotes' or 'treat someone or something in the manner indicated by the base':

concertina, dog, ghost: 'an experimental silent squad car designed to ghost about the city centre' (Guardian: 1993), *kangaroo* (1.5), *parrot, squirrel*: 'Nina's mind went on squirrelling round unhappily' (OED: 1983), 'Arlette was good at squirrelling away things in obscure places' (OED: 1981)

Boswellize: 'There was no enthusiastic curiosity about him; nobody Boswellised any playwright of his time' (OED: 1912), *bovarize*: 'people have bovarized themselves into the likeness of every kind of real or imaginary being' (OED: 1936), *cannibalize, vampirize*: 'Picasso's biographer has written of his enormous capacity to vampirize the creative energies of those around him' (Guardian: 1997).

Denominal verbs of course can have more than one sense if their bases have more than one sense, or if the referents of their bases are seen as likely to be involved in more than one kind of action. *To dust* can be ornative or privative; *gas* is ornative in 'The attendant . . . was busy gassing a pickup truck' (OED: 1959) and instrumental in 'She took a flat in a cheap suburb of Paris and tried to gas herself' (Cobuild). As Farrell (1998) points out, formations like those in 'Chris senatorized the letter' and 'Chris teacherized an A' are unacceptable because senators and teachers are not centrally conceptualized in terms of 'transfer of possession'. Yet it is quite possible for an occasional, 'nonce' verb to bring into focus an activity not usually associated with the noun, as in the following in which *handbag* is defined as an instrument and a particular way of moving identifies a *mouse* as such: 'the . . . actress . . . who handbagged Peter Cook in the face' (Guardian: 1993); 'we glimpse the cutter . . . and are about to mouse up his arm on a side trip of inspection' (V. Nabokov, *Transparent Things*, 1972, ch. 3). Occasional formations, however unexpected, can usually be seen as similar to those in the groups of established examples described – in these cases instrumental and performative respectively.

As we have seen, *-ize* verbs can be ornative, locative, resultative and performative, and, less certainly, instrumental. Examples of *-ify* verbs are not plentiful and are exemplified only under ornative and resultative. Verbs in *-ate*, with bases denoting chemical substances, have been placed under ornative, but could equally well have been labelled resultative. Prefixed formations are confined to the privative and ablative groups. Only 'zero' formations appear under every heading.

Occasional formations – like *handbag* and *mouse* – usually have no affix. The 'way' construction (*John elbowed his way to the front*), indicating movement with difficulty along a path created by the verb's action (Goldberg 1995, ch. 9), seems especially hospitable to unaffixed denominal verbs, as in: 'Henry the politician, with the shrewd business sense, Vicar-of-Braying his way from party to party...' (Guardian: 1994), and 'More than 4,000 walkers haversacked and fellbooted their way over 100 different stretches of moorland and hillside' (Guardian: 1995). 'Zero' verbs can be based on proper names, which, as Clark and Clark point out (1979, 783–5) contribute to a verb's meaning just the knowledge about who or what is referred to that is available to the speaker or writer and addressee, and is relevant in the context. Among their examples are 'we then Kleinschmidted the DNA' and 'how I was Robert McNamara'd into submission'. Plag (1999, 220), following Lieber (1998), sees 'zero' denominal verb formation as set apart from the other patterns in its semantic 'openness' and reliance on non-linguistic knowledge. However, it is worth noting that *-ize* is also productive enough to figure in unclassifiable examples like *macadamize, pasteurize, Hansardize*, 'to confront (a member of Parliament) with his former utterances as recorded in Hansard' (OED), *carmanize*: '"I have," he told Carman ringingly at one point, "been demonized by the Guardian and Carmanized by you"' (Guardian: 1997) and *Hollywoodize*: 'Puccini, that voice pervasively symbolic of the Hollywoodizing of human emotions' (OED: 1941).

2.3.2   Adjective to verb

Verbs with adjectival bases may have no affix, as is usually the case with short, non-derived adjectives, or may be suffixed by *-ize*, as often when the base is a denominal adjective, or *-ify*. Many suffixed verbs with denominal adjective bases are readily paraphrasable as if the bases were nominal, like *compartmentalize* 'divide into compartments', *contextualize* 'place in a context', *fictionalize* 'turn into fiction'.

Another suffix, *-en*, has often been noted as attaching only to bases which meet certain strict phonological conditions. Bases are monosyllabic and end in a single plosive, fricative or affricate. No other consonants occur, a restriction not shared by denominal adjectives in *-en* (*woollen*) or past participles (*fallen*): *greenen, *greyen, *pooren, *tallen. No consonant clusters are allowed: *moisten* and *soften* have no [t]. In fact, these restrictions are not absolute: *crispen* is current, cf. 'autumn's tang crispens the air' (OED: 1985), and among over thirty nineteenth-century formations recorded in OED are *dimmen* and *dullen*. Bases are occasionally nominal, as in *lengthen*, *breadthen* and the formations in: 'They [busy lizzies] have been dwarfened into ground-hugging pools' (Guardian: 1996); 'No dress youthens a girl so much as white' (OED: 1882). Jespersen (1939) places the rise of this suffix in late Middle and early modern English when inflectional final -*n* was lost in some contexts but not in others, so that variant forms became current, e.g. the verbs *fright* and *frighten*, *haste* and *hasten*. Where a non-*n* variant of a pair of verbs was homonymous with an adjective, the -*n* variant came to be perceived as derived from it, the form without an ending usually falling out of use, as with earlier *glad* and *mad*, cf. 'Hire goodly lokyng gladed al the prees' (Chaucer, *Troilus*, I. 173), 'That knowestow wel thyself, but if thou madde' (Chaucer, *Miller's Tale*, 3156). Where both variants remain current they are occasionally synonymous: *quiet* and *quieten*, *crisp* and *crispen*, but more often semantically differentiated: *black* and *blacken*, *loose* and *loosen*, *rough* (*out*) and *roughen*, *slack* and *slacken*, *tough* (*out*) and *toughen*.

Many verbs denoting changes of state can be used transitively and intransitively. Intransitive use is possible if there is no need for an explicit agent, cf. 'Cover the bowl and allow the liquid to cool' (Cobuild), 'There is no relief: the action intensifies' (OED: 1896), 'These pressures tend to equalize' (OED: 1971). Some, like *blind*, *clean*, *madden*, *deafen*, *familiarize*, *popularize*, *falsify* are only used transitively; a very few, like *pale* or *idle* are rarely used transitively – though transitive *idle* is illustrated in 'Some pursuit which idles you too much' (OED: 1892). If the adjective base of a verb is gradable, the verb can mean '(cause) to be or become more ADJECTIVE'. Context can bestow a 'manner' sense on a 'zero'-derived verb, as usually with *shrill*, used as a verb of speaking: ' "Stop!" she shrilled' (Cobuild). Two other examples are *gloom* in ' "When I have outlived my usefulness, I will be phased out," he gloomed' (Guardian: 1992), and *idle* in 'The woodbox was low and Jody idled outside to fill it' (OED: 1938). The 'way' construction illustrated in the previous section makes a verb *suave* possible in '. . . as I was suaving my way to Lingerie in a large store in the Rue de Rivoli' (Guardian: 1994). Further examples in 'zero', -*en*, -*ize* and -*ify* are:

blind, brown, clear, cool, dim, idle, muddy, narrow, open, pale, quiet, shut, slack, slim, slow, sober, steady, tan, tense, thin, warm, waterproof, yellow

blacken, brighten, broaden, dampen, deafen, darken, deepen, fatten, flatten, harden, neaten, quicken, redden, ripen, sharpen, shorten, sicken, soften, stiffen, sadden, tauten

centralize, criminalize, equalize, familiarize, formalize, normalize, popularize, radicalize, spiritualize, tenderize, trivialize, tranquillize, vulgarize, westernize

aridify, complexify, diversify, falsify, humidify, intensify, purify, rigidify, simplify, solidify.

2.4   **Nouns**

2.4.1   Verb to noun

In *the announcement of the news* (1.2.3), and other phrases of similar form like *the rapid cracking of the ice in spring, the constant barking of dogs at night, our careful examination of the evidence*, the nominalized heads, *announcement, cracking, barking, examination*, cannot be pluralized, and the only determiners possible for them are *the* or a possessive corresponding to the subject of the finite verb: *we examine the evidence*. The adjective modifiers correspond to adverbial modifiers of verbs: *rapidly cracking, barking constantly, examining carefully*. The *of* phrase, whose complement is in subjective or objective relation to the head, is obligatory. Like their base verbs, these verb-like nouns, 'process' nominalizations, denote events.

On their own, deverbal nominalizations may still denote events, as in *cycling is not allowed, translation requires skill*. Otherwise, nominalizations may denote more than just events. These we can refer to collectively as 'result' nominalizations. Their meanings, abstract or concrete, are unpredictable, and they can often be plural and indefinite, as in 'complicated *arrangements*', 'a readable *translation*', 'a large *collection* of butterflies'. Most deverbal nouns can be process or result according to context, but some, like *disturbance, information, recital* always have result meanings.

Deverbal nouns are formed with several suffixes: *-ing* can attach to any verbal base to form a process nominalization, and there are many *-ing* nominalizations with result senses, such as *building, flogging, offering, roofing, stuffing, warning, wrapping*. Verbs in *-ate* have nominalized forms in *-ion*: *oxygenation*. *-ation*, attaching to bases ending in an unstressed syllable, is the preferred suffix for denominal and deadjectival verbs in *-ify* and *-ize*: *computerization, acidification*. *-al, -ance* or *-ancy* and *-ment* all occur in modern formations, but much less often. *-al* attaches only to bases with main stress on the final syllable, as in *overthrowal*, with, unusually, a native base, *recusal* (*to recuse* is 'to object to a judge'), *referral, traversal*: 'the traversal of the fission barrier' (OED: 1955). Bases of *-ment* nominalizations can be native, as in *staggerment*: 'I was conscious of unjournalistic feelings of staggerment' (OED: 1975), *underlayment, weldment* as well as foreign: *attunement, partitionment, secondment*. *-ance* occurs in a very few established words with native bases like *furtherance* and *riddance* but most nouns in *-ance* have foreign bases. Modern formations include *absorbance, nurturance, observance, reflectance, retardance*. Forms in *-ence* are all long-established: *dependence, existence, persistence*.

Like process nominalizations, the unaffixed deverbal nouns in phrases like 'have a *bite* of the apple', 'give the cat a *stroke*', 'take a *walk* (on the beach)', synonymous with '*bite* the apple', '*stroke* the cat', '*walk* on the beach', are semantically predictable. Invariably singular and indefinite, they denote an instance of the verb's action. They always represent voluntary actions not undertaken to achieve a goal (*'have a *slip* on the ice', *'give the door an *open*'). Some nominalizations occur only in these constructions: 'have a *borrow* (of a pen)', 'have a *listen*', 'have a *think* (about the problem)', 'give the clothes a *soak*'.[6] Expressions like these are characteristic of informal registers and the nominalized items are typically native in origin. Occurrences like 'have a *consider*', 'give the patient an *examine*', seem unlikely, though not impossible, cf. 'Buchanan had a bit of a ponder himself' (OED: 1976).

A handful of 'zero' formations, typically with concrete count referents, are fully nominal and no more predictable in meaning than other result nominalizations. They can be grouped under some of the same headings as 'zero' denominal verbs, e.g. 'performative' *bore, coach, cook, guide, sweep*, 'instrumental' *catch, drill, lift, hoist*, 'locative' *haunt, hide, lounge, pass, retreat, stop* and 'resultative' *bake, brew, burn, dump, haul.*

Four suffixes, *-er, -or, -ee* and *-ant* form count nouns. Many nouns in *-er* have nominal bases (4.1), but more have verbal bases. They denote entities of various kinds connected in various ways with events. They most often name performers of actions, like *builder, programmer, surfer, racer, retriever, warbler*, or instruments crucially involved in actions, as in *blender, digger, jammer, ionizer, mixer, steamer, tourer, toaster*. Referents of *-er* nouns may be linked in some other way with the event signalled by the verb. *Cooler* and *fermenter* name vessels in which something is cooled or fermented; a *burner* is part of an apparatus near the flame, a *bedder* is a plant suitable for bedding. *Boater, diner, loafer, lounger, sleeper, trainer, wader* also denote entities associated with the (human) activity of the base. *Fermenter* 'organism', *nail-biter, page-turner, thriller* are causes of activities. The referents of *broiler* 'chicken for broiling', *cooker, eater* 'apple', *folder* 'folding bicycle', *trailer* correspond to the objects or patients of the base verbs.[7]

-er in some words corresponds to Old English *-ere: baker, singer, writer*; others have Latin and French counterparts: *painter, commander*. Related *-or* combines only with foreign bases, usually ending in [s] or [t]: *compressor, pressor, processor, contactor, conductor, reflector*. Most modern *-or* nouns have bases in *-ate: attenuator, formulator, liquidator, oscillator, plasticator, pollinator, stimulator, syncopator*. A few have stem bases: *descriptor, functor, propulsor* 'propeller', *sensor, vector*. As these examples suggest, *-or* nouns are most likely to be encountered in scientific or technical contexts.

The referents of *-ee* nouns can be quite precisely characterized. They are animate, almost always human, individuals who lack control in some degree over the event with which they are associated (Barker 1998). Often, the individual denoted corresponds to the direct object of the verbal base:

abductee, abusee, affrontee, baptizee, blackmailee, boycottee, chasee, cooptee, deportee, detainee, draftee, educatee, exploitee, internee, invitee, licensee, provokee, rescuee, selectee, supervisee, toastee, trainee.

Just over half of the OED's 167 post-1800 examples can be understood in this way. Barker, finding a similar proportion of 'direct object' examples in his study of a large corpus, regards them as prototypical (1998, 705), though, since referents of -ee nouns are invariably animate, it is no surprise that many (about a quarter of OED's examples, and of those reported by Barker) have referents corresponding to the indirect or prepositional object:

> *advertisee, borrowee, dedicatee, experimentee, gazee, grantee, licensee, offeree*: 'Provided the offer is not one which for some reason the offeree is entitled to refuse' (OED: 1952), *payee, plannee, signallee, telegraphee*.

Presentee can mean either 'person presented' or 'person to whom something is presented'.

Occasionally, the referent of an -ee noun corresponds to the base verb's subject:

> *attendee, collapsee*: 'he edges towards a collapse that is no less real for being sceptically commented on by the collapsee' (Guardian: 1995), *enlistee, embarkee, retiree, returnee* 'one who returns, or is returned from abroad to his native land' (OED), *signee* 'one who has signed a contract or register' (OED: 1953), *standee*.

Nouns in another small group have referents corresponding to something associated with the patient of an action, or with a recipient:

> *amputee* (the possessor of what the verb's direct object denotes), *chargee* 'the holder of a charge upon property' (OED), *contestee* 'a candidate for election who is in the position of having his seat contested by another' (OED), *expiree* 'one whose term of punishment has expired' (OED), *revisee* 'one whose work is subjected to revision' (OED), *snatchee*: 'Meanwhile, the Kidney Foundation, which has battled this myth for years, is asking any certifiable snatchees to step forward' (1997: example from Barker 1998, 708).

The base of an -ee noun may not be verbal, as with *biographee, patronee, pickpocketee, preceptee* 'one who is being trained by a preceptor' (OED), *redundantee, suicidee*: 'suicidees ... meet on Tower Bridge, but choose to avenge each other's tormentors instead of jumping' (Guardian: 1999), *wardee* 'an inmate of a hospital ward' (OED).

Marchand notes the 'non-passive character' (1969, 268) of some examples, cf. *cohabitee, consultee* or *quizzee* 'a panellist on a radio or television quiz programme' (OED), but as Barker demonstrates with many illustrations, lack of control is likely to be emphasized by the context of a new -ee noun, cf. 'A weightless embarkee would reel before a sudden gust, fall, and be blown about the quay' (1997: Barker 1998, 720), or *civilizee*: 'The civilizee shudders at the idea of eating wolf' (OED: 1880). New *-ee* nouns, especially those corresponding to the direct or prepositional object of the verbal base, may be contrasted with another noun with the same base, often an agent, as in: 'It is the common practice of the caller to demand the number of the callee immediately' (OED: 1959), 'A highly organized and regimented society . . . is felt by the planners, and even . . . by the plannees to be more "scientific"' (OED: 1946); 'I am not sure that the questioner could not answer that rather better than the questionee' (OED: 1953); 'the parents themselves were once the socializees instead of the socializers' (OED: 1975); 'exploiters and exploitees were gathered together' (OED: 1960). Cf. also 'The whole point of an ultimatum is to give the ultimatee some time to squirm' (Guardian: 1999).

The French provenance of *-ee* is apparent in the fact that it bears the main stress. Words with monosyllabic bases, necessarily involving adjacent stressed syllables, as in *grantee*, *payee*, *quizzee*, are not avoided, though, in longer words, the syllable adjacent to the suffix is unstressed: *èxploitée*, *sèlectée*. Bases of three or more syllables ending in *-ate* or another unstressed syllable may lose it before the suffix: *evacuee*, *nominee*, *rehabilitee*, *ultimatee*, *vaccinee*.

Some established nouns suffixed by Latin-derived **-ant** are, as Marchand notes (1969, 251), legal terms like *defendant*, or 'carry the stamp of formal procedure' like *contestant*. More recent formations of this kind include some which are likely to occur in religious contexts such as *celebrant*, *congregant*, *installant*, *officiant*, *scrupulant*, *retreatant*; terms of legal significance like *assurant*, *attestant*, *chargeant*, *disclaimant*, *movant*, *optant*, *registrant*, and others: *discussant*, *dedicant*, *matriculant*. Another definable group of *-ant* nouns denotes substances involved in biological, physical or chemical processes:

> *attractant*, *coagulant*, *colourant*, *contaminant*, *defoliant*, *depressant*, *dispersant*, *dopant*, *etchant*, *incapacitant*, *lubricant*, *propellant*, *sealant*, *suppressant*.

Euphoriant has a non-verbal base. Bases are almost always of foreign origin (*coolant* is an exception), and often, like some of the examples just given, verbs in *-ate* without their suffix.

2.4.2   Adjective to noun

'Quality' nominalizations of adjectives are comparable with process nominalizations of verbs. Quality nominalizations are non-count and paraphrasable by 'the fact that or extent to which NOUN PHRASE is ADJECTIVE' (Aronoff 1976, 38). Noun phrases within modifying *of*-phrases, obligatory or retrievable from the context, or implied in possessive determiners, are in subjective relation to the adjective bases: 'the visibleness of their wealth constituted a danger' (OED), *I questioned the legality of the decision/its legality* (cf. *their wealth was visible, the decision was legal*). Adjectival modifiers correspond to adverbial modifiers of the base adjective: *blatant visibleness, strict legality, her suitability was obvious* (cf. *blatantly visible, strictly legal, obviously suitable*). The meanings of 'entity' nominalizations, like those of deverbal result nominalizations, can be abstract or concrete, count or non-count: *an activity, a business, (a) kindness, Russianness*: 'the author's life-long affair with Russianness' (OED: 1967), *visibility: the visibility was 500 yards.*

A few adjectives ending in *-ent* and *-ant* correspond to nominalizations in *-ency* and *-ancy*, e.g. *decency, fluency, plangency, stridency, vibrancy*, or *-ence* and *-ance*: *brilliance, radiance, sentience*, though *-ence* and *-ance* more usually signal deverbal nominalizations (Marchand 1969, 294–5): compare deverbal *compliance* and *dependence* with de-adjectival *compliancy* and *dependency*. Some adjectives ending in *-ate* nominalize with *-acy*: *adequacy, delicacy, intimacy, legitimacy, obstinacy, profligacy.*

The majority of de-adjectival nouns end in *-ness* or *-ity*, two suffixes which have been focused on in discussions of 'rivalry' among affixes.[8] Bases of nouns in native *-ness* are always identical in form with the adjectives they correspond to. Attaching to foreign as well as native bases, *-ness* is generally assumed to be the more productive of the two suffixes. It can combine with almost any base which is semantically appropriate, cf. *thingness, as-suchness, off-beatness, up-to-the-minuteness, us-ness*: 'There was a pleasant feeling of us-ness in the unit' (OED: 1966). Latin-derived *-ity* attaches only to bases or suffixes of non-native origin, with the well-known exception of *oddity*. Bases are accented on the syllable next to the suffix. There are many *-ity* nouns with bases in *-able, -ible, -al* and *-ic*: *analysability, suggestibility, modality, iconicity*, and bases ending in *-ar, -ile* and *-id* are also likely to nominalize in *-ity*: *angularity, ductility, liquidity*. *-ive* and *-ous*, however, take *-ness* more readily than *-ity*: *informativeness, tendentiousness*. Adjectives ending in *-acious* usually have nominalizations in *-acity*; adjectives in *-ulous* nominalize either like *nebulosity* or like *credulity*. Many, such as *ridiculous* or *tremulous*, do not usually nominalize in *-ity*. Aronoff (1976, 43) suggests that these apparent irregularities contribute to the greater productivity of *-ness* with adjectives in *-ous*.

It is well known that *-ity* nouns are more likely than *-ness* nouns to develop institutionalized meanings which amount to more than just the quality lexicalized in the adjective base. Compare, for instance, *religiousness* and *religiosity, antiqueness* and *antiquity, capableness* and *capability*: the second member of these pairs can signal just the quality of the base adjective, but can also mean 'affected or excessive religiousness', 'ancient time', 'a faculty or property' respectively. New *-ness* nouns are likely to have only a quality sense, cf. *differentness* and *miserableness* in 'His manner was softer than at the studio, as if his differentness had been put on at the gate' (OED: 1934); '"My God! what a genius I had when I wrote that book," said Swift, half-mad and wholly miserable. Wordsworth, without any miserableness or despair, was ... of the same opinion' (OED: 1890). In a few pairs, -*ness* and -*ity* signal different senses of their -*able* bases (see 2.5.1 below). Compare *changeableness, fashionableness, serviceableness*, 'quality of being liable to change, in fashion, ready to serve, with *changeability, fashionability, serviceability*, 'quality of being able to be changed, fashioned, serviced'.[9]

2.5   Adjectives

2.5.1   Verb to adjective

Deverbal adjectives fall into two groups which we can refer to as 'subjective' and 'objective' (cf. Beard 1995, 320). The referent of a noun phrase modified or complemented by a subjective adjective corresponds to the subject of the adjective's base verb, as in 'a *squeaky* door' (a door that squeaks), or 'the air is *oppressive*'. Objective deverbal adjectives modify or complement a noun phrase whose referent corresponds to the verb's object, as in 'a *glazed* window' (a window that has been glazed), or 'the dinghy is *inflatable*'.

The present participle forms of dynamic, intransitively used verbs occur freely as premodifiers in noun phrases, and we can take them to be (subjective) adjectives when they denote a property of their head's referent, as in '*moving* parts', 'parts that move' (1.2.3). Participles of verbs denoting emotional events like *amazing, destabilizing, disgusting, fascinating, interesting, satisfying, thrilling* are gradable (1.2.3), as are those of verbs denoting mental attitudes, like *calculating, demanding, discerning, understanding*. Participles of these verbs can be fully adjectival. The present participles of other transitively used verbs can generally have attributive function, either progressive (verbal) or property-denoting (adjectival), only if accompanied by their objects, that is in compounds such as '*stone-throwing* demonstrators', '*job-seeking* graduates'. (See 7.2 for adjective compounds on this pattern.)

Past participial forms of intransitive verbs with 'patient' or 'experiencer' subjects can function as subjective modifiers in noun phrases, as in 'a *collapsed* tent', '*disappeared* civil-rights protesters', '*fallen* leaves', 'a *vanished* civilization' (Levin and Rappaport 1986, 653–5). The past participles of verbs with 'agent' subjects generally cannot function as participial adjectives: *'a *climbed* mountaineer', though there are exceptions, e.g. 'an *escaped* prisoner'.

Subjective adjectives with suffixes other than -**ed** and -**ing** can often be glossed with a modal expression: 'likely to, tending to, VERB. They may be suffixed by -**ant** and -**ent** (which correspond to Latin participial endings):

absorbent, convergent, defiant, dependent, nurturant, observant, reliant, repentant, resistant.

Adjectives in Latin-derived *-ive* have bases ending in [t], less often in [s] or [z]. Bases are often of two syllables, the second carrying the main stress:

> *addictive, appraisive, assaultive*: 'The moment the jacket was removed, she became assaultive' (OED: 1961), *completive, congestive, conscriptive*: 'a conscriptive country like this' (OED: 1906), *impactive*: 'The impactive scrutiny of strange faces' (OED: 1934), *molestive*: 'Mrs Prosser had been equally molestive to the mother' (OED: 1929), *obsessive, pollutive, replacive, supportive*.

Examples in which the base appears not to be verbal, like *instinctive* or *impulsive*, are loan words. A number of adjectives have unstressed *-at-* next to the suffix. *Collaborative, evaluative* and *propitiative*, have base verbs in *-ate*. Other adjectives, like *consultative, continuative, determinative*, have bases corresponding to Latin participial stems or to French adjectives (cf. *déterminatif*); *speculative* became current earlier than its base verb. *Talkative* and *resultative* are modelled on examples like these (11.2).

Deverbal adjectives suffixed by native *-y* have monosyllabic, usually native bases:

> *boomy, bouncy, choosy, clingy, dangly, floaty, growly, gushy, jumpy, picky, punchy, pushy, scary, weepy, wiggly, yappy.*

Objective past participial adjectives include those of 'emotional event' verbs, as in 'a *frightened* creature', 'a *satisfied* customer', and those of transitive verbs taking 'affected' objects (1.2.3): 'a thoroughly *chewed* bone'. Otherwise, the past participles of transitive verbs generally function as attributive modifiers only if accompanied by an adverb: 'a *carefully-worded* letter' (Huddleston 1984, 324), or when compounded or prefixed, as in '*architect-designed* houses' (7.3.1), '*unheard* melodies'.

Objective deverbal adjectives may be suffixed by Latin-derived *-able*. They can usually be glossed with a modal expression: 'can be VERB-ed', 'should be': *censorable*: 'My remarks ... were highly censorable' (OED: 1966), 'must be': *payable*, 'is likely to be': *murderable*: 'a man who is murderable is a man who ... desires to be murdered' (OED: 1920). *-able* attaches to native and foreign bases of any shape:

> *beddable, bombable, bookable, contactable, deterrable, downloadable, foretellable, metabolizable, microwavable, paraphrasable, telephonable, transplantable.*

The base may correspond to a verb collocated with a prepositional phrase:

> *accountable, dependable, laughable, listenable, moralizable, raceable* (of a racecourse), *skiable* (snow), *soarable* (weather conditions), *strikeable*: 'The idea of 5-day mail service is a "strikeable issue"' (OED: 1977).

Phrasal-verb bases occasionally include the particle: *roll-uppable, put-downable*. Some adjectives with bases corresponding to unfamiliar 'zero'-derived verbs are more naturally paraphrased using nouns: *jeepable* 'negotiable by jeep', *kitchenable* 'suitable for preparing in the kitchen', *sedimentable* 'depositable as sediment', *tubbable* 'washable in a tub'. In others the bases are nouns which are formally related to verbs, as in *actionable* 'subject to a legal action', *impressionable, objectionable, saleable, trailerable*: 'Boat kits – 22 trailerable models' (OED: 1980). The nominal bases of the following do not correspond to verbs, though they can of course be related to events: *cabinetable* 'fit to be a member of a political cabinet' (OED), *fissionable, overcoatable*: 'Overcoatable between 1–3 hours' (instructions on paint tin), *pelletable, roadable*: 'A "roadable" aircraft has been shown at the Detroit Motor Show' (OED: 1972), *sudsable* 'washable in soapy water' (OED), 'a *tenurable* post'.

Adjectives in *-able* borrowed from French into Middle English could be subjective as well as objective; hence the *'comfortable* [i.e. 'comforting'] words' of the Prayer Book. Other long-established adjectives which have retained a subjective sense include *agreeable* 'disposed to agree', *changeable* 'liable to change' (*changeable weather*) as well as 'can be changed' (*'changeable* arrangements'), *perishable* and *variable*. Modern subjective examples include *breathable* (of a waterproof fabric), *corrodable, recurrable* 'recurrable epithets' (OED: 1935), *unleakable*: 'A Solid [Glass] Trough . . . practically unleakable' (OED: 1902), *unflappable* and *weatherable*, seen as based either on intransitive *to weather* 'to wear well under atmospheric influences' (OED) or on the noun, and defined as 'capable of withstanding the effects of the weather'.

Bases ending in *-ate* may lose their final syllable: *allocable, cultivable, isolable* (beside *isolatable*), *manipulable* (beside *manipulatable*), *superannuable*. The related form *-ible* occurs in established loan words like *corruptible*, and occasionally in new formations: *indexible, investible* (beside *indexable, investable*), especially after bases ending in *c* representing [s]: *transducible*.

2.5.2 Noun to adjective

Foreign suffixes of denominal adjectives include *-al, -ic, -(i)an, -ary, -esque* and *-ous*. *-al* attaches to bases of foreign origin (*tidal* is a rare exception), sometimes with shift of accent:

> *accidental, behavioural, causal, cultural, dialectal, environmental, global, hormonal, institutional, operational, pivotal, scribal.*

The suffix has variant forms: with bases ending in *-ent, -ence, -ance* or *-or*, the ending is *-ial*: *tangential, residential, circumstantial, conspiratorial*; in other cases it is *-ual*: *contractual, factual, textual*. The bases of *-ic* are also foreign, and the accent is often shifted, since *-ic* requires an adjacent stressed syllable:

barbaric, cubic, democratic, geographic, heroic, historic, meteoric, Miltonic, parasitic, robotic.

Bases ending in a vowel may lose it before *-ic*: *allergic, catatonic, bibliographic.* The two suffixes are combined in many words, such as *arithmetical, geographical, poetical, tropical.* Pairs of adjectives in *-ic* and *-ical* have become differentiated in meaning, as with *analytic* and *analytical, historic* and *historical, economic* and *economical,* or one member of a pair is no longer in use: *identic, mechanic, politic; semantical, syntactical, tragical.* See Marchand (1969, 240–4) for a full account illustrated with many examples.

-ary generally has abstract noun bases: *complimentary, dietary, diversionary, evolutionary, inflationary, probationary.* The bases of *-(i)an* and *-esque* are usually proper names: *Corsican, Wordsworthian, Kafkaesque, Turneresque.* There are a few older adjectives in *-ous* with native bases, like *murderous* and *wondrous,* and many common words with bases of French origin like *advantageous, industrious, mountainous, villainous.* Newer formations are likely to be confined to scientific discourse, e.g. *arachnidous, endocrinous, migrainous.*

Most denominal adjectives with these suffixes, like *causal, Corsican, cubic, dietary, endocrinous* are non-gradable, and definable in phrases like 'relating to NOUN' in ways made clear by the context. Gradable adjectives like *Kafkaesque, mountainous,* and denominal adjectives with the native suffixes *-like, -ly, -ish, -y, -ed* and *-ful* can often be roughly glossed as 'like NOUN' or 'having NOUN'.[10] Adjectives in *-less* mean 'not having NOUN'.

-like and *-ly*, both related to the Old English noun *lic* 'body' and adjective *(ge)lic* 'similar to', suggest resemblance of some kind. *-like* can be attached to any appropriate nominal base: *dreamlike, hedgehog-like, vice-like.* Bases of *-ly* adjectives, by contrast, occupy a fairly well-defined semantic area, as these examples show:

'an *actorly* performance', '*authorly* detachment', *designerly*: 'Magazines were gaudier, more designerly' (Guardian: 1995), '*housemasterly* tones', 'a *leaderly* response', 'a *lawyerly* warning', '*musicianly* renderings', '*producerly* instincts', *writerly*: 'Dryden . . . sees his writerly obligations in new terms' (OED: 1977).

Older examples not always suggestive of 'resemblance', such as *beastly, beggarly, cowardly, earthly, ghostly, worldly* are not numerous.

New adjectives are readily formed with *-ish* and *-y*. *-ish* in adjectives meaning 'of the nature or character of, resembling NOUN', attaches much more readily than *-y* to bases denoting human beings:

demagoguish, dilettantish, fogyish, gangsterish, introvertish, lawyerish, outsiderish, playboyish, schoolboyish, tycoonish, yokelish.

Like its cognate, French *-esque*, which is much less likely to suggest disapproval, *-ish* is hospitable to proper name bases: *Beethovenish, Ibsenish, James Bondish, Heath Robinsonish, Uriah Heepish*. Adjectives in *-y* with bases denoting humans include

> *actory*: 'a very "actory" type of actor' (OED): 1967, *Bolshy, matey, hostessy, modelly*: 'Ghislaine was a bit too modelly to be true' (OED: 1961), *nerdy, officery, tarty*.

Both suffixes form adjectives with bases denoting animals:

> *apish, baboonish, goatish, mulish, owlish, pantherish, retrieverish, vulturish, weaselish*
>
> *mousy, rabbity, squirrelly, toady, snaky, spidery, vipery, weaselly*.[11]

Adjectives with both suffixes can have bases with other kinds of referent:

> *Bank Holidayish, folklorish, nightmarish, novelettish, Novemberish, prankish, red-tapeish, thrillerish*
>
> *arty, bluesy, cotton-woolly, folky, homey, trendy, Tudory, tweedy*.

Both suffixes can attach to bases other than nouns: *all-overish, stand-offish*; *iffy, ucky*.

Denominal *-y* is not confined to suggesting resemblance. An *-y* adjective often means 'having', 'abounding in NOUN':

> *busty, chocolatey, cloudy, curvy, flowery, germy, mouldy, pot-holey, strappy, toothy*,

or just 'relating to NOUN', e.g. *yachty* in 'galleries selling yachty prints' (OED: 1983). As Ljung (1970, 82) points out, the bases of *-y* adjectives meaning 'having (an abundance of) NOUN usually denote a mass, or entities which can be perceived as a mass: hence '*spidery* yard', 'yard abounding in spiders', '*treey* slope', are more likely than '*rabbity* yard' or '*housy* area'.

-ed and *-ful* also form adjectives with the general meaning 'having NOUN', but with contrasting kinds of base. Adjectives in *-ed*, usually non-gradable, are likely to have bases denoting concrete entities:

> '*binoculared* birdwatchers', 'a *blazered* team', '*cantilevered* beams', '*funiculared* mountains', '*hennaed* hair', '*knockered* front doors'.

Many such bases are compound, as in '*bottlenecked* alleys', '*blackshirted* Fascists', '*long-nosed* pliers' (7.2.3).

Adjectives in -*ful* typically have abstract noun bases:

characterful, effortful, flavourful, insightful, prestigeful, meaningful, pointful, purposeful, reposeful, resourceful, stressful, suspenseful, tactful, thoughtful.

Some bases may be more readily seen as verbal, as in *challengeful, neglectful, protectful, pushful, regretful, remindful, scornful, shudderful, sobful, thankful, thrustful.*
Some adjectives suffixed by -**less** have antonyms ending in -*ed*, -*ful* and -*y*:

'*captioned* or *captionless* picture', '*conflictful* or *conflictless* situation, personality', 'The difference between slumless Düsseldorf and slummy Glasgow' (OED: 1924).

Antonyms in -*less* often do not quite match their positive counterparts, since as Bolinger (1985) points out, -*less* adjectives are typically ungradable. Prefixation by negative *un*- (3.3) often makes a more appropriate opposite to a gradable adjective in -*ed*, -*ful* or -*y*: *unforested, unlawful, untrendy.*
Bolinger also comments on the 'strongly evaluative overtones' of -*less* adjectives, a description which certainly fits many older examples, both 'positive': *fearless, faultless, stainless*, and 'negative': *homeless, rudderless, profitless, stateless.* 'Negative' bases of course are likely to figure in 'positive' adjectives: '*problemless* hypothesis', 'a *smogless* day', '*splinterless* glass', 'a *victimless* crime', and vice versa: '*licenceless* motorists', 'a *liftless* block of flats', 'a *mythless* existence', '*vitaminless* foods', '*whipless* MPs'. The context of 'a *machineless* age' may point to either evaluative implication. *Overcoatless* is negative in 'So, overcoatless, . . . he went out into the rainy streets' (OED: 1936), and *pastless* and *televisionless* are positive in 'The perfect soldier: pastless, unhampered and complete' (OED: 1954); 'a warm and undisturbed televisionless place' (OED: 1962). Of the twentieth-century formations in -*less* recorded by OED, however, those with bases which make a neutral use most likely are the most numerous, e.g.

'*captionless* joke', '*cordless* appliance', '*crustless* bread', '*durationless* instant', '*filamentless* lamp', '*flangeless* beam', '*flapless* pockets', '*flueless* grates', '*hubless* wheels' '*inertialess* particle', '*runnerless* plant', '*sprocketless* videotape', '*vibratoless* style'.

2.6 Adverbs

Adverb-forming -*ly*, a close relative of denominal adjectival -*ly*, and here taken to be derivational, is sometimes treated as an inflectional suffix on the ground that it is obligatory with adjective bases in certain syntactic environments, cf. *slow movement*: *move slowly*, *rapid reaction*: *react rapidly*. Like plural *-s*, usually omitted in noun compounds, e.g. *caravan site*, *rabbit warren*, adverbial *-ly* is excluded from adjective compounds like *slow-moving* (7.1). But there are also good reasons for taking it to be a derivational suffix. The use of an *-ly* adverb need not be obligatory: there is often an alternative expression, e.g. *with rapidity* for *rapidly*. The correspondence of adjective and *-ly* adverb is not automatic. There are no *-ly* adverbs corresponding to some adjectives, e.g. *big*, *long*, *old*, *young*, the adverbs corresponding to some adjectives, *hot*, *cold*, *dark* for example, can only have metaphorical senses (Dixon 1982, 26ff), and the pairs *short* and *shortly*, *dry* and *drily*, *hard* and *hardly* are semantically distinct.

-ly is of course by far the most common way of forming adverbs with adjective bases. Baayen and Renouf (1996, 88–9) note that adjectives prefixed by *un-* or suffixed by *-al* and *-ing* are especially likely to figure in new formations with adverbial *-ly*, e.g. *unflappably*, *aseptically*, *demoralizingly*. (See 4.1 for examples of de-adjectival adverbs in *-ish*.)

Denominal **-ly** in words like *hourly*, *weekly*, *quarterly* (2.5.2), **-fold** with cardinal numbers and **-ward**(*s*), occur in a few words which, according to use, we can regard as either adjectives or adverbs: 'a *weekly* paper', 'the board meets *quarterly*'; 'millionfold repetitions' (OED: 1865), 'The value of this house has increased fourfold since we bought it' (LDOCE); 'the seaward edge' (Cobuild), 'He made a motion pocketwards' (OED: 1909).

Words in denominal **-like** (2.5.2) can have adverbial function, invariably relating to the subject of a sentence: 'Gnome-like he faced the umpire', 'its meaning flittered, bat-like, about my mind' (L.P. Hartley, *The Go-between*, 1953, 138, 207), 'This cactus had run wild, and, triffid-like, had taken over thousands of miles of good agricultural land' (OED: 1971). Formations with **style** can also be both adjectival: 'a Japanese-style hotel' (OED: 1934) and adverbial: 'He whistled, newsboy style' (OED: 1944), 'Some were killed execution style' (Guardian: 2000), cf. *fashion* in 'to dress *schoolboy-fashion*' (LDOCE).

Noun-based formations in native **-wise** can function as adjectives '*crosswise* streets', '*spanwise* slots', as adverbial modifiers associated with verb phrases: 'Don't hide your head in the sand, ostrich-wise' (Cobuild), 'we had to go snakewise' (OED: 1894), and as 'point of view' adverbials: 'We are mostly Socialists vote-wise' (Cobuild), 'Television-wise, his performance was more convincing' (OED: 1962), 'October is usually a very good month weatherwise' (OED: 1971). In adverbs with this function, *-wise* appears to have become noticeably productive fairly recently, from the mid-twentieth century onwards: see Houghton (1968) and Pulgram (1968), who note some warnings against it in handbooks of usage. Most cited examples are from speech, yet Pulgram suggests there is an association between 'point-of-view' *-wise* and 'advertising, business and bureaucracy' (391), a circumstance which he sees as favouring the more general acceptance of *-wise* in adverbs of this kind.[12]

Notes

1. See Plag (1999) for a detailed account of the phonology of verbs suffixed by *-ize*, *-ify* and *-ate*.
2. Plag (1999, chs 6 and 7) describes de-adjectival verbs together with denominal verbs in *-ize*, *-ify*, *-ate* and without affix under seven headings, 'locative', 'ornative', 'causative', 'resultative', 'inchoative', 'performative' and 'similative'. He summarizes the possibilities in a single semantic formulation involving the functions 'go', 'cause' and 'to', in terms of the transfer of a property or thing between the referent of the base and that of another entity.
3. This term is used by Karius (1985) and Plag (1999). The equivalent term in Clark and Clark (1979) is 'locatum'.
4. Plank (1981, 120–4) discusses pragmatic factors involved in the interpretation of prefixed verbs as 'privative' or 'ablative'.
5. Plag (1999, 137) uses this label for examples like *anthropologize* 'practise anthropology', distinguishing them from cases like *Stalinize* 'act like Stalin', which he calls 'similatives' (138f).
6. Dixon (1991, ch. 11) describes these constructions in detail. See also Wierzbicka (1982).
7. Rappaport-Hovav and Levin (1988) argue that deverbal *-er* nouns can be described as referring to the 'external arguments' of their base verbs. 'Unaccusative' verbs like *break* in *the window broke*, assumed to have no external argument, thus cannot be the bases of *-er* nouns. Examples like *broiler* 'chicken' or *eater* 'apple' are relatable to the 'middle' uses of their base verbs: *the apple eats well*. See Ryder (1999) for a critical view of this account.
8. Stimulated principally by Aronoff (1976, ch. 3). See also Aronoff (1980), Anshen and Aronoff (1981, 1988), Romaine (1983). Discussion has focused on the possible impact on productivity of phonological change in bases, and of lexicalization.
9. Aronoff (1976, 48) notes the two meanings of *fashionable*. It is not the case though, as he maintains, that denominal *-able* adjectives regularly take *-ness*: cf. *fissionability, roadability, saleability*.
10. Denominal attributive modifiers suffixed by *-type*, as in 'California-type barbecues' (OED: 1949), 'Dutch-barn-type buildings' (OED: 1960), expressing resemblance, are not gradable. See Dalton-Puffer (1999) for a discussion of this pattern, noted as very productive by Plag, Dalton-Puffer and Baayen (1999, 219).
11. Malkiel (1977), pointing out that the modern senses of *hawkish, dovish, waspish* are descriptive of people, and that *mousy* and *ratty* in 'resembling' senses are comparatively recent, suggests that *-y* has displaced *-ish* in adjectives indicating resemblance to an animal.
12. The development of the 'point-of-view' use of *-wise* is a plausible case of semantic development involving an increase in subjectivity and reference to the speaker's attitude towards the proposition: see Traugott (1989) for examples.

3

Prefixes

3.1 Scope

Prefixes are bound forms which attach initially to bases. Bases can be verbal, adjectival or nominal. Prefixed formations are often members of the same class as their bases, though verb-forming *de-*, *dis-* and *un-* can also be transpositional (2.3.1), attaching to nominal as well as to verbal bases, and there are many parasynthetic prefixed adjectives with noun bases like *multi-racial*, *non-governmental*, *anti-glare*, *non-stick* (1.2.2).

There are numerous prefixes, though comparatively few figure with any prominence in current and new formations in common use. Among those which form verbs and related participial adjectives and deverbal nouns are *de-*, *inter-*, *mis-*, *pre-*, *re-*, *un-*, and to a lesser extent *co-*, *cross-*, *sub-*, *super-*, *trans-*. Adjectives, and sometimes nouns, are prefixed by *a(n)-*, *anti-*, *bi-*, *counter-*, *dis-*, *ex-*, *extra-*, *hyper-*, *mono-*, *multi-*, *non-*, *post-*, *pro-*, *proto-*, *semi-*, *sub-*, *super-*, *trans-*, *ultra-*, *un-*. Many prefixes combine productively with stems to form adjectives and nouns which are largely confined to specialized scientific and technical registers. They include *ante-*, *circum-*, *cis-*, *demi-*, *di-*, *epi-*, *extra-*, *hyper-*, *hypo-*, *inter-*, *intra-*, *meta-*, *ortho-*, *para-*, *peri-*, *poly-*, *pre-*, *pro-*, *preter-*, *retro-*, *supra-*, *tri-*, *uni-*, *centi-*, *deca-*, *hecto-*, *kilo-*, *nano-*, *pico-*. Some of these are illustrated in 9.3.

Prefixes are semantically less heterogeneous than these lists might suggest. Almost all are related to Latin or Greek particles or quantifiers. They can be generally grouped as 'locative', 'quantitative', 'reversative' and 'negative', and there are items in each group which point to links with another group. The link between reversative and negative is clear in expressions like 'an *unlocked* door', in which the participial adjective can denote either the reversed result of an action (*unlock-ed*) or a negative state (*un-locked*). Reversative *un-* (*untie*) corresponds to Old English *on-*: its present-day form is assumed to have been influenced by negative *un-* in adjectives (*unbeaten*) (Jespersen 1942, 26.41; de la Cruz 1975, 63). Like *un-*, *dis-* is reversative in verbs (*disconnect*) and negative in adjectives (*disloyal*). *Dis-* is related to quantitative *di-* (Latin and Greek 'two'); as reversative, it can suggest 'separation' (*disconnect*), and as negative, 'division' (*dissimilar*) and 'opposition' (*disagree*). Reversative *un-* is cognate with *anti-*, which is locative ('against', 'opposite') in *anti-hunting*, *anti-particle*, but equivalent to reversative *de-* in *anti-icer*, cf. *de-icer*, and to negative *non-* in *anti-hero*, cf. *non-hero*. Negative *un-* is etymologically related to the Latin *in-* of *inactive* and the Greek *a(n)-* of *amoral*, *anhydrous*. Both these negative prefixes are homophonous with locative elements, Latin *in* and Greek *an(a)-* 'back' or 'again', as in *anabaptist* 'one who baptizes again' and *anagram*, from a Greek verb meaning 'to write back or anew'. Reversative *de-* (*deselect*) is a reflex of the Latin locative particle *de* 'down', 'from', 'off'.[1]

Prefixes as defined here are semantically distinct from stems, 'initial combining forms', like *biblio-*, *electro-*, *galvano-* (9.2). Stems represent Latin and Greek nouns, adjectives and verbs, and they have as broad a range of meanings as English nouns, adjectives and verbs. A semantic distinction between prefix and stem cannot always be made with consistency, however: the Greek stems *arch-* 'chief', *neo-* 'new' and *pseudo-* 'false', for example, occur in some words with meanings quite similar to those of the locative prefixes *post-*, *sub-* and *super-*: compare *neo-Gothic* and *post-Impressionist*, *pseudo-religious* and *subliterate*, *arch-enemy* and *super-bomb*.

Most locative prefixes exhibit polysemy in combination with bases. 'In front' is understood spatially in the nouns *forecourt*, *preabdomen*, and temporally in the verbs *forewarn*, *precook*. *Pro-*, 'in front' in Latin, has related senses in *pro-consul* ('in place of') and *pro-roads* ('in favour of'). 'Behind' and 'back' are spatial in *postabdominal* and *retro-rocket* and temporal in *post-dated* and the verb *retro-fit*. *Super-* 'above', spatial in *superstructure*, means 'superior (in size)' in *supertanker* and 'exceeding a limit' in the verb *supercool*. *Sub-* means 'below' in *subsoil*, 'subordinate' in *subplot* and 'falling short of a standard' in *subnormal*. 'Outside' is understood literally in *extraterritorial* and non-literally in *extrasensory*.

Since prefixes have some degree of semantic autonomy, it is no surprise to find many of them occurring as independent words, as in '*pre* the ceasefire', '*pro* the idea', sometimes as abbreviated forms of longer expressions, e.g. *hyper* for *hyperactive* in 'like a hyper bumblebee in seach of a bit more honey' (OED: 1985), *mono* for *monophonic*, *inter* for *intermediate examination*, *semi* for *semi-detached house*. Even reversative *dis-* has an independent homonym, explained as from *disconnect* in utterances like 'You've heard about me dissing my wireless?' (OED: 1969), though it can also be glossed as 'criticize', as in 'Whenever you're dissed, you're dealing with a bully' (Guardian: 1995).

Two prefixes, native *be-* and foreign *en-*, cognate with *by* and *in*, no longer appear in new formations. They could once be attached to verbal bases to form verbs, e.g. Old English *beridan* 'to ride around', 'surround', *enclose*, later becoming so far grammaticalized as to have only a transpositional function. Examples with noun bases, not all of them still current, can be compared with the denominal verbs of 2.3.1: 'ornative' *bedew*, *encrust*, 'locative' *bebay*, *encage*, 'instrumental' *benet*, *enmesh*, 'performative' *befriend*, 'resultative' *beprose*, *enslave*.

3.2   Verbs

Prefixed verbs as a rule are 'accomplishments' – that is, they denote situations which can be brought to a conclusion.[2] Compare stative *live* with '*relive* an experience', *control* with '*decontrol* prices', *represent* with '*misrepresent* a view', *understand* with '*misunderstand* an answer', or verbs like *continue*, *think*, *cook*, *run*, *weave*, which in intransitive use can denote 'activities' – situations with no natural endpoint – with transitively used *discontinue*, *rethink*, *precook*, *interweave*, *rerun*, denoting processes with goals, as in '*rethink* a plan', '*precook* a meal', '*interweave* the strands', '*rerun* a tape'.

De-, when transpositional, attaches mainly to short, often native, noun bases to form privative verbs (2.3.1). By contrast, the verbal bases of reversative, non-transpositional *de-* verbs, which reverse the result of an action, are predominantly foreign and often suffixed. Semantically, there is little difference between privative and reversative in some cases: compare noun-based *deflea*, 'remove fleas from', with verb-based *decaffeinate*, best glossed as 'remove caffeine from' and seen as parasynthetic (1.2.2), since a verb *caffeinate* is not likely to be much needed. Both transpositional and non-transpositional verbs prefixed by *de-* include many which are likely to be used in specialized technical or semi-technical registers:

deconstruct, decolonize, decontaminate, decontrol, decriminalize, defamiliarize, defocus, dehumidify, depollute, deprogramme, deregulate, derestrict, desaturate, deselect, desensitize.

Bases of reversative **un-** verbs are typically simple and of native origin:

unbind, uncrinkle, unfix, unfreeze, unlace, unlearn, unload, unpack, unscramble, unsettle, unsheathe, unsnib, unspool, unstrap, untangle, untense, untwist, unweave, unwind, unwrap.

Reversative **dis-** occurs with foreign bases, often with an initial vowel:

disaffiliate, disassemble, disassociate, disconfirm, disconnect, discontinue, disenfranchize, disimpale: 'holding the animal in one hand he gently disimpaled it' (OED: 1904), *disinfest, disinsecticize, disorientate, disqualify.*

A verb phrase in a negative clause is negated by a negative word, *not* or *never*. Verbs in English cannot generally be negated by means of an affix, though there are some established verbs, chiefly with stative verb bases, in which *dis-* can be seen to effect subclausal negation, cf. *John dislikes Bill* (*doesn't he*)? as opposed to the clausally negated *John doesn't like Bill* (*does he*)? Examples are:

> *disagree, disallow, disbelieve, dislike, disobey, disregard, disremember, disrespect, distrust.*

Otherwise, instances of negatively prefixed verbs are extremely rare.[3] Occasional (rather strange) modern examples of negative *un-* or *non-* in verbs are obviously backformations (11.3), based on participial or nominalized forms, e.g. 'I . . . shall be well content if it do not unbecome me' (OED: 1893), 'But the world unrecognized his visions of goodness' (OED: 1843), 'the state of trade absolutely unwarrants it' (OED: 1902), 'I had to leave the college when Gandhi ordered me to non-cooperate' (R.K. Narayan, *The Sweet-Vendor*, 1967, 33).

Mis-, generally equivalent to 'inaccurately', 'wrongly', 'badly', attaches predominantly to verbs of foreign origin which denote actions or activities demanding precision:

> *misaddress, misalign, miscalculate, miscategorize, misclassify, misconstrue, misdirect, mismanage, misperceive, mispronounce, mispunctuate, misrepresent, mistranslate.*

Re-, occasionally 'back', as in *repossess* or *rezip*, but usually 'again', occurs with numerous native- and foreign-based verbs:

> *re-activate, recheck, recirculate, recode, refry, regrout, reheat, rehydrate, remortgage, remotivate, renegotiate, re-order, repressurize, reselect, retile, re-train, rewire.*

Re- can occasionally be seen as transpositional, attaching to noun bases as in *re-lampshade*: 'they had between them re-lampshaded the entire house' (OED: 1954), *remaster* 'make a new master (of a recording)', *reneck*: 'A genuine theorbo, built as a lute in 1584 and renecked in 1730' (OED: 1967), *re-washer*: 'The local water company re-washer water taps free of charge in order to save water' (OED: 1960).

Pre- is productive with both native and foreign bases, with the general sense 'do before some other operation', indicated by the base, as in *pre-edit*, *preprocess*, or deducible from the context, as in *prearrange, precool, preshrink*. Further examples are:

precompress, precondense, precondition, predate, pre-impregnate, pre-incubate, prelubricate, preload, prepack, preprogramme, prepublish, prerecord, preselect, presell, prestretch, pretreat, prewrap.

Sprengel (1977) in a detailed study shows that many modern *pre-* verbs, whether with native or foreign bases, are (like many *de-* verbs) of a kind likely to occur in technical or semi-technical contexts, and that the synonymous native prefix ***fore-*** is to be found in only a few older but still current verbs like *forearm, foredoom, forejudge, forewarn*.

Other locative verb-forming prefixes include ***co-*** 'with, together', ***cross-***, ***inter-*** 'between', ***sub-***, ***super-*** and ***trans-*** 'across', 'over':

co-adjust, co-arrange, co-direct, co-edit, co-organize, co-produce, co-write

cross-connect, cross-date, cross-fade, cross-fertilize, cross-pollinate, cross-question, cross-refer

inter-breed, inter-communicate, inter-connect, inter-dine: 'We do not interdine [with Hindus]' (OED: 1933), *inter-link, inter-plant*: 'Fill every inch of space by interplanting one crop with another' (OED: 1942), *inter-relate*

subclassify, subdivide, sublet

supercharge, supercool, superheat, super-impose

transcode, trans-illuminate, translocate, transplant, trans-ship.

3.3   Adjectives

In predicative adjectives, the negative prefixes *a(n)-, in-, non-, un-* and *anti-* distinguish subclausal negation: *this drug is non-addictive (isn't it?)* from clausal negation: *this drug is not addictive (is it?)*. *Not* does not usually negate attributive words, unless they are negatively prefixed adjectives: 'a *not unfair* decision'. Attributive words are always negated by affix: '*non-/un-/*not scripted* interviews', 'a *non-/*not flowering* plant', '*non-tax* revenue', though progressive *-ing* participial forms like *moving* in 'the *moving* bus' represent the verbal lexeme (1.2.3) and cannot be prefixed: ***'the *non-moving* bus'. Past participles in passive clauses cannot be prefixally negated, though *John was unimpressed by the evidence* is acceptable, since *impress* is an 'emotional event' verb (1.2.3). Phrases of course can only be negated by a negative word: 'a *not very bright* light'.

Accounts of negatively-prefixed adjectives owe a great deal to Zimmer (1964). Taking up a comment by Jespersen (1917), Zimmer discusses the distinction between 'contrary' and 'contradictory' opposition. *Uncomfortable, unhappy, unwell* are contrary opposites of *comfortable, happy, well*: they 'leave some room for other possibilities between them' (Zimmer 1964, 21), as can be shown by statements like *John is neither comfortable (happy, well) nor uncomfortable*. Items like *invisible, non-rational, unpersuaded* on the other hand are 'contradictory' opposites of *visible, rational, persuaded*. The pairs in this case 'exhaust the possibilities along a given dimension' (1964, 95): *the lighthouse is neither visible nor invisible* is an unlikely statement. But the distinction is often not sharp and many items can be both contrary and contradictory. *Uninspired*, for example, as a contradictory opposite of *inspired* is equivalent to 'not inspired'; as contrary, it is a synonym of *dull*. *A(n)-* and *non-* predominantly form contradictory opposites; *dis-, in-, un-* and *anti-* are much more likely to occur in contrary opposites.

Greek-derived **a(n)-** (the *n* appears before bases beginning with a vowel and sometimes [h]) occurs in words of foreign origin exclusively. The bases of *acaudal* 'without a tail', *acardiac* 'without a heart', *achromatic* 'without colour', *anhydrous* 'without water' are nominal Greek or Latin stems. Adjectives with bases corresponding to English nouns may also be glossed with prepositional phrases: *aplacental* 'without a placenta'. Other examples can be understood as negated adjectives: *ahistorical* 'not historical', *amoral, asymmetrical, atoxic*. *Asexual* can be seen as noun-based in '*asexual* plants' but in 'women are more asexual than men' (OED: 1903) it is a gradable antonym of *sexual*.

Dis- occurs in well-established gradable adjectives with foreign bases, such as

> *disaffected, disagreeable, discourteous, dishonest, disinterested, dispassionate, dispossessed,*

but not in formations much later than the seventeenth century.

In- also attaches exclusively to foreign-derived adjective bases. The variants *il-* before [l] (*illiterate*), *im-* before [m] and [p] (*immeasurable, implausible*) and *ir-* before [r] (*irregular*) are the results of assimilation in Latin:

> *inactive, inadvisable, inconvenient, incredible, indiscernible, inedible, ineligible, inevitable, inexplicable, inexpressive, infallible, inoperable, impalpable, impermanent, improvident, intolerable, inviolable.*

Like *dis-, in-* does not generally occur in new formations. Modern examples such as *inexpellable*: 'Inexpellable was her image': (OED: 1911) or *inviscid* (descriptive of a gas or fluid) are rare. *Ineliminable, inexpiable, inegalitarian, inignominious*, identified by Baayen and Renouf (1996, 85) as innovations in their corpus drawn from *The Times*, have stem or truncated-word (9.2) bases, and are perhaps modelled on established examples like *ineradicable, iniquitous*.

As Zimmer shows, there are few adjectives with simple or lexicalized bases which are prefixed by **un-**. A possible *un-* form may be blocked (1.5) by a simple form: *nice: nasty* (**unnice*), *good: bad, evil* (**ungood*). Where prefixed forms exist there are typically restrictions on the use of one or the other member of a pair: *unclean* is only in a very limited sense the antonym of *clean*, *uncool* is the opposite of *cool* only as a general term of approval: 'anything you don't like is uncool' (OED: 1953), and the positive counterpart of *uncouth* is not in use. As he also shows, the bases of established negatively prefixed adjectives are almost always evaluatively positive: *unwell* but not **unill*, *unhappy* but not **unsad*.[4] However, 'nonce' formations with normally blocked bases: 'An unyoung "youth" leader' (OED: 1972), or with evaluatively negative bases, can easily be generated in discourse, e.g. 'This most readable and unbitchy of biographies' (OED: 1973), 'I spun round and assumed as unfurtive an air as possible' (OED: 1967), 'A man should sleep with his wife in winter. It's warm – unlonely' (OED: 1967).

Un- adjectives with neutral or evaluatively negative bases are much less unusual when suffixed by *-ed* or *-able*. *Un-* is productive with derived adjective bases of all kinds, especially verbal bases suffixed by *-able*, *-ing*, *-ed*, and nominal bases in *-ed*:

> *unbribable, uncontactable, undiagnosable; uncompelling, unthreatening, unmoving; unblemished, unchlorinated, unenlightened, unpublicized; unfootnoted, unjacketed, unscripted; unbureaucratic, unsterile, unprestigious, unchoosy, untrendy.*

In the early modern period, a number of synonymous pairs of adjectives in *in-* and *un-* were current. One or the other member of these pairs was usually lost, and whether a base now has *in-* or *un-* may seem unpredictable: *inactive* but *uncreative*, *inglorious* but *ungracious*, *irregular* but *unfamiliar*. An *un-* adjective may be unacceptable where there is an established *in-* form: **unregular*, **untolerable*, though pairs with both prefixes do occur: *in-* and *undefinable*, *in-* and *unappreciative*, *in-* and *unsubstantial*. But *in-* and *un-* pairs often exhibit a semantic difference, with the *in-* formation being the more lexicalized: *imperceptible* 'slight' vs *unperceivable*, *incómparable* 'peerless' vs *uncompárable* (Funk 1971, 376–7; Aronoff 1976, 127–8). A rare example of a base taking *dis-* as well as *un-* is *interested*: *disinterested* means 'objective' but can also, notoriously, be a synonym of *uninterested*.

Many **non-** adjectives have suffixed bases and are not gradable:

> *non-allergic, non-addictive, non-contributary, non-classified, non-ionizing, non-molecular, non-poisonous, non-recurring, non-returnable, non-salaried, non-specific.*

They may have non-suffixed noun bases, as in

> '*non-citizen* businessman', '*non-combat* duty', '*non-fat* solids', '*non-dollar* countries', '*non-title* fight',

or non-suffixed verb bases:

'*non-crease* clothes', '*non-crush* linen', '*non-dazzle* lamps', *non-iron, non-skid, non-slip, non-stick, non-stop.*

As Zimmer points out, *non-* generally 'selects the descriptive aspect of the stem for negation, while *un-* selects the evaluative one' (33). *Un-* and *non-* contrast in contrary *unremunerative* and contradictory *non-remunerative, unscientific* and *non-scientific*. *Non-* adjectives also contrast with evaluative *in-* adjectives: *insignificant* and *non-significant, impersonal* and *non-personal*. There may even be a three-way contrast, as with '*irreparable* harm', 'an *unrepairable* bicycle' and 'a *non-repairable* (throw-away) gadget', or *irreligious* 'hostile to religion', *unreligious* 'neglectful of religion' and *non-religious* 'not religious'.[5]

Anti-, with a degree of productivity approaching that of *non-*, occurs in similar kinds of formations: with derived bases, unsuffixed noun bases and unsuffixed verb bases:

anti-artistic, anti-capitalistic, anti-corrosive, anti-nationalistic, anti-scientific

'*anti-business* speeches', '*anti-fallout* pills', 'an *anti-fat* diet', 'an *anti-noise* campaign', 'an *anti-rabies* inoculation', 'an *anti-submarine* net', 'the *anti-war* party'

'*anti-flash* paint', '*anti-freeze* liquid', '*anti-glare* headlamps', '*anti-knock* fuel', 'an *anti-spin* parachute'.

A few prefixes, in particular **hyper-**, **semi-**, **sub-**, **super-** and **ultra-**, combine with a wide range of gradable adjective and participial adjective bases to form adjectives current in everyday and specialized registers:

hypercorrect, hyper-conscientious, hyper-immune, hyper-logical, '*hyper-mobile* joints', *hyper-modern, hyper-reactive,* '*hyper-saline* water', *hyper-speculative*

semi-arid, semi-conservative, '*semi-direct* lighting', 'a *semi-lethal* gene', '*semi-matt* paper', *semi-nomadic, semi-reclining, semi-skilled, semi-literate*

subaudible, subcompact 'smaller than "compact"', '*subcreative* activity', 'a *subdominant* group', '*subfreezing* temperatures', *subliterary,* '*submature* trees'

super-active, 'a *super-dense* state', '*super-heavy* matter', *super-intelligent, super-luminous,* '*supermassive* black holes', '*super-radiant* gas', *super-sensitive,* 'a *super-weak* force'

'*ultracold* neutrons', '*ultralight* aircraft', *ultra-pure, ultra-respectable, ultra-romantic,* '*ultra-short* waves', 'an *ultra-stable* system'.

Many locative and quantitative prefixes combine productively with nouns and denominal adjectives to form parasynthetic adjectives:

'*bifanged* teeth', *bicoloured, biconical, bi-weekly*;

'*cross-border* traffic';

'*extra-planetary* space', *extra-sensory, extra-systemic*

'an *inter-continental* missile', *inter-state, inter-tribal, 'inter-union* disputes'

'*mono-systemic* analysis', 'a *mono-cable* ropeway', 'a *monocausal* explanation'

'a *multi-access* computer', *multi-bladed, multi-purpose,* 'a *multi-screen* cinema'

pre-agricultural, '*pre-flight* checks',

'*post-larval* development', *post-Conquest, post-war,*

'a *pro-roads* campaign'

'a *sub-bottom* echo', '*sub-atomic* physics', '*sub-Saharan* Africa'

'a *trans-earth* orbit', 'a *trans-global* expedition', '*trans-phenomenal* perception'.

3.4 Nouns

Prefixed nouns may of course be nominalizations of prefixed verbs, like *decriminalization, disinfection, disinflation, misallocation, preselection, recirculation, subclassification.* Many prefixed deverbal nouns appear more familiar, or more likely to be used than the related verbs, which, if current at all, are likely to be perceived as backformations (11.3):

> *co-driver, counter-irritant, cross-reference, deregulation, disinhibition, hyper-ventilation, intercombination, misdiagnosis, misemphasis, multivibrator, predeliv-ery, precombustion, pre-intimation, rediffusion, resocialization, retro-analysis, sub-irrigation, supercharger, superconductor, super-infection.*

As we noted in 3.2, negatively prefixed verbs are hardly possible apart from rare cases of backformation, but deverbal nouns prefixed by *non-* are unremarkable:

> *non-adherence, non-alienation, non-arrival, non-communication, non-delivery, non-intervention, non-subscriber, non-voter.*

There are no base verbs corresponding to the following examples, which thus have to be understood as prefix + noun rather than prefixed verb + noun suffix:

co-executor, counter-espionage, misconjunction, pre-incarnation, rematch 'return match', *retrocognition, retropropulsion, superflow.*

Prefixed nouns may correspond to prefixed adjectives: *co-belligerent, counter-insurgent, non-Catholic, non-validity, semi-autonomy, supersensitivity, uninvolvement.* If the corresponding adjective is noun-based, the noun may be perceived as a backformation (11.3): *biprong* (a fork), *multi-hull* (a boat), *polyangle* (a figure with many angles), *precancer, pre-dawn*: 'So now I woke, in the pre-dawn of the desert' (OED: 1946), *prehistory, ultra-patriot, unicell* (a plant). Nouns related to adjectives and prefixed by negative *un-* are always obviously backformed, e.g. *uneducation*: 'It is not their uneducation but their education that I scoff at' (OED: 1936), 'a state of *unrepair*', *unsuccess, unsurprise.*

In formations with non-derived nouns, prefixes often have the character of modifiers, as in:

co-carcinogen 'substance that increases the carcinogenic effect of another substance', *counter-argument, hypermarket, interlanguage, interspace, pre-echo, pre-history, pre-primate, preschool* 'nursery school', *pre-verb, proto-artist, proto-planet, polyculture, poly-rhythm, monolayer, monoculture, supermind, super-cyclone, super-volcano, subcategory, sub-machine-gun.*

A non-hero is an unconventional kind of hero. Similar examples are illustrated in 'examples of Manchester non-architecture' (OED: 1960), 'Public men have learned to apply the technique of the non-answer' (OED: 1966), 'The ritual exchange of non-information' (OED: 1970), 'tarantula spiders among the bananas and other non-stories' (OED: 1973). The following nouns prefixed by *anti-* and *un-* are comparable: *anti-artist, anti-matter, anti-philosophy, anti-romance, anti-science, anti-virus; unbook*: 'Reading experts always need tricky new gimmicks to put in their unbooks' (OED: 1982), *uncountry*: 'In this uncountry there was blue sky and light' (OED: 1964), *un-death*: 'There is, every now and then, a film that escapes this sort of un-death' (OED: 1974).[6]

Dis-, or *dys-*, as this prefix is sometimes spelt in words typically confined to medical or other technical contexts, forms nouns which are antonyms of their nominalized or noun bases:

disanalogy: 'Risk is always involved in neglecting the *dis*analogy between the things compared' (OED: 1948), *disamenity* 'disadvantage of a locality', *diseconomy* 'increase in costs', *disequilibrium, disfluency, disimperialism* 'the reversal of imperialism': 'Rhodesia, where Britain faces its most painful test of disimperialism' (OED: 1962), *disincentive, disservice.*

In some cases, as in *disinformation* and *dysfunction*, the prefix is equivalent to 'faulty' or 'bad'.

Notes

1. The native prefix *with-*, unproductive since Middle English, meant 'against', hence Old English *wiðsecgan* 'renounce', 'contradict', 'deny'. In 'Sythe I have sayd it, I wyll never *withsay* it' (OED: 1530) we can see how a reversative sense could develop from a locative one.

2. See Brinton (1988, app. A) for a convenient characterization of the situation types 'state', 'activity', 'achievement' and 'accomplishment'.

3. In his account of Newspeak, Orwell does not discuss the negation of verbs, but he gives one interesting example of subclausal negation with a prefixed verb: 'Oldthinkers unbellyfeel Ingsoc', translating the verb as 'cannot have a full emotional understanding of'. The prefixed form is perhaps meant to accord with the general aim of suppressing opportunities for emphasis.

    Negatively prefixed verbs have occurred in another bizarre kind of language, 'cablese', illustrated in Evelyn Waugh's *Scoop* (1938), e.g. 'UNPROCEED LAKUWARDS STOP' i.e. 'Do not go to Laku'.

4. There are older examples of some now disused *un-* adjectives with simple stems, like *unglad*, *ungood*, *undeep*, *unwide*, but as Zimmer notes, none with 'negative' bases such as *unbad*. He points out (92) that *unsilly* was acceptable as long as its base meant 'innocent', but went out of use when *silly* could only mean 'foolish'. *Unsad* is a similar case: it was current in Middle English in the senses 'unstable', 'unserious', but only very exceptionally in the sense 'not miserable'.

5. Adamson (1990, 508–11) discusses the changing fortunes of negative prefixes in the light of a general tendency in semantic change towards greater subjectivity. *Un-*, occurring in many contrary opposites, has been productive for very much longer than *an-* and *non-*, which typically form neutral, contradictory opposites.

6. Nouns like these may once have been less marginal. A number of earlier examples are attested, e.g. Old English *unæt* 'gluttony', *uncræft* 'evil practice', *unswefn* 'bad dream', Middle English *unreason*, *unrest*.

4

Suffixes

4.1 Scope

The patterns of this chapter are chiefly non-transpositional and almost all noun-forming. There are no verb-to-verb suffixes in English, complex verbs with verbal bases being formed either with prefixes (3.2) or particles (5.2.1, 5.3).[1] The adjective-to-adjective pattern represented by adjective-based *cleanly*, *deadly*, *goodly*, *poorly*, *sickly* is not productive, but adjective bases can be suffixed by **-ish** to form adjectives paraphrasable as 'somewhat ADJECTIVE' or 'somewhat ADVERB'. Bases are generally simple, monosyllabic: *cheapish*, *clearish*, *crispish*, *loudish*, *sharpish*, *soonish*, *trueish*, or suffixed by *-y*: *busyish*, *dowdyish*, *earlyish*. Jespersen's observation (1942, 19.63) that such adjectives 'belong to colloquial language' is not quite accurate: they occur in a range of registers, though it is easy to find illustrations from speech, cf. '"True," said Bognor. "Or at least true-ish."' (OED: 1981); '"It was early," he said. "Quite earlyish."' (OED: 1968); 'Better be off sharpish if we're going to be home for tea' (OED: 1952).

As mentioned in 1.6, transpositional and non-transpositional patterns cannot always be sharply separated. In Chapter 2 we noted a few non-transpositional nouns in *-ee* (2.4.1) like *pickpocketee*, which, with noun bases relatable to events, were comparable with the deverbal examples. Alongside deverbal nouns in *-er* (2.4.1) there are numerous noun-based *-er* nouns. Like deverbal *-er* nouns, these can have a variety of referents – people: *hard-liner*, *islander*, *probationer*, animals: *porker*, *ratter*, and things: *two-wheeler*, *six-pounder*. Bases may also be adjectival (*foreigner*) or prepositional (*downer*), and phrasal bases are not uncommon (*do-it-yourselfer*).[2] Many of the noun-forming suffixes to be described below can be illustrated by a minority of transpositional examples with verbal or adjectival bases. However, it will be convenient to disregard this small degree of overlap with the patterns of Chapter 2.

The nouns of this chapter are discussed under three headings which describe their referents. Under the first are names for (human) individuals suffixed by **-ist**, **-eer**, **-ster** and **-nik** (4.2). The second heading subsumes 'diminutives', which as we shall see in 4.3 are not limited to words denoting small entities. The suffixes of this section are *-ess*, *-ette*, *-let*, *-ling*, *-oid* and a group, *-ie*, *-o*, *-sy*, *-y*, which mark the words they appear in as appropriate to very informal situations. The third group of formations, in 4.4, comprises chiefly non-count nouns belonging to various semantically related categories like 'state', 'realm' and 'collectivity' and suffixed by *-ism*, *-dom*, *-hood*, *-ship*, *-(e)ry* and *-age*. In all three sections we encounter many examples whose use may indicate an attitude: the description 'pejorative' has been used much more often in connection with noun-to-noun suffixed formations than it has in discussions of transposition or prefixation. Many patterns exhibit a particular kind of productivity – active over long periods but with comparatively few established examples.

4.2 Individuals

-ist (Greek *-istes*) is clearly genuinely productive: it is by far the most frequently employed of the suffixes in this group. The base of a noun in *-ist* is a noun or adjective which generally indicates the kind of activity or pursuit that characterizes its referent: *archaeologist, balloonist, careerist*, or a persuasion or belief of which its referent is an adherent: *behaviourist, devolutionist*. Often there is a corresponding noun in *-ism* or verb in *-ize*. Like the bases of *-ize* verbs (2.3.1), most bases of *-ist* nouns have two or more syllables with an unstressed syllable next to the suffix. Many bases are suffixed, often by *-al*, *-ation*, *-er*, *-ion* or *-ive*. Bases ending in two unstressed syllables generally lose a final vowel: *cartophilist, operettist, supremacist*. Unlike *-ize*, *-ist* attaches readily to bases ending in a stressed syllable, as in *defeatist* and *recordist*; monosyllabic bases, as in *Cubist, jazzist, stockist* are less frequent but by no means unusual.

The earliest English nouns with this suffix are medieval loans from Latin which have to do specifically with Christian concerns: *baptist, evangelist, exorcist, psalmist, Wycliffist*. The domain of *-ist* became very much wider in the course of the early modern period when the suffix combined with a great many bases relating to professional or cultural pursuits, sometimes substituting for *-er*. Nouns with *-graph-* as second element continued to take *-er*: *biographer, cinematographer*, but fourteenth-century *astronomer, astrologer, philosopher* contrast with later *economist, musicologist, theosophist*. Among many modern examples in *-ist* are:

> *activist, behaviourist, careerist, ceramicist, columnist, conservationist, descriptivist, environmentalist, existentialist, fantasist, fundamentalist, imagist, judoist, monetarist, nutritionist, projectionist, saxophonist, shootist*: 'A shootist is a man good with a gun' (OED: 1976), *trialist, voodooist, Yiddishist*.

In a small group of twentieth-century formations like *ageist, racist, sexist, sizist*, the base indicates the ground of a prejudice. Some *-ist* words may be sufficiently familiar in attributive use to be regarded as adjectives, like those in '*consumerist* outlook', '*escapist* fiction', '*leftist* rebels', '*modernist* doctrines', '*minimalist* sculpture', '*triumphalist* symbols'.

Two other suffixes, *-eer* and *-ster*, have appeared in new formations only occasionally, but over a long period of time; a fourth, *-nik* belongs to the last half-century. Nouns formed with all three reflect changing political or cultural preoccupations and are likely to have 'pejorative' overtones.

-eer (French *-ier*, Latin *-arius*) in nouns and related verbs is affixed in almost all cases to an unstressed syllable following a stressed syllable in bases which most often end in [n] or [t]: *allotmenteer, conventioneer, muleteer, puppeteer*. New formations in *-eer* have persisted since the middle and early modern English periods. OED records about 140 altogether. Coinages often evoke others with related meanings. An early sense of *engineer* is 'constructor of military engines'; other 'military' words are sixteenth-century *musketeer* and *targeteer* (1586); nineteenth-century *bayoneteer* and *cameleer*, denoting in de Quincey's definition (OED: 1837) a cuirassier mounted on a camel, and twentieth-century *pigeoneer*, 'a military pigeon-trainer', *infanteer* 'infantryman' and *weaponeer*. Words which evoke *engineer* in a modern sense are *gadgeteer, roboteer*, and *rocketeer* and *weaponeer* in the sense 'rocket or weapon scientist'. Another early sense of *engineer* is 'plotter', 'layer of snares', cf. 'that great engineer, Satan' (OED: *a* 1635), and later words in *-eer* are often similarly depreciative, like *pocketeer* (1635) 'pickpocket', *guillotineer* in 'Even persecutors and guillotineers get weary of their savage work' (OED: 1897), and twentieth-century *black marketeer* and *racketeer*. Some words concern political activity, like eighteenth-century *electioneer, factioneer, parliamenteer*, nineteenth-century *caucuseer, revolutioneering*, 'agitation for revolutions', and twentieth-century *patrioteer*, cf. 'They are quick to detect the phony and they can distinguish a patriot from a patrioteer' (OED: 1954), *pensioneering*: 'Pensioner, you can't trust the Labour Party. They are simply pensioneering . . .' (OED: 1959), *sanctioneer* and *summiteer*. Depreciatively-used words for speakers and writers include seventeenth-century *pulpiteer, sermoneer* and *sonneteer*, and eighteenth-century *garreteer* 'a literary hack'. Johnson famously notes of *gazetteer* (1611) 'journalist': 'it was lately a term of the utmost infamy' (1755). More modern examples are *conglomerateer*: 'Conglomerateers – people who buy an old bra company, change its name to Space Age Materials and go public' (OED: 1968), *coupleteer*, cf. 'The dreary coupleteers of the eighteenth century' (OED: 1927), *placardeer, leafleteer*, cf. 'The leafleteers have fairly polluted the streets this time' (OED: 1970), *jargoneer, sloganeer* and *science fictioneer* 'Some science fictioneers are plain old-style typewriter hacks' (OED: 1959).

Bases suffixed by native ***-ster*** are consistently monosyllabic. They may indicate an occupation, as in older *dyester* and *tapster*, or modern *jobster* 'jobber' and *pollster*. *Huckster* in Middle English is 'a retailer of small goods'; sixteenth-century uses carry an implication of dishonesty. Other sixteenth-century words are *bangster* 'a bully, a braggart', *gamester* 'prostitute' and 'gambler' and *lewdster*. *Gamester* in twentieth-century uses denotes 'sportsman', cf. *ringster* 'boxer'. Eighteenth-century *trickster* is still current, *shyster*, of uncertain origin, is nineteenth-century, as is another sense of *ringster* 'member of a political or price ring', cf. 'the unholy alliance of ringsters and politicians' (OED: 1875), and modern 'pejorative' examples include *fraudster*, *gangster* and *mobster*. Cf. also 'You wicked old fibster' (OED: 1861) and 'Such destruction has been launched on the face and form of England by witless plansters' (OED: 1964). Occasional coinages for speakers and writers have also persisted over a long period: *penster* (1611), 'a literary hack', *rhymester*, nineteenth-century *slangster* and *tonguester*, and twentieth-century *wordster*. Other modern formations include *jokester* and *prankster*; *bopster*, *popster*, *swingster* and *tunester*.[3]

-nik[4] appears in occasional twentieth-century loan-words from Russian and other Slavic languages, and Yiddish, e.g. *chetnik* 'a member of a guerilla force in the Balkans', *kibbutznik* 'a member of a kibbutz', *kolkhoznik* 'a member of a kolkhoz', *nudnik* 'a bore', and *sputnik*, the name of the Russian space satellite launched in 1957, the last example giving rise to various ephemeral formations such as *dognik*, its passenger, and *Yanknik*, an American satellite, which failed (*flopnik*, *goofnik*).

-nik nouns in English include *computernik*, *hold-upnik*, *no-goodnik* (cf. Russian *negodnik*), *refusenik*, a Russian calque, 'person refused permission to immigrate to Israel', *robotnik*, as in 'a society of automata, robotniks and helots' (OED: 1960), *stuck-upnik*. Another, *beatnik* (1955), the base of which, Webster (1961) suggests, evokes *beaten*, 'exhausted', cf. *dead-beat*, figured for some decades as a 'leader-word' (1.3) for formations relating to a cluster of related notions. These include the rejection of conventional standards, e.g. *far-outnik*, *way-outnik*, *straightnik*, cf. ' "Straightniks" (also known as normals) in New York City are always trying to assimilate, to be a little colored, Jewish, gay, etc.' (Alan Rinzler, *The New York Spy*, 1967, 388); the arts, as in *discothequenik*, *folknik*, *popnik*, *rocknik*, and political dissidence, as in *peacenik*, *limpnik* (in reference to the tactic of going limp in the hands of the police), *protestnik*: 'those guitar-plunking protestniks' (OED: 1965), *Vietnik* 'opponent of military involvement in Vietnam'.

4.3   Diminutives

The patterns that can be labelled 'diminutive' are various. The suffixes *-ess*, *-ette*, *-let*, *-ling* and *-oid* occur in one or more of a range of related senses to form words denoting females, or entities which are small, or entities which resemble something indicated in the base, or which are imitations. In a discussion of the relatedness of these concepts, which in many languages share a mode of expression, Jurafsky (1993, 1996) argues that the notion 'small' is central. Adjective-forming *-ish* is cognate with a Greek diminutive suffix and, as we have seen, the notions of 'resemblance' and 'approximation' are lexicalized in adjectives like *childish* (2.4.2) and *cheapish* (4.1) respectively. Other formations in this section, ending in *-ie* or *-y*, *-sy* and *-o*, invariably carry pragmatic overtones such as those of affection or contempt, which are also often evoked by words for females, small things, approximations and imitations.

English words in which a suffix indicates femaleness are not common. *-ster* often but not always in Old English indicates a female agent: *fipelestre* 'female fiddler', *lærestre* 'female teacher'; though *bæcestre* 'baker', *seamestre* 'tailor' denote individuals of either sex. Some Middle English words appear to be exclusively feminine in reference, as in Chaucer's *Pardoner's Tale*: 'And right anon thanne comen tombesteres [tumblers, dancing girls] Fetys and smale, and yonge frutesteres [(female) fruit-sellers]' (477–8), but by this time formations in *-ster* commonly denoted men as well.[5] The exclusively female-denoting suffix *-ess*, from Greek *basilissa* 'queen', via late Latin words for individuals in the ecclesiastical sphere such as *canonissa* 'canoness' and French words like *princess, hostess, lioness*, figures only in a small number of established English words for female counterparts such as *goddess, manageress, stewardess, waitress*. Words with other bases, like *clerkess* (cf. 'She was clerkess in an office' OED: 1965) are very rarely used.[6]

Words in *-ette*, also from French, are semantically varied. A few, like *proette* 'female professional golfer', *suffragette* and *usherette*, denote female referents. OED records about fifteen twentieth-century coinages denoting females, very few of which have had any sustained or serious use, cf. *bachelorette, hoboette, patrolette*. *-ette* also occurs in some words for 'imitations' like *cashmerette, flannelette, leatherette, suedette*, and in a few words whose referents resemble in some way the concept denoted by the base: *caravanette* 'a motorized caravan', *launderette, sleeperette* 'reclining seat'. More often, however, diminutive significance is uppermost, as in *balconette, brickette, featurette, kitchenette, ovenette, roomette, statuette, superette* 'a small supermarket', *terracette* 'a small natural terrace'. Bases are most often of more than one syllable, and the suffix bears the main stress.

-let is the result of the reanalysis of French diminutive *-et* suffixed to bases ending in *-l*, as in *owlet*. It occurs, more productively than the other suffixes of this section, in words for small entities, occasionally animate, e.g. *chieflet* 'a petty chief', *mouselet, shrikelet, swiftlet*, but much more often inanimate, e.g. *bomblet, booklet, cloudlet, filmlet, flatlet, plantlet, spinelet, streamlet*. *Starlet*, unusually, has female as well as diminutive significance. Bases are usually of one syllable, though cf. *chamberlet* 'a minute chamber or cavity', *pinnaclet* 'a small pinnacle'.

-ling is also reanalysed, from Old English *-ing* indicating an individual, as in *flyming* 'fugitive', added to bases ending in *-l*, as in *lytling* 'little one'. Old English nouns in *-ling*, like *ræpling* 'prisoner' (from *ræpan* 'to bind'), are

not diminutives: their bases indicate only something which characterizes the individual named. *Gutterling* 'one bred in a gutter' is a nineteenth-century formation on the Old English pattern: 'After a week's experience as a gutter-ling of the fashionable world' (OED: 1846). Forming words with diminutive significance in Middle English (*youngling, nestling*), the suffix subsequently appeared in a series of nouns denoting young animals or plants like *duckling* and *oakling*. Similar modern formations include *spiderling, waspling, seedling, sporeling* 'a young plant developed from a spore'. Like *-let, -ling* attaches pri-marily to words of one syllable: a number of bases of this kind occur with either suffix: *crablet* and *crabling, fruitlet* and *fruitling, sharklet* and *sharkling*.

   -oid, from a Greek element meaning 'having the form or likeness of', forms adjectives and nouns, often in combination with stems (9.4.2). Nouns in *-oid* have referents which resemble or approximate in some way to those of their bases. Examples are *factoid* 'something accepted as a fact but prob-ably not the case', cf. 'A record not of the actual truth but a series of semi-fictional factoids' (OED: 1987), *meteoroid, mineraloid, planetoid, spheroid*. Among those with stem bases are *hominoid* 'an animal resembling man', *schizoid* 'person with schizophrenia-like symptoms', *vocoid* 'vowel-like sound', *satelloid* 'a satellite with an engine', *toxoid* 'a modified toxin'.

   Not surprisingly, diminutive formations are liable to figure in contexts in which there is an implication of affection, irony, playfulness or contempt. The implication 'inferior' is now part of the meaning of *novelette*, earlier 'a short novel', 'a story'. Cf. also the use of *lecturette* illustrated in 1.5. *Earthling* in a sixteenth-century use denotes a lowly being in 'Wee (of all earthlings) are Gods vtmost subiects' (OED: 1593), as it does in 'An Earthling has no good way to estimate the age of a Martian' (OED: 1949). Some examples are clearly created just for such contexts:

> 'the pretty little cataractettes playing at leap-frog' (OED: 1849); 'the kind of stuff that émigré rhymsterettes wrote after Akhmatova' (OED: 1957); '"How about a drinkette?", said Helen' (cited by Bauer 1998, 68); 'The gossamer conceits of our bardlet' (OED: 1867); 'Very serviceable in teach-ing some dukelets and their good ladies better manners' (OED: 1870); 'The strong able-bodied ones go off to the Colonies and only the weedlings remain' (OED: 1911).

   The formations considered so far in this section, however, are unlike the 'situational' diminutive expressions common in some other languages like German, Greek, Italian and Polish. Such diminutives occur regularly in – and only in – certain affective and interactive situations, e.g. Italian 'Non supporto i tuoi trucch*etti*', 'I can't stand your little tricks', Greek 'perimenete ena lept*aki*', 'wait a minute', Polish 'pomidor*ka*', '[would you like a] tomato?'[7] Situational formations – which include 'augmentatives', expressive of 'large-ness' and related concepts, as well as diminutives – are often taken to be the products of a distinct kind of word formation with its own rules. Their meanings are predictable: they are synonymous with the neutral words that form their bases. Bases are not restricted as to word class, and a sequence of suffixes within a word may have a cumulative effect. As Dressler and Merlini-Barbaresi put it, such words 'modify the whole speech act in the given speech situation' (1994, 395). This kind of word formation is not found in English, but there are some English formations which are comparable in that they are confined to informal affective or interactive situations and very often have more formal non-suffixed synonyms.

-kin, from Dutch or Flemish, in a few long-established words like *catkin* and *manikin* and older names like *Watkin* and *Perkin*, may occasionally occur in utterances like 'our domesticated tigerkin' (OED: 1849), 'He'll be with me most of the time – the lovekins will' (OED: 1925).

'Hypocoristic' nouns suffixed by *-ie* or *-y*, often with shortened bases (see 11.5), are always associated with informality and with an attitude, of affection, contempt, or familiarity. The term *hypocoristic* is from a Greek word meaning 'pet name'. Hypocoristic nouns are often animate, e.g. denominal *bookie, cabby, chappie, clippie* '(female) bus conductor', *doggie, druggy* 'addict', *groupie, foodie, townie,* and de-adjectival *baddie, fatty, lefty, meany, toughie.* Examples with inanimate referents include *nightie, quickie, thingy.*

-o with noun and adjective bases evokes various attitudes according to context, as in the nouns *boyo* and *kiddo*: 'Have I ever let you down, kiddo?' (OED: 1938), *thicko, scruffo, wino, wrongo,* cf. 'You look like a couple of wrongos to me' (OED: 1985), and *yobbo,* adjectival or adverbial *cheapo,* cf. 'You can buy that cheapo, cos no one wants it' (OED: 1967), *sleazo, starko* 'naked', *stinko* 'drunk', and the noun and adjective pairs *pinko,* cf. 'He made Ronald Reagan look like a pinko liberal' (OED: 1972), *weirdo* and *whizzo,* cf. 'a proper whizzo party with marks on the ceiling' (OED: 1968).

Adjectives *comfy, pervy* and *sarky* have shortened adjective bases. Adjectives in *-sy* are adjective-based, e.g. *cutesy,* or noun-based: *ballsy* 'spirited', *booksy*: 'I'm going to . . . snitch him away from your booksy conversations' (OED: 1958), *folksy, homesy*: 'A homesy, folksy account of a small town boy called Jason' (OED: 1953), *palsy, pubsy*: 'the pubsy, Fitzrovian atmosphere of Lord Longford's party' (OED: 1977), *tricksy.*

Non-plural *-s,* as in *ducks,* sometimes attaches to another attitudinal suffix, as in *lovekins* (above) and *walkies.*[8]

4.4 States, realms and other non-individual entities: *-ism, -dom, -hood, -ship, -(e)ry, -age*

The nouns of this section do not name individuals. Most have a range of non-count senses, and a minority of count nouns have senses relatable to these. The contribution to the vocabulary of words formed with these suffixes – with the exception of -*ism* – is moderate or low,[9] though new formations can always be found, a situation reflected in comments like the following in OED under -*hood*, -*dom* and -*ship* respectively: '-*hood* can be affixed at will to almost any word denoting a person or concrete thing . . . so that the number of these derivatives is indefinite. Nonce-formations are numerous'; '-*dom* is . . . freely employed to form nonce-derivatives'; 'In certain uses the suffix [-*ship*] lends itself more or less freely to the formation of nonce-words'. Some examples (from OED) of words with the same base and different suffixes suggest a degree of substitutability:

'This critical cocksuredom' (1883); 'That magnificent cocksureism' (1899); '. . . in something very like pariah-hood' (1936); 'Forgetful of the gaol and his pariahdom' (1887); 'its absence set a stamp of servility and pariahship on the prescribed caste' (1920); 'I . . . joined in the dreadful rebelry' (1893); 'never mind his rebeldom of the other day' (1859); 'The mere clerkage . . . hundreds, perhaps thousands of them' (1829); 'The worst of bureaucracies, a permanent clerkery' (1885).

Coordinated examples also point to some interchangeability.

'Crushed down in the struggles of authorship and artistdom' (1861); 'The winning ways of catdom and kittenhood' (1890); '. . . one who has come up in the world from sneak-thiefery and gangsterdom' (1923).

The polysemy exhibited by words with this group of suffixes is more extensive and more complex than in any other area of word formation. Examples are very often interpretable only in relation to a context. OED's definitions in fact often do not quite match the illustrations given, relying implicitly as they do on the reader's familiarity with a range of possible senses. In the following pages we shall look at the extent to which the suffixes are really interchangeable, and at the relationships linking the various senses of words containing them, drawing extensively on OED's illustrations of items dated between 1800 and 1985. Examples are from OED except where otherwise indicated. Some of the 'nonce' examples given may appear unfamiliar, but I have assumed that there has been no essential change in the uses of these suffixes during this period. In demonstrating the polysemy of nouns formed with each suffix, I have distinguished 'major' and 'minor' senses. Major senses are defined as those represented by more than fifty examples recorded in OED since 1800. Each suffix is associated with two or three major senses and one or more minor ones, found in smaller groups of examples.

-ism

Bases of *-ism* nouns are, like those of *-ize* verbs and *-ist* nouns, predominantly foreign-derived nouns and adjectives. 'State' or 'condition' is a common meaning of nouns in *-ism*:

> Blondism in Europe may be less than 10,000 years old. (1965)

Examples like these include those denoting a pathological condition, e.g. *adrenalism, euthyroidism, Parkinsonism*. Another sense of *-ism* nouns is 'activity':

> Will *Pravda's* rash critic now be found to have indulged in right-wing diversionism and petty-bourgeois wrecking? (1955)

A third major sense, virtually peculiar to *-ism*, occurs in nouns like *Marxism, revisionism, rightism*, which can be defined with the use of expressions like 'system of belief', 'theory', 'principles':

> He suggested a philosophy of the absurd, and his subsequent work has been an affirmation of 'absurdism' in politics and ethics, as well as in metaphysics. (1954)

The independent use of *ism* corresponds to this 'belief' sense, cf. 'Movement towards "Communism", or "totalitarianism", or . . . whatever one's preferred "ism" . . . happens to be' (1963).

In a few 'belief' words (cf. the comparable examples in *-ist* in 4.2), the base indicates the ground of a prejudice, like *ageism, sexism, bike-ism*: 'So my next resolution is fixed, to continue to work against "bike-ism", discrimination against any kind of cyclist . . .' (Guardian: 1998) and *speciesism*: 'Animals have rights . . . There are forms of "speciesism" as corrupting as "racism" or "sexism"' (1982). Another minor pattern is that of count nouns denoting an instance of a kind of activity, usually a peculiarity of expression, like *colloquialism, Devonshirism, Edwardianism, Micawberism, Westernism*. These represent a readily extendable group.

-dom

Nouns suffixed by native *-dom* have as bases everyday words of one or two syllables, whose referents are usually animate, though cf. *cabdom, oildom, motordom, slumdom. -dom* nouns often denote 'state':

> '[They] had not yet emerged from this early condition of apedom' (1853); '. . . as men leave brutedom behind' (1890); 'the increasing cipherdom of

its young tormented hero' (1964); 'During my father's clerkdom' (1886); 'Discomfort . . . that goes with the bondage of . . . lodgerdom' (1927); 'She was withering towards old-maiddom' (1920); 'She emerged from this Ripvanwinkledom feeling and sounding better than she has in ten years' (1956); 'Today the possibilities of social refugeedom are just as great' (1968); 'Most of [the estate] has reverted to slumdom' (Guardian: 1997); 'Yuppiedom does not conduce to a realistic view of the human condition' (1984).

Many -*dom* words refer to animate 'collectivities':

'Cabdom is furious against the railway companies' (1868); 'Manhattan dollardom trooped into the Ritz-Carlton carrying flasks' (1920); 'An age when organized gangdom had no voice in the government' (1935); '[He is] the darling of North London luvviedom, who mention his name approvingly' (Guardian: 1998); 'the manners of youth being . . . superior to those of grown-updom' (1900); 'Its long combat with German Professordom' (1870); 'Restrictions . . . are such as to drive the whole of Russian studentdom into a common camp of protest' (1899); 'touristdom in flocks' (1888).

Many examples have a sense exclusive to -*dom*: the non-count sense of 'realm' illustrated in:

'the oldest inhabitant of cameldom' (1885); 'a careless young athlete's adventures in crookdom' (1929); 'This . . . championship, most prestigious in golfdom' (1971); 'a voice that was recognizable throughout maoridom' (1974); 'The "progressive" metropolises of motordom' (1961); 'The new order immediately precipitated a fresh quarrel in oildom' (1926); 'She . . . spread her unconscious influence throughout teacherdom' (1908); 'His directions are easy enough; but applying them to his bit of south-east London villadom involves finding a Chinese chip shop' (Guardian: 1997); 'this was a gathering of the kings of wastreldom' (1931).

A fairly small number of count nouns in -*dom* (about twenty recorded since 1800) have the minor sense of '(politically or otherwise) defined territory':

'Into this huddledom . . . came a youth' (1923); 'Reverence has few dedicated Temples in the Babeldom of nineteenth century England' (1882); 'The early Aryans [were] . . . split up into a number of small states or citydoms' (1862); 'Cook is fond of the animal, because he has cleared her cookdom of this insect pest' (1874); '. . . provinces, susceptible of being easily broken off the Shahdom' (1884).

An obvious model or leader-word for these is *kingdom*.[10] *Earldom* can fit this pattern but is more likely to be used in another minor sense, 'title', like the formations in 'All old quartermasters . . . look forward to the cookdom, as the cardinals look to the popedom' (1929).

-hood

Like -*dom*, native -*hood* attaches generally to one- or two-syllable bases. Most bases have animate referents, but there are a very few words with inanimate noun bases like *islandhood*: 'It is the insularity (the islandhood, so to say, of the islands . . .' (1862) and *sentencehood*: '. . . an adequate theory of English 'sentencehood' (1961). 'State' is the most frequent meaning of nouns in -*hood*, as in:

> 'They were citizens . . . longing to return to their citizenhood' (1871); 'the reality of our own ego-hood' (1873); 'A man . . . cannot glide into complete farmerhood' (1890); 'Sentenced to a compulsory hermithood in a hideous African desert' (1938); 'Genuine outsiderhood, as experienced by . . . a whole host of people' (1958); 'A sense of peoplehood is growing' (1958); 'the contemporary cult of victimhood' (Guardian: 1997).

'State' examples include an appreciable number which, like *childhood*, denote a stage of life, as in 'their years of flapperhood' (1921); 'those who had left studenthood behind' (1910); 'Little Froggies which have just emerged from tadpole-hood' (1891); 'the physical transition from infancy to early toddlerhood . . .' (1976).

The other chief meaning of -*hood* nouns is '(animate) collectivity':

> 'A mass of struggling anthood' (1879); 'Attitudinising creatures, like too many of the companionhood' (1877); 'an extensive cousinhood was already settled there' (Dan Jacobson, *Heshel's Kingdom*, 1998, 62); 'The well-preserved dowagerhood of Hampton Court' (1891); 'The powdered footmanhood of London' (1862); 'The belief . . . that he had sufficient influence with the officerhood of Gordon's force to buy them over' (1884); 'There is another side to this story, which the suburbanhood of Manchester would like greatly to tell' (1879).

As most of these examples suggest, 'collectivity' -*hood* nouns are typically definite and modified, unlike the majority of -*dom* formations with the same sense, which are usually indefinite. Compare for example 'Benedictions delivered gratis from the beggarhood of the city' (1843) with 'The kindly hospitality of the farmers on whose charity beggardom mainly throve' (1882), and 'If the girlhood of the Pacific slope are half as innocent as they are insolent . . .' (1883) with 'His house was ringed all day and half the night by gazing girldom' (1955).

Knighthood is established in the minor sense of 'title'; *fatherhood* has this sense in 'The House decided informally that the Fatherhood rested with whoever had been longest in the House' (1899). One well-established example in *-hood* fits no pattern: *neighbourhood* in the sense 'area', perhaps a development from the sense 'vicinity' as in the phrase *in the neighbourhood of.* The first clear case in OED, 'All the camps in this neighbour-hood quite quiet', is dated 1813.

-ship

-ship is a native suffix, but its bases are often foreign in origin, as in *accompliceship, commissionership, librarianship, musicianship, partisanship.* Nouns in *-ship* often refer to 'states':

'This House sees no reason to abandon bipartisanship in British foreign policy' (1952); 'I, who left fanship when I was seventeen, started out on the goose chase for Menjou' (1928); 'the development of his ghostship into godship' (1891); 'The flour industry gave the late Mr. Charles A. Pillsbury the means of millionaireship' (1901); 'That other fiction, the Pope's prisonership in the Vatican' (1906).

A number of 'state' nouns have bases which suggest such leader-words as *friendship* or *relationship*, e.g. 'united by the ties of guestship' (1868); 'His long, intimate palship with Marlon "Bud" Brando' (1974); 'The premature sweetheartship that existed between them' (1898).

Another major sense of nouns in *-ship* is 'activity', often relating to the exercise of skill. The referents of base nouns are often agents or roles:

'it was his axemanship that was needed' (1961);[11] '. . . his vigorous batsmanship (OED: 1907); 'feats of drivership' (1860); 'Entrepreneur-ship . . . might be common to all developing economies' (1959); 'This is indunaship – this is ruling' (1955); 'His . . . irrepressibly assertive mentorship' (1905); 'It was indeed a triumph of reportship: they gave the artiste's *rôles*, her lap-dog's photo' (1912); 'some masterly ringmastership on the part of the party chairman' (1966); 'a sine qua non of successful tycoonship' (1976).

Many count nouns in *-ship* denote an office, and usually also the title associated with it:

'The public esteem for the institution of the Kabakaship in Buganda' (1960); 'The out-ridership was claimed by two Fellows' (1901); 'The Kaisership is the old Presidency of the Bund plus the warlordship' (1913).

There are a few nouns in *-ship* with a 'collectivity' sense, as we saw in 1.3. *Contributorship, listenership, readership, subscribership* and *viewership* have bases associated with a particular area of activity. Other examples are *butlership* (1.3), *landownership*: 'England's landownership will never be without the representatives . . . of her ancient Aristocracy' (1867) and *leadership*: 'We had an early dinner this evening . . . for . . . the Leadership on both sides and their wives' (1964). Another minor group of *-ship* formations are mock honorific expressions such as 'their Dollarships' (1869), 'her elephantship' (1882), 'your youthship' (1966).

-e(r)y

In words of French provenance this suffix represents either *-erie*, or *-er*, *-ier* + *-ie* (Latin *-ia*). In modern English words it may appear to be one suffix, as in *birdery* 'a collection of birds', or a sequence, *-er* + *-y*, as in *fibbery* 'the practice of a fibber'. Formally, the suffix in *antlery* 'antlers collectively' and *cindery* 'a cinder-heap' is just *-y*. I have included cases like all of these, but not examples on the pattern of words whose ending represents Latin *-arium*, like *aviary* or *signary* 'an arrangement of signs', or examples like *bardolatry*, in which *-ry* is part of a Greek compound element. Bases of *-ery* are nouns and occasionally verbs and adjectives often of one syllable, which may be part of a longer expression: *control freakery, tit-for-tattery*. *-ry* occurs after an unstressed syllable, though not one containing a diphthong: *comradery, missilery, gradgrindery*, or, usually, one which constitutes a compound-element: *blacksmithery, eggheadery, whizz-kiddery, windbaggery*. Bases do not usually end in a vowel, though *cherryry* 'a collection of cherry-trees', *gewgawry*, and *gypsyry* are attested.

Many *-(e)ry* words have an 'activity' sense:

'The tale of back-stabbery in an Oxford college' (Guardian 1998); 'The ponderous banditry which the Chinese dignify by the name of war' (1924); 'I was engaged in some boffinery in a blasted back-room unit' (1960); '. . . while Tom's up to crookery of some sort' (1962); 'The now familiar recipe of aggressive demagoguery and muck-raking' (1959); 'Some road-hoggery was due to the imperfect construction of the motor car' (1965); 'a reign of snoopery and an encouragement of informers' (1981); 'The Western dislike of time-wasting summitry' (1958); 'Falk decided to indulge in a bit of extracurricular tycoonery' (1956); 'The visit was a mixture of old-fashioned glad-handing and soapboxery' (Guardian: 1997); 'a parliamentary year which has seen . . . a handsome output of windbaggery' (Guardian: 1996).

Many denote 'collectivities', often (unlike *blackguardry* and *wagery*) of inanimates:

'amongst the blackguardry of London' (1853); 'Artificial componentry . . . is a great deal faster than the natural mechanism of the brain' (1959); 'Senator John's subcommittee also had attacked what it called excessive "gimmickry and gadgetry" in today's war-planes' (1952); 'sixteen musket-balls, besides smaller missilery in profusion' (1990); 'Two generations of wagery were to live their squalid life . . . before we find singers . . . grasping the true meaning of industrial oppression' (1917).

-(e)ry nouns may also name locations connected in some way with the entities or activities indicated by their bases, as in: 'Large fibro-tiled Home, 3 bedrooms, . . . toolshed, fernery, garage' (1969). Further examples include places connected with eating: *carvery* 'buffet or restaurant where meat is carved', *eatery, noshery, servery, snackery*; with commercial activities: *bindery, cannery, cokery* 'coke-furnace', *cocoonery* 'place for rearing silkworms and obtaining cocoons', *packery, smeltery, washery*; with animals: *cattery, mousery* 'place where mice are bred or kept', *piggery, quailery, rabbitry, rookery, snakery*. In some cases the notions of 'collectivity' and 'place' are not separable, as in 'The occasional disturbance of this populous mousery by the visits of Owls' (1888); 'The Adélie penguinry was but a mile or two away' (1921).

Count nouns in *-(e)ry* name the result of activity, or an instance of it: 'There were none of the peacockeries, whims and fancies, . . . gimcrackeries . . . which proclaim the chamber of a young man' (1882); 'some ill-tempered snideries' (1978).

-age[12]

Bases suffixed by *-age* may be verbal or nominal; they are often mono-syllabic. Many *-age* nouns, like *breakage, coverage, leverage, outage, seepage* and *spillage*, denote 'activity', its result, or an instance of it:

> 'under the chaperonage of a guide' (1857); 'Special oil throwers are pro-vided to prevent the creepage of oil along the shaft' (1903); 'This place had many accidents by floodage and by fire' (1864); 'Other films employ a method known as narratage, in which one of the characters . . . is depicted as telling the story' (1948); 'Scrappage of passenger cars in 1948' (1948); 'Screenage of eye applicators by substances of low or medium atomic weight' (1940); 'The basement-beds below it, formed of the strewage of older land-surfaces' (1940).

Among nouns in *-age* that can be glossed 'collectivity', the majority have a meaning like 'amount of some entity seen as a substance or mass', as in *acreage, roughage, voltage, wattage* and *yardage*:

> 'The figures . . . showed the daily gallonage achieved' (1936); 'The dark slates that form the universal roofage' (1867); 'More than half the total

seatage' (1889); 'the slender tubage heaves and throbs' (1896), 'Our rail-roads have about 170,000 miles of trackage' (1896); 'The umbered purple loom of the birch twigage' (1923); 'to fill the voidage left by the natural depletion' (1966); 'The weedage, leafage, and flowers have been painted white' (1866).

Conforming to an old pattern represented by a small number of exam-ples, and illustrated in the medieval phrase *tonnage and poundage*, formations in *-age* can indicate an amount of something charged for, or the charge itself:[13]

'Each company was put to the expense . . . of several thousand pounds in clerkage' (1883); 'Normal day rate together with a plusage for reaching a certain level of output' (1962); 'From April 2 imported tinned marmalade will be available on points . . . The pointage will be announced later' (1944); 'Costs . . . such as . . . harbour dues, warehousage' (1915); 'telegrams will carry a fixed charge irrespective of wordage' (1958).

As these illustrations show, each suffix has a different range of major senses.

	'state'	'activity'	'belief'	'collectivity'	'realm'	'place'	'office'
-ism	+	+	+				
-dom	+			+	+		
-hood	+			+			
-ship	+	+					+
-(e)ry		+		+		+	
-age		+		+			

A number of familiar, and troublesome, problems of lexical semantics are raised by the polysemy of words with these suffixes. One question is whether we can identify some senses as basic, and others as extensions of them. In identifying the basic sense of single words, we may choose the earliest, or the most securely established. We may choose the most frequent sense, or the sense which we feel to be most closely related to human experience, or the sense from which the development of others may be most naturally traced (Cruse 2000, 199–201). In considering the relatedness of derivational patterns, it seems reasonable to see the last three as especially relevant.[14] 'Activity' seems more basic than 'office' in *-ship* nouns, many of which are found in both these senses, e.g. 'I felt that a little saleswomanship might be a good thing' (1977) and 'Gloria held the assistant pet-food saleswomanship in . . . a Shepherds Bush emporium' (1973). Among nouns in *-(e)ry* and *-age*, 'activity' is the most frequently occurring sense. The 'collectivity' sense of *snobbery* and *vagabondage* in 'The admiration of all the "snobbery" of London' (1887) and 'the whole vagabondage of the country' (1855) can be seen as metonymically related to the 'activity' sense, as in 'Snobbery, like murder, will out' (1943), and 'he . . . betook himself to vagabondage' (1871). Dickens's definition of *growlery* points to a similar kind of connection between 'place' and 'activity': 'this, you must know, is the Growlery. When I am out of humour, I come and growl here' (*Bleak House*, 1853, ch. 8). It seems clear that the count senses of nouns in -*ism* and -*dom* in words like *Americanism* and *kingdom* are derivable from non-count senses rather than the other way round, though whether speakers feel that there is a connection is a matter for doubt.

To take another case, compare the 'realm' uses of *oildom* and *motordom* illustrated above with the 'collectivity' uses in 'At the news all oildom rushed into the streets' (1904) and 'Fashionable motordom halted at the Hôtel des Grottes' (1916). In this case both are non-count and it is not clear that one sense is more basic than the other. Rather, like the meanings of words such as *newspaper*, 'institution' or 'copy', and *window* 'opening' or 'frame', the relationship is bidirectional. Each guarantees the possibility of the other, and this conclusion is supported by the fact that an appreciable number of -*dom* nouns are found in both senses.

The examples given so far in this section have been chosen to illustrate distinct senses, but many others remain ambiguous in their contexts. Illustrations of many examples in -*ism*, such as *consumerism* or *conformism*, do not force a choice between 'belief' and 'activity'. *Blimpism* and *outsiderism* in the following may be seen as exemplifying more than one of the 'state', 'activity' and 'belief' senses: 'Blimpism, plus the Cairene climate, are two of Hitler's strongest weapons' (1943); 'His "outsiderism" made him enjoy shocking the professional scientists' (1958). In some illustrations of -*dom* nouns it is hardly possible to decide whether 'collectivity' or 'realm' is more salient, as in 'One of filmdom's finest mansions is Pickfair' (1927), 'Even dingy lodgerdom would disclaim the place' (1905), 'the most comprehensive documentary I have seen so far about West Coast hippiedom' (1969). We can regard such examples as genuinely ambiguous, or, alternatively, as having a single vague sense which in many circumstances need not be made more precise.

We began this section by noting that, on the evidence of synonyms, the six suffixes seem to be to some degree interchangeable. Complex words are not usually formed if a word in the sense required is already available (Rainer 1988). *Authorship* is sufficiently well established to make the appearance of *authorhood, authordom or authorism* not very likely. But, as we have seen, there are many occasional, infrequently used and therefore little known formations with these suffixes. Consequently (allowing for the difficulty of pinpointing sameness of meaning) it is not surprising that we find synonyms, *pariah-hood, pariahdom* and *pariahism* for example, beside *pariahship*, all with the sense 'condition of being a pariah'.

We sometimes also find a word with a suffix used in a sense not customarily associated with that suffix. The 'belief' sense normally unique to -*ism* for example can occasionally be seen in nouns suffixed by -*dom*: 'The trouble with Outsiderdom as a philosophy is the squalid assortment of fellow travellers it attracts' (1961). (Compare *outsiderism* above.) Nouns in -(*e*)*ry* are also occasionally comparable with -*ism* nouns with the 'belief' sense. Compare 'There have been too many episodes . . . which reflect the spirit of kluxery' (1949) with '. . . carrying the flambeau of kluxism' (1929). Cf. also 'I doubt whether even a twelfth of the astronomers of our time favour "Sunspottery"' (1882), and 'Wenzel gave no support to Wycliffry' (1900).

Nouns in -*dom* and -*hood* rarely denote 'activity', but some examples can be found:

'. . . goaded to frequent outbursts of savagedom by hunger' (1889); 'the practice of spydom' (1859); 'the sublime art of scribbledom' (1887)

'Margaret would not spoil the boy by over-fosterhood' (1834); '. . . to put an end to the system of robberhood in this part of the country' (1863); 'To decipher a double palimpsest calls for the masterhood of a Tischendorf' (1875).

Nouns in -*ery* and -*age* denoting 'state' are unusual, but attested:

'It will be Clinton's fate to watch his own descent into lame-duckery' (Guardian: 1998); 'the result depends largely on whether the overdog has stopped believing in his own overdoggery' (1962); 'He had fallen . . . to the lowest depth of the most snubbed hen-peckery' (1838); 'I wonder when people will begin to realise what wagery means' (1917)

'In the days of his recruitage' (1884); 'many a man is reduced to a state of dronage' (1875).

There are a very few count nouns in -*ship* denoting 'territory' on the pattern of the established sense of *kingdom*, but they do occasionally occur:

'Lugdunum became . . . the favourite cityship and ordinary abiding-place of the emperors' (1870); 'Until then the nation had consisted of a number of separate stateships' (1917).

The degree of variation shown by these suffixes is much greater than that found with other patterns of word formation. Among the major senses distinguished, 'state', 'activity' and 'collectivity' are each associated with four suffixes. -*dom* and -*hood*, attaching to bases of the same kind, appear especially substitutable for one another in nouns with the 'state' sense. But otherwise, there are some limits to intersubstitutability. As we have seen, there are appreciable differences among 'collectivity' nouns in *-dom*, *-hood*, *-(e)ry* and *-age*. Some combinations of pattern and sense appear not to be allowable at all: no suffix other than *-dom* occurs in words with the non-count 'realm' sense; an *-ism* noun cannot denote a 'collectivity', and only *-(e)ry* nouns can denote 'places'. *-ism* almost has a monopoly on 'belief', and *-ship* on 'office'. Despite the many cases of overlap, we can conclude that the domains of these suffixes remain largely distinguishable.

Notes

1. A few pairs of verbs like *fall* and *fell*, *lie* and *lay*, *rise* and *raise*, *sit* and *set* are relics of an earlier derivational relationship between causative and non-causative verbs. Changes in transitivity, as for example in *John is cooking the rice* and *the rice is cooking*, are now of course not a derivational matter.
2. In a comprehensive description of *-er* noun formation, Ryder (1999) discusses the various kinds of meanings that *-er* nouns can have, and the cognitive factors involved in the selection of verbal, nominal and other bases. (See also 12.1.)
3. Lubbers (1965) cites and discusses a great many examples of nouns suffixed by *-ster*.
4. Bauer (1983, 256–66) discusses a number of coinages and investigates the formal and semantic characteristics of their bases.
5. In Jespersen's view, *-ster* was originally neutral as to gender. Von Lindheim (1958, 494ff) disagrees.
6. Nouns marked as feminine are of course not necessarily associated with disparagement, especially in languages in which they are frequent. See Malkiel's (1966, 356–61) discussion of male and female agentives in a number of languages.
7. Examples from Dressler and Merlini-Barbaresi (1994, 114), Sifianou (1992, 161) and Wierzbicka (1984, 128). See Dressler and Merlini-Barbaresi (1994) for an extended and detailed discussion of such situations, collectively characterized by them as 'non-serious' (395). Scalise (1986, 131–3) discusses some Italian diminutive suffixes. Wierzbicka (1984) includes a short discussion of Australian 'depreciatives' like *prezzie* and *barbie* in an account of Polish diminutive names and other expressions used in contexts of intimacy or solidarity. Sifianou (1992) discusses Greek diminutives in requests, offers, compliments and other speech acts for which politeness is important.
8. Mühlhäusler (1983), with a wealth of illustrative examples, discusses some reasons for linguists' neglect of such 'situation-creating' (76) phenomena.
9. The numbers of examples recorded in OED since 1800 are approximately 380 (*-dom*), 260 (*-hood*), 260 (*-ship*), 390 *-(e)ry*, 140 (*-age*). *-ism* examples are much more numerous: there are about 580 twentieth-century examples.
10. The earliest use of *kingdom* in the count 'territory' sense is dated 1300 in OED. In Old English, *cynedom* means 'power of a king'.

11. OED lists *-manship* as a suffix and points out that words like *brinkman* are backformations.

12. Words like *briquetage* whose pronunciation (brɪkə'tɑːʒ) clearly reveals them to be French loans are left out of account, even though their meanings may be comparable with English *-age* (ɪdʒ) formations.

13. In a detailed study of the development of *-age* in a number of European languages, Fleischman (1977) shows how feudalism – involving as it did many new kinds of social relationship dependent on payments, services and obligations – gave rise to numerous noun + *-age* words such as *baronage*, *cellarage*, *pasturage*, *vassalage*. This suffix, descended from a Latin adjectival ending, as in *silvaticus* 'of woods' (> *savage*), already occurred in some late Latin words relating to payment, like *pulveraticum* 'payment for hard agricultural labour', > Old French *pulverage*, and was thus well placed to increase its productivity in new words for feudal relationships. The spread of feudalism meant the spread of these words to other languages, including English. Fleischman shows that a later cultural event, the Industrial Revolution, occasioned many semi-technical denominal and deverbal formations in English such as *drainage*, *pumpage*, *siphonage*, *spillage* and *wastage*.

14. Givón (1967, 1), in an interesting account of *-dom* and *-hood* words based on the structure of their definitions in Webster (1961), suggests that derivation and semantic extension should not be thought of as distinct processes. He notes two other elements which occur in polysemous formations: *-archy* and *-cracy*, cf. *squirearchy* 'squires collectively' and 'rule or dominance of squires', as in 'The form of polity in Brendon was a kind of Squirearchy' (1861), *bureaucracy* '(powerful) group of bureaucrats' and 'government by bureaucrats'. Recent formations include *meritocracy*, *quangocracy* and *punditocracy*. Compare also nouns in *-ate* like *directorate* 'office of director' and 'body of directors'.

5

Particles

5.1 Scope

Complex words containing native elements with spatial meanings like **down, in, off, on, out, over, under** are usually referred to as compounds (cf. Jespersen 1942; Marchand 1969; Meijs 1975), since such elements also function independently, in prepositional phrases and phrasal verbs. In discussing their role in word formation, we shall use the traditional term 'particle'. Particles figure both as initial elements of verbs, adjectives and nouns like *downplay, inbuilt, upkeep* (5.2), and as final elements in nouns like *playback* or *pay-out* (5.4), complex words transpositionally related to phrasal verbs (1.2.2). As initial elements of words, particles have much in common with the prefixes of Chapter 3, many of which are related to Latin and Greek prepositions and adverbs (and many of which, as we noted in 3.1, can occasionally be used as words). Both prefixes and particles are attached to verbal bases to form verbs (*precook, overlook*), to verb-related adjectival stems (*interleaved, under-mentioned*) and to verb-related nominal stems (*subcontractor, onlooker*). Both attach to nouns in attributive and predicative expressions '*intercity* train', '*offshore* island', 'the policy is *anti-car*', 'editing is *on-line*', and both can modify non-derived nouns (*super-volcano, outfield*). Certain initial particles, semantically distinct from their independent homonyms, occur productively in series of items and are thus even more like prefixes. These particles are *out* in verbs, and *over* and *under* in verbs, adjectives, and deverbal and de-adjectival nouns (5.3).

5.2   Particle + base compounds

5.2.1   Verbs

Old English locative particles included *ut* 'out', *up*, *on*, *of* 'off', *ofer* 'over' and *under*. In Old English sentences, a particle could precede or follow the verb with which it was associated. Often it occurred before the verb, especially in subordinate clauses and when the verb had a non-finite form, e.g. *siþþan ic up aweox*, 'after I grew up' ('The Wife's Lament', 3); *wæs se cyng inngongende to him*, 'the king went (lit. was going) in to him' (Bede 438.5). But sometimes, especially in main and independent clauses it followed the verb: *wurpaþ hit ut on þæt wæter*, 'throw it out on the water' (Exodus 1:22); *ceorf of þæt lim*, 'cut off that limb' (Ælfric Homilies, I.516.4). The changes in word-order which took place between the Old English and late Middle English periods meant that the particle came regularly to follow the finite verb: hence the phrasal-verb and prepositional-verb collocations of modern English.

Especially in poetry, however, even in the nineteenth century, the particle can sometimes still be found before the verb, as in 'Like water-dimples down a tide Where ripple ripple overcurls' (George Meredith, 'The Lark Ascending', 1883); 'The helmsman steered, the ship moved on; Yet never a breeze up-blew' (Coleridge, 'The Rime of the Ancient Mariner', 1798); 'Duke Leopold outleant And took the oath' (E.B. Browning 'Casa Guidi Windows', ii, 1851). Despite appearances, the verbs in these examples are best seen as inverted representatives of the verb + particle collocations *curl over*, *blow up*, *lean out*.[1] The prevalence in modern English of verb–complement order ensures the virtual confinement of such particle + verb expressions to poetic contexts which favour archaism.

Particle + base verbal compounds are still formed in modern English, but very restrictedly. Bases are typically native and monosyllabic.

back-comb, *back-cut* 'to make a back-cut (in cricket)', *backdate*, *back-pedal*, *backfill*, *backtrack*

download, *downface*, *downplay*, *downsize*, *downshift*, *downturn*, *downwash* 'to deflect (an airstream) downward'

inbuild: 'The sect often in-builds a hard core of suspicion' (OED: 1961), *infill*, *input offbreak*, *offdrive*, *offload*, *offprint*

outbreed 'to breed from parents not closely related', *outcrop*, *outcross* 'to cross (an animal or plant) with one not closely related), *outfit*, *output*, *outsource*, *outwinter* 'to keep (animals) in the open during winter'

overdub 'to impose (additional sounds) on a recording', *overdye*, *overfly*, *overhang*, *overlay*, *overpaint*, *overpunch*, *oversew*, *overstamp*, *overwrap*, *overwinter*, *overwrite undercarve, underplant, under-ride* 'Sediment-charged rivers spread material out over the lake by under-riding the lake water' (OED: 1977), *underseal*

uparch 'So soon as the lava can uparch the strata it does so' (OED: 1877), *upgrade, uprate, upshift, upstage, upwell* 'Hot molten rock, called lava, upwells through tubes in the upper layers of the earth' (OED: 1973).

Many of these items are not commonly used in finite form. Some have base + particle synonyms: *face down, play down, shift down, build in, fill in, fit out, fly over, shift up, well up*. The accentuation on the first element of some examples, like *backfill, backtrack, infill, input, offprint, outcrop, outfit, output, underseal* shows them to be derived from the nouns of the same form.

5.2.2   Adjectives

Participial adjectives with initial particles are also rather infrequent. Established items include *ingrowing, ongoing, outbound, uplifting, under-mentioned*. Adjectives may correspond to particle + base verbs, as in '*overflying* aircraft' or 'an *upgraded* rail link', or they may have verb + particle counterparts, e.g.

'a *down-blowing* fan', '*incoming* mail', '*infalling* debris', '*outjutting* precipices', '*over-curling* cornices of snow', '*upcoming* events'

'a *downturned* face', 'an *inbuilt* device', '*off-shed* fragments', '*out-turned* pockets', '*upswept* hair'.

5.2.3   Nouns

Established particle + deverbal noun compounds include *downslide, incomer, input, off-cut, out-take* 'length of film or tape rejected in editing', *throughput, upkeep, uptake* 'take-up of water by plants', *upturn*, and the nouns corresponding to the transposed verbs noted in 5.2.1. Cf. also the following (all from OED):

'the backswing of the pendulum' (1948); 'a fierce in-catch of his breath' (1895); 'A period of intensive learning – of intaking rather than outputting' (1959); '. . . through the outblowing of the winds from the icesheets' (1928); 'the lonely halts of the long upclimb' (1920); 'The upshine of a street lamp' (1934); 'I missed one upshift and smashed gears' (1978); 'an upthrusting of castles, belfries and white walls' (1984).

Examples in which the base is not related to a verb and the particle has modifying function are rather more commonplace, e.g. *down-pipe, in-joke, out-tray, under-dog, up-trend*. Prepositional phrases very occasionally become established as nouns, e.g. *underchin*: 'The geese [had] . . . jet-black head and neck, snow-white under-chin' (OED: 1978); *underfoot*: 'No flame could lick far into the forests so long as their underfoot was moist' (OED: 1959).

5.3   *Over, under, out*

5.3.1   Verbs

Over occurs in a number of established verbs in senses related to its spatial sense,[2] e.g. 'dominate': *overpower, overrule*, 'upset': *overbalance, overturn, overthrow*, 'go beyond a limit': *overflow, overreach, overshoot, overstep*. In another related sense, 'do to excess', it attaches to a variety of native and foreign verb bases, and this is the sense most likely to occur in new formations today:

> *over-act, overbook, overcharge, overcompensate, overdress, over-extend, overestimate, overfish, over-react, over-simplify, over-sleep, over-use, over-work.*

Verbs like these appear to have paved the way for antonymous verbs in **under**, meaning 'do insufficiently', which are not recorded earlier than the sixteenth century:

> *underachieve, under-capitalize, under-determine, under-dress, under-perform, under-report, under-spend, under-tip, under-use.*

Out in the sense 'go beyond a limit': *outgrow, outlive,* and the closely related sense seen in many modern examples, 'surpass or get the better of (someone or something) in an activity indicated by the base', is productive:

> 'The Russians outachieved the United States in launching earth satellites' (OED: 1960); 'he outboxed and outpunched me' (OED: 1950); 'a case of the chick outguessing the experimenter' (OED: 1913).

Unlike *over* and *under*, *out* can be transpositional, combining with noun and occasionally adjective bases:

> 'Like all smart crooks, he outsmarted himself' (OED: 1975); 'even Antonia had been outmonstered' (OED: 1955); 'the lawyers outstar the headline stars themselves' (Guardian: 1997).

As long as the resulting verb can be understood as an 'accomplishment' (3.2) – *outweigh* is a notable exception – any verb, adjective or noun is an eligible base. Marchand (1969, 96) accordingly notes that the pattern is 'of almost unlimited productivity'. In fact, however, established examples, such as *outdo* and *outwit*, are scarce. The expression 'it outHerods Herod' (*Hamlet*, II.ii) has been the pattern for a number of others, such as 'She outmoderns the moderns' (OED: 1935), 'The range of the tartans outrainbowing the rainbow' (OED: 1956), 'a realism which outZolas Zola' (OED: 1887).

5.3.2   Adjectives

Over, intensifying in adjectives, attaches to adjective bases:

over-articulate, over-concise, over-confident, over-friendly,

and to participial-adjective bases:

over-demanding, over-cultivated, 'an *over-arranged* occasion', 'the *over-controlled* personality', 'The organization . . . is over-structured' (OED: 1971).

Under, 'insufficiently', attaches hardly at all to non-participial adjectives – *under-ripe* is a rare and often cited example – though formations with *-ing* and *-ed* do occur:

'*under-achieving* pupils', *under-developed, under-employed, under-powered, under-publicized,* 'We're under-garrisoned and under-policed' (OED: 1936).

Such formations not infrequently occur in contexts which explicitly contrast them with corresponding *over-* formations, as in 'Swards were overgrazed in winter and spring and undergrazed in summer and autumn' (OED: 1977).

Out in the 'surpass' sense is confined to verbs and consequently there can be no *out* + base adjective without a possible corresponding *out* + base verb. *-ing* adjectives are scarce, since generally only the present participles of intransitive verbs can function as adjectives (2.5.1) and verbs prefixed by *out* are transitive. *-ed* adjectives, though, are easily formed. They may have verbal or nominal bases:

'I felt tired and out-gambited' (OED: 1962); 'They were just out-foxed, outmaneuvered, and out-organized' (OED: 1976); 'The police are outnumbered and outgunned' (Guardian: 1998).

5.3.3   Nouns

Over and **under** attach to deverbal nouns:

overcapitalization,   overcompensation,   overdramatization,   over-expansion, overplanning underconsumption, underfulfilment, underfunding, under-registration, under-ventilation.

Over also attaches to noun bases related to adjectives:

over-ambition, overdominance, over-intensity, over-optimism, over-susceptibility.

Prefix-like **out** can occur in process nominalizations (2.4.1), as in 'the *outmanoevring* of the enemy', but formations based on result nominalizations are impossible: **'an *out-achievement*', **'an *outguess*'.

5.4   Base + particle nouns

Verb + particle combinations are phrases, and as we saw in 1.2.2, nominalized formations related to them are untypical complex words in that the right-hand element is not clearly the head. The phrasal character of deverbal noun + particle formations is especially obvious in non-count uses like those in 'We were supposed to keep out of the pilot's way at blast-off' (1952), 'Gas will be liberated . . . during pumpdown' (OED: 1971), 'All engines were prepared for opening and for tick-over' (OED: 1931), and uses in which they denote an instance of the verb's action following *have/give/take a* (2.4.1): 'give (something) a *rub-down*, 'make a *get-away*', 'have a *fry-up*, a *punch-up*, a *sleep-in*', 'I had only been here two days when we had our first sort-out' (OED: 1972).

Nevertheless, final particles are very much more frequent in deverbal nouns than initial ones. Berg (1998, 258–9) suggests that the productivity of deverbal noun + particle nouns, surprising for a left-headed pattern, can be explained by various factors: the frequency of verb + particle collocations, the tendency for collocated verbs and particles to lose their semantic independence, and the productivity of 'zero' verb-to-noun derivation. Nouns formed since 1800 with final *off*, *out* and *up* – such as *kick-off*, *turn-off*, *opt-out*, *shoot-out*, *carve-up*, *flare-up* – are more numerous in OED than those with other particles – such as *take-away*, *throwback*, *clampdown*, *lead-in*, *add-on*, *change-over*, *break-through*.[3] Some examples, like *roll-away* (e.g. furniture), *ride-on* (e.g. lawn mower), *live-in* (servant), *see-through* (fencing), *stand-up* (comic), are always or nearly always used attributively.

A verb + particle collocation which corresponds closely in meaning may not be current, as with examples like *hide-out*, *lease-back*, *play-off*, *showdown*, or may occasionally be derived from the noun + particle formation, as in 'I think like a white man, and when I get out into the world, that is maybe going to hang me up a bit' (Evening Standard: 1971). It is rare, however, for a base + particle noun to have no perceivable relationship with a verb (cf. Berg

1998, 247), as with *dust-up* 'fight', *stock-out* 'state of being out of stock', *ton-up* 'speed of 100 miles per hour', *voice-over*.

Other cases in which the relation with a verb is indirect or non-existent are formations in series, such as:

> *brown-out, dim-out* 'partial black-out', *white-out* 'heavy snowstorm with low visibility', based on *blackout* 'covering of lights'; *greyout, red-out* 'reddening of vision' based on *blackout* 'loss of consciousness'; *rain-out* 'incorporation into raindrops of radioactive debris' based on *fallout*; *sick-out* 'industrial action on the pretext of sickness' based on *walk-out*.

There are a number of formations with *in* as final element, denoting initially 'group protest' and later 'group activity'. The earliest 'protest' example noted by OED is *sit-in* (strike) (1937); others, from the 1960s and later, include *teach-in* 'informal debate', *work-in* 'occupation of the workplace', *sick-in* 'sick-out', and those illustrated in:

> 'left-wing Catholics staged a pray-in' (OED: 1967); 'various groups staged "die-ins" to simulate the effects of the gas' (OED: 1970); 'College catering would be disrupted by students . . . holding mass eat-ins' (OED: 1973).

Besides 'protest involving discussion', *talk-in* has been used to denote simply 'conference', like *think-in*. Connotations of 'protest' have sometimes been absent from uses of words like *be-in* (1967), defined by OED as 'A public gathering of hippies', *love-in, smoke-in* and *swim-in*. See OED *-in*, suffix 3 and Harder (1968) for many other examples.

Notes

1. Some older particle + verb sequences are established as such, e.g. *overarch*, *uproot* (beside *arch over, root up*). The sequence *upwell*, on the other hand, in lines by Robert Bridges: 'Out of the topmost stone / Of yonder hill upwells a fountain head' (OED: 1885) is best seen as inverted, and distinct from the more recent formation *upwell* in a very different register illustrated in 5.2.1.
2. Old English had prefixes *ofer-* and *under-* as well as particles of the same form. *Ut* was a particle only. See Brinton (1988, 208ff) for an account of semantic developments in *over, under* and *out* in combination with verbal bases. There are verbs in Old English like *oferdrincan* 'to overdrink', but the senses 'do inadequately' and 'surpass' in *under* and *out* verbs appear later.
3. OED records nearly one hundred nouns ending in *up*, over seventy in *out* and around fifty in *off* since 1800. There are considerably fewer nouns with other final particles.

6

Noun compounds

6.1 Scope

A noun compound has a final element which is nominal, modified by one or more elements which in independent use may be nominal, adjectival or verbal. We begin by identifying five patterns, exemplified by *bicycle-repairing* (noun + deverbal noun), *refugee camp* (noun + noun), *potter's wheel* (noun-genitive *s* + noun), *greenhouse* (adjective + noun), and *spoonbill* (exocentric). All these sequences, except the last, prompt questions about their status as words.

6.1.1 Noun + deverbal noun

In *bicycle-repairing went on in the back room* and *tax evasion is easy if you know the ropes*, the nominal characteristics of the compounds are as limited as those of the heads of the paraphrases *repairing of bicycles* and *evasion of taxes*: they are process nominalizations (2.4.1). No plural is possible; only *the* or a possessive corresponding to the verb's subject (*John's bicycle-repairing* ...) is allowed as determiner; modifiers like *careful* or *frequent*, corresponding to adverbs (*frequent bicycle-repairing* ...) are acceptable. The deverbal head of the compound cannot stand alone unless its modifier, corresponding to the similarly essential object in a paraphrase, is clearly implied in the context. The term **synthetic** is often used for compounds like these, in which the verb–object relationship is conditional on the verb being nominalized (Bloomfield 1933, 231–2): there is no independently-formed verb *to bicycle-repair* (see also 8.1). Since many compounds containing result nominalizations are also appropriately called synthetic, we shall use the term 'syntactic' for compounds containing process nominalizations as heads and embodying a verb–object relationship. Compounded process nominalizations cannot easily exhibit relationships other than that of verb–object: compare the subject–verb expressions in **'unexpected guest-arriving is a nuisance'*, **'frequent* *dog-barking* disturbs the neighbours', **mechanic-repairing* of bicycles', **tycoon-evasion* of taxes'. Adjuncts and complements of the verb other than direct objects also appear strange when compounded with process nominalizations: **guest-cooking* of meals', **council-sending* of letters'. Syntactic compounds like *bicycle-repairing* are phrase-like in that they are as readily formed and as semantically predictable as transitive verb + object collocations, but word-like in that their non-final constituents are typically understood as generic and non-referential, and are not fully 'available' syntactically.[1] They can be coordinated – *bicycle- and car-repairing* . . . – but they cannot easily be antecedents of pronominal forms: compare *repairing of bicycles is necessary to keep them on the road* with *?bicycle-repairing is necessary to keep them on the road*. The accentuation of syntactic compounds (*bícycle-repairing*) contrasts regularly with that of phrases: (*repairing of bícycles*).

Synthetic compounds in which the final, deverbal, element is suffixed by *-er*, and the accented modifier corresponds to an object, like *bícycle-repairer*, differ from syntactic compounds as defined above in that their correspondence with phrases is less close: modifiers like *careful* and *frequent* can occur in phrases (*a frequent repairer of bicycles*) but not (in the same sense) with compounds: **a frequent bicycle-repairer* (Rappaport-Hovav and Levin 1988, 138). Moreover, compounds of this form are not semantically predictable. *Drug-users* and *fire-fighters* are people who use drugs and fight fires, but *nutcrackers* and *shock absorbers* are things; a *coffee-maker* could be either.[2]

In other noun + deverbal noun compounds the modifying noun is comparable with an adjunct: *cycle commuting* 'commuting by cycle', *night flying*, *bungee-jumping*, *sports commentator*, *water-skier*. Relationships within noun + deverbal noun sequences are various, e.g. *insect repellant* 'repellant for insects', *picture writing* 'writing which uses pictures' or 'writing which consists of pictures', and of course deverbal nouns can be countable: *flea-bite, telephone call, ice fall*. In all synthetic compounds the modifier is accented.

6.1.2   Noun + noun

Sequences of nouns like *refugee camp* can, like sentences, be indefinitely extended in principle. Most examples have two elements, but if *refugee camp* is a compound, so is *UK film industry task force appointment controversy*. As with phrases and clauses, the make-up of noun sequences can be shown by bracketing: [*student* [*advice centre*]] or [[*student advice*] *centre*], [[*nicotine patch*] *success rate*], [[[[[*UK*] [*film industry*]] [*task force*]] [*appointment*]] [*controversy*]]. Elements may often be coordinated: *garden seats and ornaments*; *radio and television personalities*. It is occasionally possible to substitute *one* for a head element: *Do you want a teaspoon or a jam one?* (Example from Bauer 1998, 77 who notes, however, that clearly acceptable instances are hard to find.)

On the other hand, noun + noun sequences can be modified, prefixed and suffixed as units: [*busy* [*student advice centre*]], [*ex-*[*education minister*]], [[[*South*

Sea] *island*]*er*]. They are pluralized as units: [*refugee camp*]s. Modifiers are typically generic and cannot easily refer independently to a pronoun: ?*cat flaps allow them to go in and out as they wish*. If modifiers are pluralized, it is usually because they are 'pluralia tantum', nouns which in plural form have particular senses: *fees controversy, clothes cupboard*, or because they refer in the context to a collection of individuals or items (Pinker 1999, 185), cf. *buildings insurance, communications satellite, weapons system*, in contrast with *roads sign, *trains timetable, in which there is no reason to differentiate among particular roads or trains. Modifiers can be proper names: *Brontë country, a Dickens biography*. As Kay and Zimmer (1990) point out, the modifier in *a Wittgenstein argument* can be either referential: 'an argument advanced by Wittgenstein' or generic: 'one of the kind associated with him'.

Noun + noun compounds are often accented on the modifier noun: *advice centre, succéss rate*, but by no means always: *carrier pígeon, garden páth*.[3] They can be lexicalized, one element as in *breezeblock* and *penknife*, or both, as in *hedgehog* and *pigeon-hole*, having little relation to the noun in independent use. In such cases, coordination and anaphoric reference to the elements separately is obviously impossible. Varying degrees of lexicalization mean that we cannot clearly identify a class of 'compound words' distinct from phrasal sequences of two or more nouns – which in any case behave partly like words. It is convenient therefore to refer to all such sequences as 'compounds'.

6.1.3   Noun-genitive *s* + noun

There is a clear distinction between the phrase *the potter's wheel* in *the potter's wheel was in his back yard* and the compound *potter's wheel* in *John bought a second-hand potter's wheel*. In the first case, the noun phrase *the potter* as antecedent of *his* refers to a specific individual. In the second, *second-hand* modifies the compound *potter's wheel*, in which *potter's* identifies a kind of wheel.

But inevitably there are intermediate cases. Taylor (1996, ch. 11) discusses a number of these. *Newton's Law* or *Valentine's Day* may appear to identify a specific individual, but the modifier in these cases serves rather to identify the particular principle and date. In Taylor's example *The archaeologists discovered fragments of a man's skull*, the phrasal reading [*a man*]*'s skull* and the compound reading *a* [*man's skull*] do not differ appreciably, since *a man* is non-specific. Taylor notes that compounds are likely to have genitive *s* if they resemble phrases with genitive noun phrase modifiers (like [*the potter*]*'s wheel*) in some way: if they have a modifier with a human referent: *shepherd's pie* but not *car tyre*, or a modifier evoking a single individual: *driver's seat* but not *passenger seat*, or one which can be construed as a possessor (*women's magazine* but not *girlie magazine*) – though all three of these – *shepherd's pie, driver's seat, women's magazine* – are like *potter's wheel* in the second example above, and must be analysed as compounds.

6.1.4   Adjective + noun

Non-gradable denominal adjectives with foreign bases like *military* and *rural*, and those derived from English nouns like *herbal* and *editorial*, are comparable with modifying nouns (Levi 1978, ch. 2). Compare *military* sales and *arms sales, country pursuits* and *rural pursuits, herbal tea, editorial chair* and *herb tea, editor's chair*. As Bolinger (1967, 31) remarks, 'There seems to be no good reason . . . why . . . a man with a tin hat uses *construction materials* while one with a cap and gown uses *instructional materials*'. As with the examples of 6.1.2, we shall assume that all these sequences are compounds.

Many sequences of gradable adjective and noun, on the other hand, seem to have little claim to be considered compound words. The nominal head can be substituted for: *a complex problem and a simple one*. Premodifying adjectives can be coordinated: *long and rough grass*, or themselves modified: *a still outstanding claim, an imaginatively converted warehouse*. Sequences like these are regularly accented on the final element.

The adjective in an adjective + noun sequence often signals a characteristic property, in contrast to its 'temporary' significance elsewhere (Bolinger 1967): contrast *a responsible person, the visible stars, the late chancellor* with *the stars visible tonight, the person responsible for this error, the chancellor is late*. Related to this is the susceptibility of attributive adjective–noun collocations to lexicalization (cf. Sadler and Arnold 1994), which involves loss of independence in the constituents, e.g. *hothouse, magic lantern, tight rope, wild fowl*. We can add a modifier to the first elements of *guided missile, flying saucer, moving image*, but probably not without a sense that the sequence must be reanalysed: *a [carefully guided] missile, a [high flying] saucer, a [fast moving] image*.

Some lexicalized adjective + noun sequences are accented on the adjective: *happy hour, hothouse, smart card, tight rope*. Others are accented on the noun: *big bang, blue moon, cold war, heavy metal, high court, magic lantern*. Most participial adjective + noun sequences, and adjective + deverbal *-er* noun sequences, lexicalized or not, are accented on the noun: *bad loser, best-seller, fast breeder, high flyer, loudspeaker, rough sleeper*. Again we have no firm criteria separating compound and phrase.[4]

6.1.5   Exocentric compounds

So far we have considered endocentric compounds or sequences, in which the final element is functionally and semantically equivalent to the whole and can be considered its head. A *coffee-maker* is a kind of maker, a *refugee camp* a kind of camp, a *hothouse* a kind of house. Exocentric or 'headless' compounds, a comparatively small group in which the final element is not of the same kind as the whole (1.2.2) are formed on three patterns. The relation between the elements of *pickpocket* and *rotgut* is analogous to that of verb and complement; *highbrow* is adjective + noun and *spoonbill* noun + noun.[5]

Compound Nouns which in independent use have irregular plural forms lose this characteristic as final elements in exocentric compounds: *coltsfoots, low-lifes, walkmans, fig-leafs*: 'Surely we don't want to see doctors as fig-leafs to the pharmaceutical dealers?' (Guardian: 1998). Compounds like these are generally accented on the non-final element. Many examples are likely to be encountered as modifiers within noun phrases, as in 'a *free-lance* writer' '*long-nose* pliers', ' a *maidenhair* fern', '*break-neck* speed', '*stop-gap* measures' (see 7.3.3).

accent

6.2   Meaning

Compound nouns vary in the degree to which the relations between their parts, and hence their meanings, are likely to be clear to a hearer or reader encountering them for the first time. Only syntactic compounds present no problems of interpretation arising from their status as words. In other synthetic compounds the relation between the deverbal element and its modifier is usually clear, and a sufficient guide to the meaning of the whole. In gradable adjective + noun sequences the relation between modifier and head does not vary except in becoming obscured through lexicalization. Noun + noun compounds with relational heads like *animal doctor, car thief, crew member, probation officer, roads lobby, table leg* are not likely to present difficulties.

The terms 'appositional', 'copulative' or 'equative' are often invoked in discussions of noun + noun compounds (cf. Bauer 1983, 202; Jespersen 1942, 8.21; Spencer 1991, 312; Warren 1978, 98f). As we saw in 1.2.2, expressions containing coordinated elements are phrases. Noun + noun examples in which both elements denote roles, like *author-illustrator, producer-director* are arguably also phrases, not complex words. *Absentee landlord, carrier bag, demon barber, fossil fuel, killer virus* by contrast, might be seen as 'appositional' compounds, on the basis of a paraphrase containing *be*: 'the bag is a carrier', etc., though there are differences among these examples. In *carrier bag*, the modifier indicates the purpose of the head's referent, in *fossil fuel* its nature and in *killer virus* its effect. *Demon barber* could also be paraphrased 'barber like a demon'. For many noun + noun compounds there is no obvious single interpretation that everyone is likely to agree about.

However, a classification in terms of semantic categories of the kind already encountered in connection with denominal verbs (2.3.1), may cast some light on how we make and understand new noun + noun compounds.[6] The examples below include some in which the modifier is a denominal adjective (*tidal wave*), and some with modifiers that could be seen as verbal (*search engine*).

In the following, the heads denote 'instruments' and the modifiers what they are for:

divining rod, gas mask, ignition key, magnifying glass, mosquito net, protection money, search engine, sheep dog, stop cock, swipe card, think tank, traffic lights, tranquillizer gun, tugboat, visitor centre, weather balloon.

The modifying element may indicate how the referent of the head, and hence the whole, functions:

air gun, axe killer, cable car, charm offensive, computer game, correspondence course, herbal remedy, postal ballot, radio transmitter, vacuum cleaner.

The head may indicate the location of an activity or entity:

amusement park, battlefield, call box, caravan site, checkpoint, fruit market, launch pad, observation post, polling booth, swimming pool, towpath, wildlife sanctuary.

The referent of the compound may be characterized by its modifier in terms of where it comes from or where it can be found:

field mouse, land mine, mountain ash, polar bear, space station, tropical fish, web site, zoo animal.

The head is 'cause' in:

horror film, influenza virus, sneeze weed, tear gas.

The modifier indicates a cause in:

anxiety neurosis, emergency stop, emotional tie, gas blast, hunger strike, lottery millionaire, panic buying, sex discrimination, sunburn, tax exile, tidal wave, traffic congestion.

A 'source' is head in *beef cattle, car factory, honey bee, silk worm* and modifier in *bird droppings, cane sugar, coal dust, goat cheese, press release, whalebone.*

The modifier's referent may be a 'possessor' in some sense, signalled by *s*: *beginner's luck, carpenter's level, dogs' home, driver's seat*, or with an uninflected modifier: *ant heap, company policy, rabbit warren, state archive, minority rights, national debt, student loan.*

The modifier may say something about the content of the head's referent (concrete or abstract): *arms cache, cheque book, current bun, film festival, fruit cake, media circus, miracle play*; or its composition: *butter mountain, compost heap, prose poem, rail link*; its material: *carpet bag, ivory tower, smoke screen*; or its form: *bar code, bow tie, chain reaction, documentary evidence.*

It may denote something the second element resembles: *bell jar, box kite, demon barber, fan vaulting, garter snake, mackerel sky, weaver bird, zebra crossing.*

The modifer of a head with an abstract referent usually indicates what the latter is about (Levi 1978, 103ff):

border dispute, cold war thriller, financial report, identity crisis, redundancy notice, scare story, tax law.

This attempt at classification, like many others, relies on rather loosely defined distinctions, and these groupings may not seem particularly homogeneous. *Anxiety* is a 'cause' of *neurosis*, but not in the same way that the *tide* 'causes' *waves*. A *carpenter* can 'possess' a *level*, but *dogs* do not own their *home* or *beginners* their *luck*. The concept of 'source' has to be stretched to cover both *coal dust* and *goat cheese*. It may not be obvious where to place many familiar compounds, such as *camera angle, exclusion zone, keyhole surgery, rainforest, war crime, World Cup*. Entities have more than one aspect, and the semantic groups set up by the classifier of noun compounds are unlikely to be mutually exclusive. The second elements of *sleeping bag* or *springboard* can be seen either as 'instruments' or 'locations'. *Rabbit warren* appears above in the 'possessor' group, but could also be placed in the 'location' group along with *wildlife sanctuary*. Compounds which evoke 'resemblance' often illustrate other relationships as well, like the 'appositional' *demon barber*, and 'possessor' examples like *catcall* 'call like a cat's call', *crocodile tears, horse laugh*. There seems to be some justification for Sweet's observation (1891, §1560):

it is only by leaving open the logical relations between the elements of compounds that we are able to form them as we want them without stopping to analyse exactly the logical or grammatical relations between the words we join together, as we might have to do if we connected them together by more definite means.

A factor which may cause problems for the compound-classifier (though not of course for the compound-user) is analogy. A new compound can be formed on the model of a familiar one, like *brush name* for an artist's alias on the pattern of *pen name* or the antonym of *blacklist* in 'a Government whitelist of allegedly safe states' (i.e. states whose citizens are not entitled to political asylum), *earth legs*, after *sea legs*: 'After months in orbit [the cosmonaut] had recovered his earth legs' (Guardian: 1997), *planet-fall* after *landfall*: 'Smoking was strictly prohibited from take-off until planet-fall' (OED: 1954), or *greenwash* after *whitewash* in its metaphorical sense 'something that conceals faults': 'Disinformation disseminated by an organization so as to present an environmentally responsible image' (COD: 1999).

As Ryder (1994) convincingly demonstrates, groups of compounds with a common first element, like *sea*: *sea chest, sea cow, sea cucumber, sea weed* . . . or a common second element like *man*: *cave man, camera man, clergyman, weather man* . . . play an appreciable part in the creation and use of compounds. Cf.

also the following *rage* compounds. *Road rage* ('rage directed by motorists at others in difficult driving conditions') provided a pattern for several analogous words, including *tube rage*, *alarm rage* ('rage prompted by car alarm noise'), *rod rage* (of anglers), *trolley rage* (of supermarket shoppers) and *golf rage*. These examples are not linked by a common relation between the elements, and *rod rage* at least would be difficult to paraphrase and accommodate in any of the groups mentioned above.

Compounds like *airport*, *fire sale*, *nuclear trigger*, which may be hard to place in the kind of classification attempted above because they seem to imply a 'missing link', can often be related to other compounds with the same first elements and a more direct relation (Ryder 1994, 147ff). *Airport* is part of a group including *airman*, *airplane*, *airship*, *airspace*; *fire sale* is understood against a background of *fire alarm*, *fire drill*, *fire engine*, *fire extinguisher* and others; *nuclear trigger* depends in a similar way on *nuclear bomb*, *nuclear physics*, *nuclear power*.

Levi (1978) interestingly proposes that certain relationships seen in compounds and in other kinds of expression are privileged. They are 'recoverable' and need not be expressed, and ambiguity is to be expected. She identifies nine relationships, with verbal or prepositional labels, which any noun + noun compound can potentially embody, though one of them will usually be the customary one. They are 'cause' (*tear gas*, *viral infection*), 'have' (*picture book*, *lemon peel*), 'make' (*honey bee*, *daisy chain*), 'use' (*steam iron*), 'be' (*soldier ant*), 'in' (*field mouse*), 'for' (*horse doctor*), 'from' (*olive oil*) and 'about' (*tax law*).[7] A corollary of this is that any other relationship must be overtly expressed if a compound is to be comprehensible, as in *fish-eating dinosaurs*, *moss-covered rocks*, *under-the-table deals*.

Fish dinosaurs may not be a familiar combination, but it is surely allowable: Chaucer speaks unproblematically of *seed fowl* and *worm fowl* in the *Parliament of Fowls*. A *moss house* is a house or shelter covered or lined with moss. (This example, and *moss rocks* if it happened to occur, could be accommodated in any case under the 'have' label: Levi's groupings are no less elastic than others.) And there appear to be other relationships which at least on occasion, and especially with contextual support, need not be expressed. The presence of *pro-* or *anti-*, for example, can depend on whether the context makes them necessary. A *speed table* is a raised area of road designed to reduce the speed of traffic, i.e an *anti-speed table*. *Witch doctor* has more than one definition – 'doctor who is a witch' and 'doctor who detects witches' – because witches conventionally have more than one aspect: they can cure illness, but may also inflict it. Context dictates which interpretation is the more appropriate, as in: 'Our consternation would be complete when our witch doctor, who evidently should really be called an anti-witch doctor, insisted that each herb he prescribed for us had its own individual incantation' (Sunday Times: 1971). The context of a Guardian headline 'West pins hopes on Serbian sanctions' made it clear that this meant sanctions *against*

Serbia. It was assumed that *sleaze rules* in another Guardian headline, 'PR boss peer promises to follow sleaze rules' was meant to be understood as 'rules designed to *check* sleaze', though the potential ambiguity of a similar example, *burglary campaign* was seen as amusing in the following context:

> Dear Resident, says this interesting letter issued by Newcastle West Crime Prevention Panel, 'You will no doubt by now be aware of the burglary campaign being undertaken by Northumbria Police . . . ' (Guardian: 1990)

Most new compounds, however, can be seen in terms of one or more of a few general relationships of the kind illustrated earlier, or listed by Levi. Encountering new items like *robbery anguish, credit card gold, forklift raiders* (in newspaper headlines : 'Robbery anguish in Greek church', 'Pawnbrokers hit credit card gold', 'Forklift raiders held'), we can reasonably interpret them in terms of general notions like 'cause', 'source' and 'instrument'.

But, as Downing (1977) shows, such interpretations necessarily leave out of account most of the specific knowledge that makes compounds intelligible. A paraphrase like 'lights for traffic' is no less cryptic than the compound *traffic lights* – unless supplemented with the knowledge of what traffic lights are. In *briefcase* and *watchcase* the idea of a 'case' is adjusted, or 'accommodated'[8] in accordance with what we know of briefs and watches. Since *zebra crossing* is not likely to mean 'crossing for zebras', its interpretation enlists the idea of 'resemblance', possibly a last resort, brought into consideration if no other relationship seems plausible (cf. Downing 1977, 830).

In most circumstances, compounds, as Downing shows, are easy to invent, use and understand because they name entities in culturally relevant ways. We expect the modifier of a compound to provide needed information about its head's referent and to subclassify it in a useful way. Though the semantic relationships between the elements of compounds may not be confined to a limited set, we can expect some to be 'favoured' because they reflect the ways speakers find it useful to refer to people and things. A compound whose head has a human referent will probably indicate something about the occupation or identity of the person referred to. Compound names of animals and plants are likely to carry indications of appearance, habitat or location. Names of natural objects will often say something about what they are made of, their origin or where they are found. Names of man-made objects are likely to encode a relation of 'purpose'.

6.3 Contexts

Noun compounds are so freely formed and used, often with little or no effect of novelty, that any discussion of them should consider their role in discourse, and the ways in which context contributes to their interpretability. (See, e.g., Kastovsky 1982, 1986b.) As well as expressing a new lexical concept, a compound often serves as a compact version of a longer expression in its neighbourhood which furnishes a full gloss for it. *Clock-tinkering* and *fountain cavort* in the following encapsulate material in earlier sentences:

> It seems to be that time of year again for the Guardian leader to make its ritual misguided suggestion that tinkering with the clocks could save lives on the road. . . . what about the many people who are currently being killed in broad daylight? . . . Your clock-tinkering would not have saved them. (Guardian: 1993)

> There is a story that Ernest Hemingway once saw Zelda and Scott Fitzgerald cavorting in the fountain outside New York's Plaza Hotel and felt challenged. He cried: 'I can do a fountain cavort twice as good as Scott's . . .'. (New York Times)

In the next example a series of statements has its culmination in the compact summary of the final sentence:

> Machines are an increasingly important part of our lives. . . . I do not know how any of them work. I am frightened of handling them and I cannot mend them when they go wrong. I am a machine cripple. (Observer: 1983)

Compounds may (less often) be followed by material which defines them, a stylistically effective arrangement illustrated in 'My salad days, When I was green in judgment, cold in blood' (*Antony and Cleopatra*, I.v). Cf. also Charles Tomlinson's *fox gallery* and its accompanying explanation:

> A long house –
> the fox gallery you called
> its upper storey, because
> you could look down to see
> (and did) the way a fox would
> cross the field beyond   'The Fox Gallery'

or the more prosaic *discomfort gazumping*:

> Most of us have experienced the problem of discomfort gazumping. It is never wise to announce in an office that you are suffering from flu because at least three other people will be struggling on with pneumonia. (Guardian: 1998)

Such forward-pointing compounds are often encountered in newspaper headlines and may be enigmatic without the accompanying text:

Test-tube gift
Australia will send Mzuri, the first gorilla born through in-vitro fertilisation, to Britain for breeding. (Guardian: 1993)

Snake girls' record
Two Chinese girls set record living for 12 days in a room with 888 snakes. (Guardian: 1993)

Similarly, no specific glosses can be devised in the absence of explanatory contexts for 'Disaster skipper faces retrial', 'Murder youth detained', 'Crash train "braked"'. Only the following context will reveal the nature of the skipper's, the youth's and the train's involvement in the events. Examples like these furnish clear illustrations that a compound guarantees only the fact of a connection in some context of the referents of its components.

Notes

1. Syntactic compounds are of particular interest for the relationship between morphology and syntax. Spencer (1991, 324–44) and Carstairs-McCarthy (1992, ch. 4) usefully summarize some recent discussions, though they do not distinguish between what are here called syntactic compounds and other synthetic compounds. See Oshita (1994) for a distinction similar to that adopted in this chapter.
2. Rappaport-Hovav and Levin (1988, 131–2) note the contrast between -*er* nouns in postmodified noun phrases, which are typically unambiguous like *a wiper of windshields* (a person) and in compounds, which are not: *a windshield-wiper* can refer to a person or a thing.
3. Marchand (1969, 20ff) adopts stress as the deciding criterion for compound status: *áircraft carrier* is a compound but not *government offícial*. Liberman and Sproat (1992), in a detailed investigation of stress in noun sequences, analyse modifier-accented cases as nouns (N^0) and head-accented cases as intermediate between word and phrase (N^1), though regarding both as 'word level objects that are formed in the syntax' (175).
4. For Marchand, stress distinguishes compounds (*bláckbird*) from non-compounds (*black márket*). In parallel with their treatment of noun sequences, Liberman and Sproat correlate modifier and head accent in adjective + noun sequences with N^0 and N^1 status respectively.
5. Exocentric compounds can be compared with metonymical expressions confined to particular situations, like the subject noun phrase in *the mushroom omelette is waiting for his bill.*

6. See especially Jespersen (1942, ch. 8), Marchand (1969, ch. 2), Levi (1978) and Warren (1978) for similar groupings.
7. 'Like' is specifically excluded on the ground that the metaphorical reading of combinations like *imperial bearing, lunar landscape, summer sunshine* (in March) is regularly dependent on the literal reading (Levi 1978, 106–18).
8. Langacker (1987, 485) defines accommodation: 'The adjustment in details of a component required when it is integrated with another to form a composite structure.' See Ryder (1994) for further discussion of accommodation in compound elements.

Syntactic compounds
Synthetic compounds

-er ending phrase → unambiguous
-er ending compound → a person or thing

N + N
initial-stressed → compound
final-stressed → phrase

Adj + N, / N + N
modifier-accented → compound
head-accented → phrase

7

Adjective compounds

7.1 Scope

The final element of an adjective compound may be a form ending in *-ing*: *life-threatening*, *suspicious-looking* (7.2) or *-ed*: *male-dominated*, *security-coded* (7.3). It may be a derived adjective with another suffix: *cycle-friendly*, or a non-derived adjective: *street-wise* (7.4). Non-heads are nouns, adjectives and occasionally adverbs.

Sequences of adverb + adjective or participial adjective raise the question of the distinction between compound and phrase. *-ing* participles can be progressive, as in 'the train was *slowly moving*' (or '*moving slowly*'), or property-denoting, as in 'the administrative apparatus was *slow-moving*' (1.2.3, 2.5.1). Within a noun phrase, both kinds of sequence can be hyphenated, as phrases within noun phrases generally are, but '*slow-moving* apparatus' has a claim to compound status, unlike '*slowly moving* train'. A property-denoting participial adjective can be modified by an adverb without its suffix which must still precede the participle when the combination is predicative, at least in standard English. Other compounds like *slow-moving* are

> 'a *free-flowering* bush', '*heavy-tipping* customers', 'all *right-thinking* people', 'a *slow-burning* fire', '*tough-talking* delegates'.

-ly adverbs can premodify property-denoting participles without forming compounds with them (Roeper and Siegel 1978, 227). A combination like *visually-haunting* in 'a visually-haunting experiment in early Technicolor' is clearly seen not to be a compound in 'the experiment was visually haunting'. A few adverbs which never have *-ly* precede non-attributive property-denoting participial adjectives: *fast-moving*, *hard-drinking*, *late-flowering*, and generally follow progressive participles and other forms of the verb: 'the bus was *moving fast, running late*'. Others, like *ever* and *ill*, precede participial elements in

established combinations which we can call compounds: '*everlasting* flowers', 'the windows are *ill-fitting*'.

Combinations of *-ly* adverb and *-ed* participle like those in 'a *closely-cut* lawn', 'a *severely-depressed* patient', 'an *efficiently-operated* machine' need not be regarded as compounds, even though the adverb is likely to precede the participle in other positions: 'the machine was *efficiently operated*', and some combinations consist of items often found together: 'a *centrally-heated* house', '*genetically-engineered* oil-seed rape'. By contrast, established combinations with non-*ly* adverbs in which the order cannot vary are plausibly compounded: '*hard-pressed* local schemes', 'a *long-established* traditional band', 'the community is very *tight-knit*', '*widespread* damage'.

Combinations of *-ly* adverb and adjective as in '*environmentally-conscious* individuals', 'a *politically-sensitive* decision' also do not make convincing compounds, unlike combinations of non-*ly* adverb and adjective: 'an *ever-present* worry'. In predicative position, sequences like those in 'a *three-year-old* boy', 'the *centuries-old* Arab presence in the Iberian peninsula', are clearly seen to be phrases: '*the boy is three years old*' (cf. Meijs 1975, 110).

7.2   *-ing*

7.2.1   Noun + verb-*ing*

In a very commonly encountered pattern, the first constituent, a noun, corresponds to the direct object of the transitive verb represented in the head constituent. As with simple *-ing* adjectives (2.5.1), the referent of the noun phrase modified or complemented by the adjective corresponds to the verb's subject:

> 'a bisexual *axe-wielding* murderess', '*job-seeking* graduates', 'that *match-saving* innings', 'hypocrisy of a more than usually *nausea-provoking* kind', '*muesli-eating* liberals', '*ozone-depleting* CFCs', '*victim-blaming* magistrates', 'a *self-locking* car'.[1]

Other possibilities for the formation of noun + *-ing* adjective compounds are limited. Some examples with nominal elements corresponding to adjuncts appear to be ill-formed, or at least unlikely: *'a *library-working* student', *'a *neighbour-complaining* resident', *'a *witness-tampering* defendant', though a few, with first elements referring to place or time, like '*flat-dwelling* students', '*ground-nesting* birds', 'an *ocean-going* ship', '*street-running* trams', 'a *winter-flowering* cherry' are quite acceptable.

In '*bomb-making* equipment', *equipment* is not equivalent to the subject of *make*, and *bomb-making* is not an adjective. It is a noun compound and the phrase can be glossed as 'equipment for bomb-making'. In 'a *confidence-building* gesture' and 'a *path-breaking* mission', though, the compound modifiers may be seen as ambiguously nominal or adjectival, as are some non-compound modifying *-ing* forms like that of *answering machine*, 'machine which answers' or 'for answering'.

Adjectives like those in

> 'a *carpet-bagging* opportunist', 'a *finger-painting* artist', '*hunter-gathering* communities', 'a *jet-setting* expert'

which do not embody a verb–object relationship correspond to potential compound verbs derived from compound nouns: *carpet-bagger, finger-painting, jet set, hunter-gatherer*.

In compounds with body-part nouns, such as:

> 'an *eye-watering* injection', '*foot-tapping* music', 'a *heartbreaking* situation', 'a *toe-curling* spectacle', '*pulse-pounding, spine-tingling* sexy psychological thrillers' (example from Oshita 1994, 193)

the participial element has the 'involuntary change of state' sense associated with the intransitive use of the corresponding verb (Oshita 1994, 193).

'Emotional event' verbs like *appal, depress, encourage* do not compound easily to form adjectives. Grimshaw (1990) argues that the role of a noun inside a compound must be lower on the hierarchy agent–experiencer–goal/source/location–theme than that of a noun outside it. Hence she regards expressions like 'a *parent-appalling* exploit', in which *parent* is experiencer and *exploit* is theme, as impossible (15f). But this and similar cases, like 'a *patient-depressing* ward', 'a *traveller-encouraging* signpost', 'a *child-boring* show', do not seem entirely ruled out, though perhaps they are not very likely since the noun may well appear redundant.

A subject–verb relation within an *-ing* compound adjective is obviously impossible, since VERB-*ing* adjectives are always 'subjective'. Also ruled out are compounds from which an element – indirect object or complement – obligatory in the corresponding phrase is omitted. Thus, 'a *story-telling* teacher' is acceptable, but not *'a *class-telling* teacher', or *'a *defendant-finding* court'. Compounds in which the *-ing* form corresponds to the verb in a phrasal verb are also unacceptable: *'a *light-turning* caretaker'.

7.2.2   Adjective + verb-*ing*

Adjectives can be compounded only with present-participial adjectives corresponding to verbs of perception:

> '*crazy-looking* people', 'a *bitter-tasting* brew', '*strong-smelling* herbs', '*strange-sounding* names', '*suspicious-looking* packages'.

As with noun + -*ing* formations, there are no combinations in which a lexical element which would be obligatory in a corresponding phrase is omitted: *'a *guilty-finding* court', *'a *happy-making* partner'.

7.3   *-ed*

[handwritten: complement / adjunct]

7.3.1   Noun + verb-*ed*

In a very frequent pattern, nouns compounded with past participles correspond to nouns in prepositional-phrase complements:

'*alcohol-related* incidents' ('incidents related to alcohol'), 'a *coral-encrusted* wreck', '*car-dominated* streets', '*drought-ravaged* areas', '*fear-fuelled* fantasies', '*foil-packed* coffee', '*formaldehyde-exposed* workers', 'a *grime-streaked* car', '*inflation-linked* repayments', 'a *loophole-riddled* treaty', 'the *rat-infested* trench', '*tortoiseshell-framed* spectacles',

and to nouns in adjunct prepositional phrases, with various roles:

'agentive': 'an *architect-designed* house', 'a *chauffeur-driven* car', 'a *government-inspired* panic', 'a *self-inflicted* injury'[2] 'a *solicitor-prepared* will kit', 'the industry remains *state-controlled*'

'instrumental': '*drug-induced* wisdom', '*satellite-borne* pornography', 'a *spring-powered* trap'

'locative': 'a *London-based* company', '*home-distilled* petrol', 'his *jail-painted* portraits', '*night-scented* stock', 'a *Northumberland-born* poet'.[3]

[handwritten: X V O]

A verb–object relationship within a compound is excluded, since adjectives based on the past participles of transitive verbs adjectives are 'objective' (2.5.1): the modified or complemented noun phrase corresponds to the verb's object. Examples like *rent-controlled* may appear to represent such a relationship – 'the rent is controlled', but a more appropriate paraphrase would be 'controlled in rent' (cf. Roeper and Siegel 1978, 234–5). Similar examples are *heartbroken*, *hidebound*, *tip-tilted*, *tongue-tied* and:

'you sit *browfurrowed* over jigsaw puzzles', 'his edited and *colour-enhanced* tape', 'the *skin-stretched* look of the exhausted', 'the village is a *time-stopped* spot'.

[handwritten: related to compound noun]

Other cases, such as 'an *air-conditioned* room', '*gift-wrapped* parcels', '*flavour-sealed* coffee', '*traffic-calmed* streets' can be understood as related to compound nouns: *air-conditioning*, *gift-wrapping*, *flavour sealing*, *traffic calming*, or to compound verbs corresponding to them.

In examples with 'emotional event' verbs, the cause-denoting noun is likely to seem redundant: '*teacher-inspired* student', '*conjurer-enthralled* children'.

7.3.2   Adjective + verb-*ed*

Adjectives cannot be compounded with passive participles, with the exception of a narrowly delimited group: those in which the first element is based on the proper name of a national or social entity, an 'agent' or 'location', as in 'a *British-based* company', 'a *French-developed* missile', 'the *Israeli-occupied* Left Bank' (Mackenzie and Mel'čuk 1986).[4]

Compounds such as *'*raw-eaten* eggs', *'*flat-hammered* metal' corresponding to a resultative or depictive phrase: *John hammered the metal flat, John ate the eggs raw* are usually not acceptable (Levin and Rappaport-Hovav 1995, 44–5). *Clean, close, fine* and *thin* in *clean-shaven, close-cropped, fine-ground, thin-sliced* can be explained as adverbial without the *-ly* suffix, like some of the examples in 7.1. Other cases, like *blue-rinsed, short-cropped, white-painted* are plausibly analysed as compound-noun base + denominal *-ed*, like some of the examples in the next section.

7.3.3   'Bahuvrihi' compounds

Sequences analysable as two-element nominal base + *-ed* are common:

'*clear-sighted* realism', 'the culture is anarchic and *free-spirited*', 'a *glass-fronted* building', 'two *great-coated* figures', 'a *low-powered* airgun', 'his *many-pocketed* fishing vest', '*security-coded* doors'.

Similar examples with other suffixes are occasionally found: '*art-historical* references', 'our *light-industrial* heritage', 'the *military-industrial* complex', 'an *other-worldly* attitude'.

These are sometimes called 'extended bahuvrihi compounds'. The term 'bahuvrihi' is worth pausing over, since it is used for more than one kind of sequence. In 6.1.5 we noted a group of exocentric, 'headless' compounds whose meanings are at variance with those of their second elements. The adjective + noun and noun + noun varieties (*highbrow, spoonbill*) are often labelled 'bahuvrihi' (cf. Jespersen 1942, 8.6; Marchand 1969, 5.11). Some writers, like Spencer (1991, 311), include 'verb–complement' compounds like *pickpocket* and *rotgut* under the label of bahuvrihi. These differ from the adjective + noun and noun + noun kinds in having no 'extended' forms.[5]

Adjective + noun and noun + noun 'bahuvrihi-compounds proper' (Kastovsky 1992, 395) can be found in Old English. Besides a few exocentric noun compounds similar to *spoonbill* which correspond to Latin formations, e.g. *anhorn* 'one horn', 'unicorn' (Latin *unicornis*), *fifleaf(e)* 'five leaves', 'potentilla' (Latin *quinquefolium*), Old English has a more numerous group of adjectival formations which match the pattern of Sanskrit *bahu-vrihi-*, literally 'much rice'. *Vrihi-*, 'rice', is a noun but the compound is declined as an adjective and means 'having much rice'. Comparable Old English adjectives in which the second element has the form of a noun include *anræd* '(of) one mind', 'resolute', *bærfot* 'barefoot', *brunecg* '(with) a bright edge', *eaðmod* '(of) a humble mind', *yfelwille* '(with) an evil will', 'malevolent'. Some of these have synonymous 'extended' forms with adjectival or participial suffixes, e.g. *anrædlic, eaðmodig, yfelwillende*. Old English adjectives like *bærfot* can be compared with modern English noun compounds which are typically used as modifiers, like those in *'copper-plate* handwriting', *'long-range* forecast'. Exocentric adjective + noun and noun + noun compounds are sometimes matched by extended forms in *-ed*: *'bareback(ed)* rider', *'duckbill(ed)* platypus', *'long-nose(d)* pliers'; *bighead* (noun) and *bigheaded, faint-heart* (noun) and *faint-hearted*. Thus the range of compounds referred to as 'bahuvrihi' straddles the noun–adjective divide and includes suffixed forms, which of course are not headless (1.2.2).

Exocentric noun	Nominal attributive	Extended bahuvrihi adjective
	bareback (rider)	*barebacked* (rider)
	brushtail (possum)	
dimwit		*dimwitted*
	duckbill (platypus)	*duckbilled* (platypus)
featherbrain		*featherbrained*
	long-nose (pliers)	*long-nosed* (pliers)
paperback	*paperback* (book)	*paperbacked* (book)
redskin	*redskin* (warrior)	*redskinned* (warrior)
bluebell		
		hairy-nosed (wombat)

Bahuvrihi compounds are typically descriptive labels for living things. Earlier examples include nicknames, like Old English *Widsið*, 'wide journey', *Bluebeard, Hotspur, (Harold) Harefoot*. A number of extended bahuvrihis have body-part second elements and first elements which are metaphorical or indicate resemblance, e.g. *cool-headed, clear-headed, level-headed, pig-headed; almond-eyed, eagle-eyed, lynx-eyed; lantern-jawed, pigeon-toed, sharp-eared, straight-faced, tight-fisted, wasp-waisted*. Endocentrically-used phrases which are idiomatic in the same ways, like *a lantern jaw, a straight face*, may well be based on the extended forms.

Some *-ed* compounds in which the base of the second element may be either nominal or verbal are open to more than one analysis: 'Are the British *colour-prejudiced*?': 'imbued with colour prejudice' or 'prejudiced with regard

$$[x + N] - ed$$
$$[x + V] - ed$$

to colour'; 'his *oak-panelled* study': 'having oak panels' or 'panelled in oak'; 'the *pedal-powered* drive chain': 'having pedal power' or 'powered by pedals'. Other combinations in which -*ed* is either denominal or deverbal include sequences like *well-intentioned*, and pairs of compound and phrase like *strange-shaped* and *strangely shaped*, *deep-rooted* and *firmly rooted*, *short-sighted* and *partially sighted*, *lighter-hearted* and *more light hearted*, *internationally minded* beside *single-minded* and *liberal-minded* (see Jespersen 1914, 15.34–15.36, for many more examples).

7.4   Adjective

7.4.1   Noun + adjective

The noun in a noun + adjective compound corresponds to the complement of a prepositional phrase:

'the *Balkan-weary* troops', 'Central Europeans have gone *bike-crazy*', 'a *car-dependent* culture', '*commission-hungry* advisers', '*dishwasher-safe* plates', 'everyone is *computer-literate*', '6,500 *cycle-friendly* miles', '*energy-efficient* buildings', 'the *fossil-rich* sands of the Gobi', '*labour-intensive* methods', 'a *media-shy* financier', 'a *self-confident* performer', 'large areas of the world are *radar-blank*', 'the car-thief is being challenged to become *victim-aware*'.

As Marchand (1969, 86) notes, a few examples, like *colour-fast*, *foot-loose*, *top-heavy*, appear also to reflect a subject–complement relationship ('the colour is fast').

Some final elements of noun + adjective compounds appear in series of forms like *colour-blind*, *night-blind*, *snow-blind*, *class-conscious*, *style-conscious*, *football-mad*, *power-mad* (Marchand 1969, 84, 87). In such circumstances they may take on a suffix-like character, as happened with -*less* (2.5.2), from an Old English adjective *leas* 'lacking', 'free (from)'. Further examples are *ice-free*, *smoke-free*, *sugar-free*, *accident-prone*, *drought-prone*, *gaffe-prone*, *blame-worthy*, *noteworthy*, *praiseworthy*. *Proof* attaches to verbal as well as nominal elements: *jam-proof*, *snow-proof*, *sound-proof*, *tamper-proof*, *thief-proof*. *Happy* has undergone some semantic modification, appearing in a variety of twentieth-century adjectives descriptive of demoralized states: *bomb-happy*: 'many troops . . . were rendered "bomb-happy" and fell easy prisoners' (OED: 1943), *battle-happy*: 'two thoroughly frightened battle-happy guys' (Russell 1947), *queue-happy*: 'They were tired and "queue-happy" from months of waiting in line' (Russell 1947). Other examples mean 'enthusiast': 'election-happy campaigners' (Russell 1947), 'a hi-fi-happy neighbour' (Guardian: 1996), or something like 'too eager to resort to . . .': 'bark-happy watch-dogs' (Russell 1947), 'PC denies that he was truncheon-happy' (Guardian: 1996).

Examples like '*continent-wide* deflation' and colour adjectives like *ashblond, blood-red, bottle-green, peacock blue* can be seen as embodying a comparison, and in some older examples the first element has acquired the character of an intensifier: *dog-tired* (OED notes also *dog-drunk, dog-hungry, dog-lean, dog-mad*), 'a *rock-solid* Labour seat'; *paper-thin, razor-sharp, skin-tight, stone-blind, stone-cold, stone-dead, stone-deaf.* OED defines *brand-new* as 'new, as if fresh and glowing from the furnace', and *cock-sure* more tentatively: 'the sense ought to be "as sure as a cock"' (OED *cock-sure*).

7.4.2   Adjective + adjective

A few examples have denominal and participial first elements which are intensifying in effect, like *icy-cold, silky-soft, snowy-white*, and *freezing cold, hopping mad, piping hot* (explained by OED as 'so hot as to make a piping sound'), *wringing wet, yawning dull,* and there are colour expressions such as *bluish-green, pearly grey.* We noted in 1.2.2 that expressions like that in '*public–private* partnership', in which neither element is the head, are not complex words. Word-like antithetical combinations on this pattern can however sometimes be found: 'The ironic cruel-compassionate exposition of the everyday life of the English middle classes' (Observer: 1968), 'Into this much admired pantheon . . . Krim, eager for the American Experience, muscled his humble-surly way' (Sunday Times: 1970).

7.5   Attributive and predicative

The object–verb-*ing* formations of 7.2.1 are comparable in transparency and ease of formation to the 'syntactic' nominal *bicycle-repairing* kind of 6.1.1. With other kinds of adjective compound – 'bahuvrihi' cases aside – potential uncertainties and ambiguities of meaning are much less likely to arise than they are with noun + noun compounds (6.2, 6.3), since the head is always a relational element. New, occasional, formations are frequent, and typically lack any appearance of novelty.

Most of the examples in the preceding sections were encountered in texts, chiefly in newspapers, and most of them are attributive. Biber (1988, 104ff) identifies a number of features associated with the concise presentation of information in texts, including nouns, prepositional phrases and the use of a varied vocabulary, reflecting precise lexical choice. Attributive adjectives, as he observes, 'are a more integrated form of nominal elaboration than pre-dicative adjectives' (105), and longer words are likely to have more specific meanings than shorter words. It is thus not surprising to find that texts, predominantly written, which are concerned with the presentation of information, are prolific sources of compound adjectives. The 'information-packing' function of attributive compound adjectives is obvious in:

> He tells the story of Hippasus, who discomfited the Pythagoreans. These bean-eating, island-dwelling, soul-migrating, mathematics-revering Greeks believed in a universe made up of whole numbers . . . (Guardian: 1999)

A potential disadvantage of predicative compound adjectives is that the modifying element may point to salient information which might be more effectively placed after the relational, head, element; cf. the following examples:

> Politically it is not vote-winning to talk about measures that might actually make the public suffer. (Guardian: 1997)

> We're at this time water-critical in the L[unar] M[odule]. We'd like to use as little as possible. (Astronaut, quoted in Sunday Times: 1970)

A predicative adjective compound may be prepared for in the preceding context, so that the information in its modifier is more appropriately defocused:

> More scarily, sleep deprivation can be blamed for accidents such as the Challenger disaster when the space shuttle exploded during take off in 1986. The ground crew had been sleep-deprived as had some of the managers. (Guardian: 1998)

In this example, and in other predicative examples containing past participle forms interpretable as either verbal or adjectival, like *starved* in 'my son was oxygen-starved at birth' (Guardian), or *harvested* in 'The ferns available are all salvage harvested and therefore do not contravene environmental ethics' (plant shop leaflet), the distinction between compound adjective and compound verb is tenuous. As we see in Chapter 8, the inappropriate defocusing of salient information is likely to be a factor which decreases the acceptability of compound verbs.

Notes

1. In response to Chomsky's (1970, 214ff) comment on the 'variety and idiosyncrasy' of *self* compounds, Meijs (1975, 46ff) points out that the idiomatic appearance of many examples is also a feature of corresponding sentences and therefore not to be ascribed to the compounds themselves. In

'a *self-clearing* cafeteria', '*self-effacing* charm', 'a *self-justifying* excuse', *self* represents an entity associated in some way with the head of the noun phrase, much as the modifier in 'a *dishonest* excuse' describes the maker of the excuse.

2. *Self* occurs as modifier in both *-ing* and *-ed* adjective compounds, since it can be understood as corresponding to either agent or patient.

3. Other relationships seem unlikely: ?'*fog-glimpsed* figures', *'*bed-stored* boxes' (i.e. 'glimpsed through the fog', 'stored under the bed') (cf. Roeper and Siegel 1978, 242).

4. Mackenzie and Mel'čuk (1986) suggest that the participial element must be that of a verb with a meaning in the areas of 'create', 'maintain', 'support', 'control', 'permit'. However, some of their starred examples, such as *'*Israeli-opposed* dictatorship' or *'*Japanese-captured* fort' do not seem unacceptable.

5. Marchand regards all exocentric compounds as 'pseudo-compounds'. He describes them under 'zero-derivation', assuming, for example, *paleface* to be derived from a phrase, 'a person with a pale face' (1969, 113ff, 386ff).

8

Verb compounds

[handwritten annotation] Verb compound → √ derived from adjectival/nominal expressions
→ X combination of two lexical items

8.1 Scope

A compound verb has a final verbal element, modified usually by a noun, sometimes by an adjective: *to handweave, to parcel-bomb, to cold-call*. Verbs, however, should not be thought of as compounded – formed by the combining of two lexical items – in the same way as noun compounds and adjective compounds. Verb compounding is a productive process in some languages, but English is not one of them. Despite some suggestions to the contrary (e.g. Brömser 1985, Lehrer 1996b), there will almost always be an intermediary nominal or adjectival expression from which an English compound verb is derived. For this reason, Marchand's term for all formations of the kind illustrated in this chapter is 'pseudo-compound verb' (1969, 100–7). It is convenient, however, to go on referring to 'compound verbs' here.

Some compound verbs are derived, like the verbs in 2.3.1, by transposition from nominal expressions, e.g. *to litmus-test*: '[They] elected to litmus-test the first night of their new lives with a high-profile outing' (Guardian: 1996); *to rugby-tackle*: 'The trouble appears to have started after a protester rugby-tackled a police officer' (Guardian: 1999). Further examples of this kind are:

to cannonball, handcuff, honeymoon, machine-gun, mastermind, mountain-bike, pitchfork, rubber-stamp, sandbag, sandpaper, shipwreck, short-circuit, snowball, wheel-clamp, wrongfoot.

Other compound verbs do not correspond to homonymous nouns:

Hogarth will literary-edit the proofs for me: & Kennington art-edit the books (OED: 1923).

St Petersburg talent-spotted Wright of Derby when he was hardly known in England. (Guardian: 1998)

They are felt to be based on suffixed compound nouns or adjectives, and are generally agreed to be the products of backformation (11.3), which involves a reanalysis of constituent structure. *Literary editor, art editor* and *talent-spotter*, or *talent-spotting* are noun compounds consisting of adjective or noun + [verb + suffix], but *to literary-edit, to art-edit* and *to talent-spot* presuppose an analysis [adjective or noun + verb] + suffix.[1] Similar cases are:

> *to brainwash, computer-generate, deep-fry, dive-bomb, drink-drive, earmark, free-associate, ghost-write, globe-trot, guest-edit, housekeep, sleep-walk, spoonfeed, spring-clean, stage-manage, tape-record, window-shop.*

Where more than one related nominal or adjectival form is familiar, there may appear to be more than one source of a verb: *to proof-read* joins a family with the nouns *proof-reader* and *proof-reading* and the participial adjective *proof-read* among its members. *To big-game-hunt*: '[He] . . . big-game-hunted, smoked a pipe, enjoyed being thought a spy' (Guardian: 1996) might be based on *big game hunter* or transposed from another nominal, *big game hunt*.

As with noun and adjective compounds, verb compounds may be formed by analogy with others of the same kind: *to chain-drink* (Pennanen 1966, 115) and *to sight-translate* (Hall 1956, 85) are modelled on *to chain-smoke* and *to sight-read*. Verbs in a small group appear to have a verbal first element and to share the pattern of *to drink-drive*: *crash-land, dry-clean, fly-drive, freeze-dry, shrink-wrap, strip-search*.

Verbal expressions with *-ly* adverbs as modifiers may correspond to established nominal expressions, as in:

> '[They] rejected his charge that Cambridge University had constructively dismissed him' (Guardian: 1996); '. . . the plight of refugees who have been ethnically cleansed from the kingdom' (Guardian: 1998); 'One possibility is to genetically-engineer oil seed rape' (Guardian: 1995); 'The RSC version has been politically corrected' (Guardian: 1998).

These, though, are not plausible compound verbs, in contrast to *conventional cook*: 'For best results, conventional cook' (instruction on packet) or *part-privatize*: 'government plans to part-privatise the tube' (Guardian: 1999), which have non-*ly* adverbial modifiers. (Compare the adjectival phrases and compounds in 7.1.)

In striking contrast to noun and adjective compounds, verb compounds are uncommon. Seen out of context, a verb compound may be judged doubtfully acceptable, or even ill-formed, and when encountered in context it is likely to strike the hearer or reader as rather conspicuous. Verb compounds are of interest, however, for a number of reasons, and in this chapter we shall look at numerous examples, shown wherever possible in context. We shall consider why the formation of compound verbs should be so restricted, and look at some circumstances which may discourage or favour their use.

regular inflections
irregular inflection

8.2 Inflection

verb – same meaning – follow the past tense form
verb – not same meaning – not follow the past tense form

Uncertainty about the past tense forms of irregular verbs is sometimes mentioned as a factor inhibiting the use of compound verbs, or at least restricting them to infinitive, gerund or present-participle form, though in fact not very many examples are affected. Compound verbs perceived as transposed without affix from compound nouns often have the regular past tense ending: *joyrided*: 'We joined forces and captured a motor-ambulance which joy-rided us back here' (OED: 1915), *lipsticked, moonlighted* (*to moonlight*: 'to work at a secondary job, especially at night'), *potshotted*: 'And what the deuce of your punctuation? ... How much the fine careless rapture and therefore to be potshotted at ... ?' (OED: 1918), *soundbited*: 'And Ross Perot thought he couldn't be soundbited' (example from Harris 1993, 139).[2] Compounds like these are comparable with headless, exocentric noun compounds like *lowlife*, *figleaf* (1.2.2, 6.1.5): they have no constituent which is of the same kind as the whole. As heads of the noun compounds from which the verb compounds are derived, *ride, stick, light, shot* and *bite* are no longer related to irregular verbs (cf. Kim *et al.* 1991) and thus cannot be irregularly inflected. Similarly, simple nouns based on irregular verbs are themselves the bases of regular verbs, cf. *to cost*, 'to work out the cost of', as in 'John costed the equipment' beside the non-derived verb in 'the book cost £10', *to cast*, 'to put a cast on': 'the doctor casted his arm' (example from Kim *et al.* 1991, 179) beside 'John cast his vote', 'the ecologists hided the forest' (example from Spencer 1991, 184) beside 'John hid from the police'. Compare also denominal particle + base verbs like *input* (5.2.1) 'data verification is done by the computer's reflecting back to the user ... exactly what has been inputted' (OED: 1967).

Compounds perceived as backformed from a noun or adjective compound with a suffixed deverbal head will inflect in accordance with the non-compounded verb: *book-kept*: 'He book-kept for the camp' (OED: 1917), *browbeat, button-held*: 'Charles Lamb, being button-held one day by Coleridge ... cut off the button' (OED: 1880), *ghost-written*: 'The autobiographical boloney ghost-written by Samuel Crowther for Ford' (OED: 1932), *gold-dug*: 'I'll bet she just gold-dug Eddie' (OED: 1947), *hand-wrote*: 'To prove that Francis hand-wrote the Junian letters is not to demonstrate that he composed them' (OED: 1871). Kim *et al.* (1991) show experimentally that, for instance, the verb *to line-drive*, 'to hit a line-drive', is more likely to have the regular past tense form *line-drived*, while the homonymous verb meaning 'to drive along a line' (presumably from *line-driving*) is more likely to have the past tense form *line-drove*. Some variations can be explained as the consequence of alternative analyses. *To spotlight* for example can be seen as transposed from the noun *spotlight*: 'His understanding of the jazz idiom spotlighted the "bluesy" features of the Concerto beautifully' (OED: 1963), or as backformed from *spotlighting*: 'I feel that my future career as a painter stands spot-lit and exposed' (OED: 1976).

Not all cases fall into these two groups. Compounds corresponding to noun compounds with a 'zero' derived deverbal head like *deep-freeze, free-fall* retain the irregular inflection of *freeze* and *fall* in 'If the cook deep-froze the body, he knew about the murder' (OED: 1957) and 'I free-fell an eternity' (OED: 1959), no doubt because *freeze* and *fall* are far more common as verbs than as nouns or heads of noun compounds. *To hairweave* is plausibly based on *hairweaving*, but the following newspaper example admits the possibility of regularized inflection: 'One man we heard of had, sadly, to have his hair unwoven (or de-weaved) as he was posted to a country where hairweaving was unknown.' *Wove* as a rather infrequent form, may be obsolescent: it is displaced by the regular form also in 'George Carman QC . . . said Mr Aitken had "weaved a tangled web"' (Guardian: 1997).

Prescriptive considerations may also sometimes play a part, since regular inflection is apt to be seen as 'lazy' or uneducated (cf. Marcus *et al.* 1995, 244–5). They may account for *hunger-struck* rather than *hunger-striked* in 'She has hunger-struck in prison' (OED: 1914). The particle + base verb *to input* sometimes retains the irregular inflection of *put*: 'At regular intervals, the day lists are input to the computer' (OED: 1968). The form *broadcasted* is to be expected since, as Pinker (1999, 168) points out, the noun *broadcast* is much more common than the verb and likely therefore to be felt as basic. The same may well be true of the noun and verb *forecast*. Fowler however finds both *broadcasted* and *forecasted* 'ugly' (1965, 206).[3]

8.3 Focus

Tennis-playing as a noun compound allows an event to be referred to as an entity: *John prefers tennis-playing to studying for his exams*; as an attributive adjective compound it constitutes a description: *a tennis-playing student*. Both are unproblematic: we can easily imagine suitable contexts, and as we have seen, noun and adjective compounds like these are very freely formed. By contrast, a context in which an infinitive or finite verb *tennis-play* would be more felicitous in describing an event than *play tennis* (*John tennis-plays*) is comparatively unlikely. Pennanen (1966, 131) gives an example which nicely illustrates the appropriate avoidance of a finite compound verb:

I think you enjoy it because your wife enjoys it. She does not enjoy paintings, so you do not paint. If she enjoyed snake-hunting I think you would hunt snakes.

'I think you would snake-hunt' in this context would of course mean the loss of end-focus for *snakes*.

One reason why compound verbs are so often judged unacceptable or non-occurring may be that it is the citation form, the infinitive, that comes first to mind, and the simple finite form which is imagined in a context. Estimates of the frequency and acceptability of compound verbs may depend on what forms of the verb are being taken into account. Non-finite examples which approach the status of nominal or adjectival compounds may appear comparatively natural:

> First women are consumers, clothes-buying as college girls ... then appliance-buying as housewives. (P. Macpherson, *Reflecting on The Bell Jar*, Routledge 1991, 17)

> One of Marcus Plantin's first jobs in television was gift-wrapping presents for the conveyor belt on the BBC's Generation Game. (Guardian: 1997)

> Brown has been working hard to ensure his friends and allies are promoted, relentlessly empire-building. (Guardian: 1997)

> The images were taken on 35mm film, then computer scanned and printed on an Iris ink jet. (Guardian: 1996)

> the animals will be mercy-killed (Guardian: 1997)

> [She] failed to get legal aid in Germany where claims are means-tested. (Guardian: 1996)

> The site was password-protected to avoid alarming innocent Web surfers. (Guardian: 1997)

However, as we noted in 7.5 with predicative compound adjectives, the information conveyed by the modifying element can sometimes appear inappropriately defocused, and the same is likely to be true of some examples like these. Compound verbs in progressive or perfect participle form, and those in infinitive form, may be more likely to seem awkward for this reason:

> I was cabinet-making in the garage. (Hall 1956)

> she could have guest-edited any number of women's magazines (Guardian: 1996)

> she has cold-called presidents and film stars (Guardian: 1997)

> These obvious facilities for cyclists around Seattle are backed up by extensive campaigns to stop driving to work, to car-share, and to cycle. (Cycle Touring and Campaigning: 1996)

> Harris insisted on pursuing the strategy even after it became possible to 'precision bomb' military or industrial targets. (Guardian: 1994)

Why shouldn't I back-seat-drive? (Hall 1956)

If I put a hilt on the other sword, will you sword-fight me? (Hall 1956).

The problem of inappropriate de-emphasis of 'new' material which we expect to find following the verb, may seem especially acute where the verb is a simple finite or imperative form:

> As they rock-climb, learn to swim and gear up for the end-of-term performance . . . (Guardian: 1997)

> remove the eggs when you spring prune the roses (Guardian: 1997)

> If you want to create cloud-like drifts of pale blue or pink, direct sow some forget-me-nots. (Guardian: 1998)

> pull out the old electronic organiser and time-manage the rest of your week (Guardian: 1998).

8.4   Lexicalization

The content of a modifier in a compound verb may be more naturally defocused if the nominal or adjectival expression which is the source of the verb is a familiar one, like *guest editor*, *cabinet-maker*. Compare the compound verb, corresponding to the established nominal expressions *fund-raising* and *fund-raiser*, with the verb–complement collocation in 'Tom had to learn to fundraise and organize accounts' (Hackney Gazette).

A number of writers have suggested in fact that only lexicalized compounds can give rise to backformed compound verbs: 'the more idiosyncratic the base compound's meaning is, the more likely the two major constituents . . . are reanalyzed as one semantic unit. . . . the internal semantics is the driving force behind the structural reanalysis' (Oshita 1994, 200). Conversely, a transparent, or relatively transparent, synthetic noun compound is not thought to be a suitable base for a verb compound. This is said to account for the ill-formed nature of verbs like *to peace-make*, or *to tennis-play* (noted as clearly unacceptable by Roeper and Siegel 1978, 217–18) or *to train-ride* (condemned by Scalise 1986, 118).

It certainly seems reasonable to suppose that the lexicalization of a noun or adjective compound is among the conditions favouring the formation and use of a compound verb. Cases like the following are not especially hard to find:

> 'We're as likely to ghetto-blast at 3 am as we are to run naked down the Strand' (Guardian: 1993); 'intellectuals who fellow-travel the Communist line' (OED: 1949); 'Mr Bullock . . . was headhunted from Flymo to revive

Neill' (OED: 1985); 'A man who kerb-crawls is not committing an offence' (OED: 1971); 'I couldn't bring myself to muckrake details of the guard's murder' (OED: 1973); 'She fought the steering-wheel as though she were shadow-boxing' (OED: 1924); 'Can that! Soft pedal on that chatter, Ben!' (OED: 1916); 'Some think he is trying to tailor-make a monarchy' (OED: 1959); '"We would like doctors who have any cause for concern about colleagues", demanded the Patients' Association, "to whistle-blow on them"' (Guardian: 1997).

Many examples, however, are not noticeably lexicalized, and we can point to other factors which can contribute to the acceptability of a compound verb.

8.5 Acceptability in use

Compound verbs can be effectively used in situations where it is appropriate to focus a constituent other than the one which figures as the compound's first element. It may be appropriate if the compound combines or is based on items or notions introduced in the preceding context:

> The second important display is 'head-shaking' . . . Birds already paired together frequently head-shake together. (OED: 1959)

> Please note, we will be undertaking random police checks on our applicants. If you are not prepared to be police-checked, we cannot accept your application. (Instruction to charity volunteers 1998)

> Our fragile landscape is essentially man-made – and much of it could be just as easily man-destroyed by discordant intrusion. (Cycle Touring and Campaigning: 1999)

> She has spent the day exploring various old churches in Périgueux. . . . Day of the general mobilization she had been cathedral-looking at Avignon. (Arthur Koestler, *Scum of the Earth*, 1941, 179)

In the following, with the noun corresponding to the direct object of the simple verb placed out of the way inside the compound, new or focused information can be indicated in the compound verb's object:

> Please have clerk weigh and price mark bananas. (Hall 1956: sign in supermarket)

> The row started when shop stewards complained that the women had queue jumped a union waiting list of people wanting to become ferry drivers. (OED: 1976)

Like Chaucer, he role-plays himself. (D. Howard, *The Idea of the Canterbury Tales*, 1976, 376)

The U.S. Army may not wire-tap American civilians in foreign countries. (OED: 1976)

They need only a movement on the flank to panic-strike them. (OED: 1898).

An adjunct or prepositional complement may gain from being the sole element, or the sole weighty element, to the right of the verb:

. . . a 76-year-old who has lost both legs, but still parachute jumps for charity (Guardian: 1996)

As we stagger about in disbelief at the government's idea to road-build us out of recession . . . (London Cyclist: 1993)

Location-filmed in the pile which inspired it, it's a tale of secrets . . . in a crumbling castle. (Guardian: 1996).

Compound verbs may be motivated by a need for compactness, as in instructions like 'hand sort and wash before use', 'shallow fry for 10 minutes' or the message 'Word is preparing to background print the document'. Cf. also 'Robert Newton stars as the doctor planning to acid-bath murder his wife's lover' (Guardian: 1996, from a summary of television programmes).

In many less stylistically-marked cases, a first element usefully renders a compound verb's meaning more specific than that of the corresponding simple verb, provided in general that it does not introduce information which is too unexpected. The verb in 'many people will probably never cycle-commute regularly' (Cycle Touring and Campaigning: 1996) was found in an article about cycling, and *cycle* had been prepared for in the context. The improbability of the verb in a made-up example, *John knife-cut the loaf*, on the other hand, can be ascribed to the fact that *knife* can normally be taken for granted and needlessly narrows the verb's meaning. 'John finger-painted a landscape' or 'Chancellor tongue-lashes Free Democrat' (examples from Hall 1956) sound much better: *finger* and *tongue* tell us something relevant about the nature of the actions, as do the first elements in many of the examples already given. Further illustrative cases are:

The clubs offer members . . . the chance to bulk purchase branded goods. (Guardian: 1993)

Let's charcoal-broil a steak! (Hall 1956)

On [the cell door] had been chalk-marked a very poor representation of a skull and cross-bones. (Brian Keenan, *An Evil Cradling*, Vintage, 1992, 53)

> In 1993, *The Sun* confessed it had computer manipulated a picture of a Franciscan monk with his girlfriend to show the monk wearing a habit. (Guardian: 1998)
>
> New tourists come in and say 'Are you the place that deep fries Mars Bars? (Guardian: 1996)
>
> In California, . . . Hollywood executives are even teaching themselves to dream-solve problems while they sleep. (Guardian: 2000)
>
> If you must night-drive, keep the dash-lights as dim as possible. (OED: 1956)
>
> If your dog had been obedience-trained he would not have been stolen so easily. (OED: 1971)
>
> At home, I often wish to scan and optical character read German text. (Guardian: 1997)
>
> a German patrol that had radio-located the aircraft (OED: 1943)
>
> It [a banana] is imported through Southampton, road freighted to Lancashire for ripening, and then on to Somerset. (London Cyclist: 1994)

In the last example, the inclusion of *road* in the verb allows the writer to maintain the series of locative adverbials which underlines the point about the unnecessary transport of goods.

8.6   Frequency

It is sometimes suggested that compound verb formation in English is a modern phenomenon. Earlier examples can be found in OED, e.g. *to law-break*, *to bloodsuck* and *to jail-deliver*: 'I wot forsothe for law breking thou shalt lawe breke' (OED: 1382); 'Howe ought he to be ruled that hath ben blode sucked' (OED: 1541; *bloodsucker* 'leech' is recorded in 1347); 'It dissolves the very workes of the devill, Iaile-delivers his prisoners' (OED: 1631; the noun compound *jail-delivery* 'deliverance from jail' is dated 1592). Kastovsky (1992, 375) suggests that Old English verbs like *ellencampian* 'to campaign vigorously' and *morgenwacian* 'to rise early' 'may represent sporadic attempts at verbal composition'. But a number of writers perceive verb compounding as having greatly increased in productivity in the last two centuries, and especially in the twentieth (see e.g. Hall 1956, Kastovsky 1986a, Marchand 1969, 102, 104). It is true that most examples to be found in dictionaries are modern, but this must largely reflect the greatly-increased chances in modern times of a new 'nonce' word, especially a noticeable one, being preserved. Lexicographers now frequently update dictionaries, include appendices of new words, and make far greater use of newspapers and journals than the earlier editors of the OED did. Hall also felt that compound verbs were on the increase, but his judicious estimate in the 1950s that 'an attentive reader and listener comes across a new one at least every two weeks' (1956, 87) hardly needs revising at the end of the century: compound verbs are still rare.

Genuine verb compounding – a typologically rare phenomenon, as noted by Gerdts (1998, 99) – has been discussed and illustrated with examples from a number of languages: see especially Mithun (1984, 1994) and Rosen (1989). These discussions indicate that the factors favouring it are similar to those illustrated above for English pseudo-verb compounding – the need to background known information, to allow a constituent to occupy a position of salience, or to narrow the meaning of a verb. But Kastovsky's speculation (1986a, 419) that increased numbers of examples might be a factor in the future development of genuine verb compounding in English does not seem well founded.

We can expand on Jespersen's observation that English compound verbs 'are felt to some extent as contrary to idiom' (1942, 9.71). They exemplify a conflict: with the verbal element on the right, they conform to the 'right-hand head rule' (1.2.2), but the preferred position of salient information is to the right of the finite verb. As we saw in 5.2.1, compound verbs with locative particles as modifying elements, like *backfill, downshift, upgrade*, are also rare – in marked contrast to left-headed verb + particle collocations such as *cut up, take away, turn off*. The conclusion must be that genuine verb compounding is not likely to develop in modern English.

Notes

1. 'Syntactic' noun compounds like *bicycle-repairing* (6.1.1) can be analysed as either [[bicycle repair]ing] or as [[bicycle] [repairing]], since they are in effect parasynthetic formations (1.2.2).
2. Harris's explanation for the form of *soundbited* is functional; *bited* reflects the writer's concern not to draw attention to the usual sense of *to bite*, a likely consequence of using the form *soundbitten*.
3. Fowler (1925) cautiously advocates the compromise of a past tense form *broadcasted* to avoid confusion with the present tense, but a past participle *broadcast*. *Broadcasted*, he thinks, is 'less wrong than *forecasted*', but (oddly) 'less right than *roughcasted*'.

9

Stem formations

9.1 Scope

We have defined stems as lexical elements which cannot be used on their own (1.2.1, 1.4). The examples in 9.4 will illustrate stems in combination with prefixes and suffixes, e.g. *pericarp* 'seed vessel' (Greek *carpos* 'fruit'), *amorphous* (Greek *morphe* 'form'), *ovoid* 'egg-like' (Latin *ovum* 'egg'), and stems in combination with one another, e.g. *carnivore* 'flesh-eater' (Latin *caro-* 'flesh', *vorare* 'to devour'), and with words, e.g. *photoallergy* 'allergy caused by light'. Stems belong exclusively to the Latin- and Greek-derived area, or stratum, of the vocabulary. In 9.2 we shall look at more precise uses of the term 'stratum', and in 9.3 at dependent bases like those in *optimize* or *ventriloquist*, which can be related to English words, as well as stem bases like *-carp-*, *-morph-* and *-vor-*, which cannot.

9.2 Strata

There are no native affixes which will not attach to foreign base words (aside from the odd historical relic like the *-th* of *warmth* or *growth*, unlikely to occur with new bases of any kind), but some foreign affixes, like *-ity*, *-ive*, *a(n)-*, *dis-* attach only or preferentially to foreign base words and to stems. Native base words are invariable in form (again, words with *-th* provide fossilized exceptions: *width* and *depth*), whereas foreign base words may, when combined with some foreign suffixes, be different, in vowel or consonant sounds, or in accentuation, or both, from the corresponding independent forms; compare *employee*, *visibility*, *prestigious* with *employer*, *visibleness*, *prestigeful*. Stems take only foreign affixes, cf. *acardiac*, *haloid*, *hydrous*, *dental*, *thanatist*, *opacity*, *luminize*, *vitrify*. In the preceding chapters we have noted in passing a few characteristics of words with foreign affixes, such as the occurrence of stems with *-oid* (4.3), the loss of a final syllable in bases combining with *-ize* (2.3) and *-ist* (4.2), and of final *-ate* in words suffixed by *-ant* (2.4), the invariable placement of main stress immediately before *-ic* (2.5.2).

Differences of form between native and foreign words are prominent in generative studies aimed at accounting for the knowledge speakers have of the make-up and pronunciation of complex words. A precisely-defined concept of 'stratum' figures in work of the last two decades on lexical phonology (or lexical morphology). A standard assumption of such work is that some affixes are assumed to have effects on the bases they attach to. According to whether there is an effect or not, affixes are assigned to two groups, those of 'stratum 1' or 'non-neutral' or '+' affixes, and 'stratum 2', or 'neutral', or '#' affixes. + indicates a 'morpheme boundary' across which certain phonological rules are seen to operate, and # a 'word boundary', which blocks rules designed to alter the shapes of bases. Many – not all – foreign affixes are non-neutral, while all the native affixes are neutral.

Different sets of interacting phonological and morphological rules operate on different strata, or levels. We have just noted some examples with *-ee, -ity* and *-ous*, stratum 1 suffixes, contrasting them with *-er, -ness* and *-ful*, stratum 2 suffixes, whose bases never vary from their independent forms. Further examples of stratum 1 affixation are *-ic* (*allergy, allergic*), *-ify* (*rigid, rigidify*), *-al* (*accident, accidental*). Affixes on stratum 1 may themselves be subject to variation in form, as with the endings of *diminution, explanation, premonition*, and compare stratum 1 *in-* (reflecting assimilation in Latin, cf. 3.3) in *illegible* with stratum 2 *un-* in *unlikely*. Rules involving stratum 1, or non-neutral, affixes apply first, thus offering an explanation for the fact that these affixes are (often) unable to occur 'outside' neutral, stratum 2, affixes: the 'Affix Ordering Generalization'. **Carefulity* and **hardenation* are impossible: they contain a stratum 2 suffix inside a stratum 1 suffix. Stratum 1 affixes tend to be more restricted in their application, and the outputs of rules attaching them to bases are said to block those of later, more general rules. Thus *advantageous* and *decency* preempt the possible words *advantageful* and *decentness*, illustrating the operation of the 'elsewhere condition', a general principle which says that general rules apply only where specific rules do not – elsewhere.[1]

An embarrassment for such frameworks is that affixes are resistant to classification in this way. Two very frequent sequences, for example, *-ize* and *-ation* as in *Westernization* and *-able* and *-ity* as in *washability*, involve a suffix usually judged to be neutral before a non-neutral one – though in fact the nature of both *-able* and *-ize* is problematic. According to Aronoff (1976, 121ff) there is one kind of *-able* (sometimes taking the form of *-ible*) in idiosyncratic *tolerable, divisible* and *cómparable* and another in fully analysable *toleratable* and *repairable*. Katamba (1993, 114–15) judges *-ize* to be neutral, on the ground that its attachment has no effect on stress in its bases, but it qualifies for non-neutrality in that it attaches to stems as well as words, as in *anodize, embolize, iridize*, and to dependent bases like those of *Bolshevize*, *diarize, feminize,* which are identifiable with words. There are several other affixes which in combination with word bases display the kind of predictability and productivity usually associated with stratum 2, but which also attach to dependent forms, behaviour which is generally agreed to belong only to stratum 1. Examples are: *-ant,* cf. *colourant, sealant, propellant* beside *celebrant, defoliant, postulant; -ee,* cf. *experimentee, supervisee, trainee* beside *amputee, evacuee, biographee; -ism,* cf. *absurdism, Americanism, sexism* beside *cladism, heurism, feminism.*

In a recent proposal in which these difficulties do not arise (Giegerich 1999), strata are defined with reference to bases, not affixes, and affixes are not exclusively associated with either stratum. Stratum 2 accommodates word bases and affixes which combine productively with them in ways which can be stated in terms of a rule such as 'attach *-able* to a word base corresponding to a transitive verb'. Stem^2 and affix combinations, and word and affix combinations which are subject to phonological variation, are listed on stratum 1: their partially systematic relationships are not seen as statable in terms of rules. Stratum 1 combinations are all assumed to be formally and semantically unpredictable, but a stratum 1 affix, if it occurs frequently enough, can sometimes 'transfer' to stratum 2 and figure in a productive pattern. Examples include *-able, -ant, -ee, -ism* and *-ize,* stratum 2 combinations of which, as Giegerich notes (52), are likely to feature native as well as foreign words as bases.

A different approach, that of Raffelsiefen (1996, 1998), dispenses with strata altogether. Raffelsiefen (1998) points out that bases attaching to suffixes with initial consonants never exhibit any formal variations, whereas those in combination with vowel-initial suffixes often do. (Suffixes with initial vowels are often foreign: *-able, -ant, -ette, -ify, -ist, -ize, -ity,* though not *-en, -ish, -y,* and native suffixes often have initial consonants: *-dom, -hood, -like, -ly, -ness, -ship,* though *-let* and *-ment* are foreign.) A combination of base and initial-vowel suffix constitutes a phonological word: the final syllable has as its onset the final consonant of the base. Phonological effects associated with suffixes are seen only within phonological words.

The forms, and sometimes the ill-formedness, of new words with vowel-initial suffixes can be explained as resulting from the interaction of various constraints. Phonological constraints include the prohibition of adjacent stressed syllables (**fraudeer*), the restriction of the size of the word-final foot to a dactyl (*radicálity, medícinal*), the prohibition of identical adjacent onsets (**acutity*). Constraints such as these interact with identity constraints which ensure a degree of recognizability to the bases of derived words, for example the requirement that a stressed syllable in a derived word should correspond with a stressed syllable in the base, or that the segments in a derived word should be identical with the corresponding segments in the base. Raffelsiefen shows that constraints interact in ways which are specific to each suffix. Adjacent stressed syllables are acceptable in nouns suffixed by *-ee,* for example (*grantee*), but not in nouns suffixed by *-eer* or (usually) in verbs suffixed by *-ize*: (**boldize*, **corruptize*). *-able* adjectives may have matching adjacent syllable onsets (*describable*), but *-ify* verbs and *-ity* nouns may not (**deafify*, **sordidity*). *-ish* and *-able*, unlike *-al* and *-ity*, are not restricted to bases which end in a dactyl: there is no stress shift in *vínegarish* or *ínjurable*, as there is in *medícinal* and *radicálity*. As Raffelsiefen argues, a description based on rules associated with strata could not account for the differing effects exhibited by the range of vowel-initial suffixes in combination with their bases.

9.3   Stems

The productive formation of new words in English is usually taken to be **word-based** – that is, the base of a regularly formed new complex word must be able to occur also as an independent member of a major word class – noun, adjective or verb. Only lexical words can be depended on to have identifiable meanings and only meaningful elements can be manipulated in regular ways to form new complex words.

We have already encountered many complex words with bases which cannot stand on their own. As we have seen, in Giegerich's framework, complex words with bases relatable to independent words but not identical with them (*economize*, *evacuee*, *stimulant*) are treated in the same way as those with stem bases (*capable*, *holism*, *vector*). Both kinds of combination are listed at stratum 1 and assumed not to represent productive patterns.

Earlier attempts to 'save' affixed words with incomplete word bases for word-based word formation have involved 'adjustment rules' to take care of alternations like those in *defend*: *defensive*, *curious*: *curiosity*. Adjustment rules also account for variations in the form of affixes like *a(n)-*, *in-* (*il-*, *im-*, *ir-*) and *-ation* (*-tion*, *-ion*). Aronoff (1976, ch. 5) proposes a particular kind of adjustment rule, 'truncation rules', which allow complex words with incomplete bases to be seen as word-based and as the output of productive rules. Truncation rules delete a suffix after some stems when another suffix is added. So we can say that in pairs like *aggression* and *aggressive*, *locomotion* and *locomotive*, the noun serves as basis for the adjective (Aronoff 1976, 28ff). Words in *-ize*, *-ist* and *-ism* sharing an incomplete word base (*eulog-*, *plagiar-*) might be accommodated in the same way, assuming one member of the pair or trio could be identified as basic.

An objection to truncation as conceived by Aronoff is that it assumes subtraction, and subtraction is a rare process in word formation because it reduces analysability (cf. Plank 1981, 209–10). As Plank suggests (207), we need not assume truncation of *aggression* and similar words if we concede word status to the potential verbal bases, *aggress* and *locomote*, since there are noun–adjective–verb series like *repulsion*, *repulsive*, *repulse*, and backformations are always possible (see 11.3). This is after all comparable to assuming the existence of a verb *McDonaldize* on the evidence of the noun *McDonaldization*. In other cases, this solution is not available, as with the 'deletion' of *-ate* before some words in *-ee* (*nominee*), *-ant* (*celebrant*) and *-able* (*allocable*).[3] Without a device like truncation, recognizing elements like *celebr-*, *alloc-* or *nomin-* is more problematic, since they cannot be assigned with certainty to any word class, despite the fact that *-ant*, *-able* and *-ee* generally attach to verb bases. For this they need what Marchand calls an 'adaptational' suffix (as opposed to a derivational suffix), in this case *-ate*, which adapts Latin verbs in *-are*: words like *celebrate* are not complex for an English speaker (1969, 209).

Truncation has a part also in Raffelsiefen's account, in which the final syllable of a base word is sometimes lost to satisfy a phonological constraint. Examples are *optimize* and *appetize*, which avoid the identical onsets in *optimumize, *appetitize. *Dictatee and *mutatee are avoided for the same reason, but in this case the alternatives *dictee and *mutee are also unacceptable since they sacrifice too much of the base and make it difficult to recognize (1998, 243–4).

It is clear that some affixes combine productively with incomplete word bases. As long as incomplete bases can be seen as alternant forms of current independent items, the word-based principle of word formation is not seriously challenged. But it is worth asking whether English word formation is in fact invariably word-based. Can stems, elements not identifiable with words at all, have any meaning for speakers? Giegerich (1999, 74) reasonably observes that to say that the base of *mollify* is adjectival because *-ify* attaches to adjectival bases is to argue in a circle. This verb, a loan from French or Latin, first appears in English at the beginning of the fifteenth century. *Moll-* is not very likely to figure in new words, even if speakers with a knowledge of Latin might understand it as meaning 'soft' and make a connection with *emollient*.

Yet there is a body of prefixed, suffixed and compounded words, formed in modern times with bases of the same kind as *moll-*, and it includes many which we can see as formed on productive patterns. We shall assume that alongside the major, word-based system, English has an alternative **stem-based** one (cf. Scalise 1986, 76). This secondary system resembles those of Latin and Greek, but is distinct from both. As Jespersen observed nearly a century ago, 'one needs only a smattering of science to be acquainted with technical words from Latin and Greek that would have struck Demosthenes and Cicero as bold, many of them even as indefensible or incomprehensible innovations' (1905, 113).[4]

Speakers and writers have differing degrees of lexical knowledge. Some stems, like those in older words such as *mollify* or *tangible*, may not mean much to most speakers, but the meanings of many other stems are likely to be much more accessible, for example those in *emulsify* and *emulsive*, *toxic* and *toxophobia*, *viral* and *viroid*. Moreover, a great many modern stem-based complex words like *lactase* or *capsid* are coined and used by scientists and technicians in command of specialized vocabularies of stems and affixes. It is not unusual for stems to figure in a variety of complex-word patterns, for example *-phyt-* (Greek *phyton* 'a plant') in the adjectives *phytal*, *phytic* and *phytiform*, the suffixed nouns *phytane* and *phytase* and the compounds *phytobiology*, *sporophyte*.

Although they cannot be assigned to word classes, the stems that appear in modern coinages have meanings for some speakers at least. The assumption that the base of a productively formed complex word must be syntactically specified, as only words can be in English (Aronoff 1976, 48), seems insecure on the evidence of many word-based cases – verbs in *-ize* whose bases might be nouns or adjectives (2.3, and cf. Plag 1999, 128ff), nouns in *-er* and *-ist* with nominal, adjectival or verbal bases (4.2), adjectives in *-able* (2.5.1) and verbs in *un-* with nominal or verbal bases (2.3.1, 3.2). On such evidence, semantics has more to do than syntax with the potential combinability of formative elements.

9.4   Stem combinations

Some prefixes and suffixes attach predominantly to stems to form words usually confined to scientific and technical registers. Stems combine with one another to form compounds, which are common both in specialized registers and in everyday contexts. Verbs based on stems are rare: the great majority of stem-formations, affixed words and compounds, are nouns and adjectives.

9.4.1   Prefixation

As we saw in Chapter 3, many prefixes can be generally characterized as 'locative', 'quantitative' or 'negative'. One negative prefix, *a(n)-* (3.3) attaches to stems as well as words in parasynthetic adjectives and related nouns, e.g. *acaudate* (Latin *cauda* 'tail'), *anhydrous* (Greek *hydros* 'water').

Locative prefixes like Greek **epi-** 'upon', 'close to', **hypo-** 'under', **meta-** 'with', 'behind', **ortho-** 'straight', **para-** 'beside', **peri-** 'around' and Latin **intra-** 'inside' and **supra-** 'above' occur in words relating to many specialized areas of knowledge, notably in anatomical, botanical and geological names and parasynthetic adjectives descriptive of organs, parts and features. Examples are:

> *epicyte* 'membrane of a cell' (Greek *cytos* 'receptacle'), *epilimnion* 'upper layer of water' (Greek *limnion* 'lake'), *hypoblast* 'inner layer of cells' (Greek *blastos* 'sprout', 'germ'), *metabranchial* 'relating to part of a crab, located

with reference to the *branchia* 'gills' (Greek)', *orthocarpous* 'having straight fruit' (Greek *carpos* 'fruit'), *paravesical* 'beside the bladder', *perivenous* 'around a vein', *intradermal* 'under the skin', *suprafoliar* 'above, or on, a leaf'.

Quantifying prefixes also occur in such words:

> *monobranchiate* 'having one set of gills', *triannulate* 'having three rings', *polyadenous* 'having many glands', *tetracanthous* 'having four spines'.

In the names and descriptions of many chemical substances and compounds, locative and quantitative prefixes indicate positions of molecules or atoms, or the place of a compound in a series. In *ortho-*, *meta-*, *paracoumaric* (acid), the prefixes relate to different locations of hydrogen atoms on the benzene ring; *metatungstic* describes an acid with fewer molecules of H_2O than an *orthotungstic* acid; *hypovanadic oxide* is an oxygen compound with fewer oxygen atoms than *vanadic oxide*. *Triplumbic* means 'containing three atoms of lead'; *dithionic* acid has two atoms of sulphur (Greek *theion* 'sulphur'); *polytheonic* acid has several.

These examples give a very limited illustration of the versatility of these prefixes, some of which are polysemous; e.g. *para-* 'beside' can mean 'disordered', as in *parakeratosis* 'skin disease', *hypo-* 'under' means 'deficient' in *hypocalcaemia*, *meta-* 'behind' means 'later' or 'consequent' in *metapneumonic*.

9.4.2   Suffixation

A few verbs coined in the twentieth century have stems combined with *-ify* and *-ate; -ize* verbs are slightly more numerous according to OED, though it records only a handful. Some verbs, like *alluviate*, may be backformations from earlier nouns in *-ation*; others are probably also backformed, e.g. *ecize* from *ecesis* (Greek, 'inhabiting'), or *quaternize* 'to convert into quaternary form'. *Erotize* may owe its existence to *erotism* or *erotic*, *embolize* to *embolism* and *technify* to *technical*. *Mucify* 'become mucus-secreting' and *opacify* 'become/ render opaque', have bases which also occur in stem compounds, e.g. *muciduct*, *opacimeter*. Further examples are *quantize*, *sinify* 'invest with Chinese character', *technify*, *pupariate* 'form a puparium'.

There is much more evidence of genuine productivity in stem-based adjectives. In many modern coinages, *-al*, *-ic*, *-oid* (or *-oidal* if the word suffixed by *-oid* is a noun) and *-ous* are attached to stems, as in:

> *paucal* (Latin *paucus* 'few'), *phytal* (Greek *phyton* 'a plant'), *axenic*, of an organism, 'free from other organisms' (Greek *xenikos* 'alien'), *hygric* 'relating to moisture' (Greek *hygros*), *mucoid(al)* 'resembling mucus', *peloidal* (Greek *pelos* 'clay'), *citrous*, *ferrous*, *cuprous* (Greek *citron* 'lemon', Latin *ferrum* 'iron', *cuprum* 'copper').

Many such stems, like the ones in these examples, occur also in stem compounds (9.4.3). Another ending, *-form* 'having the form of', 'resembling', attaches only to stems, as in *bacilliform, pupiform, rubelliform* (Latin *bacillus, pupa, rubella*). OED records over 450 such words since 1800.

-ic is often attached to certain final elements in stem compounds, such as *-troph-* and *-gen-; -ous* is common with others, like *-gam-, -phil-, -zyg-, -vor-* and *-fer-*. Some combinations of stem and suffix, appearing together often, have taken on the character of a single suffix. An example is *-ferous* (Latin *ferre* 'to bear'). A few words, like *luciferous* and *vociferous* are loans or analogical formations of the early modern period, but OED records over two hundred adjectives in *-ferous* formed during the last two centuries, noting '*-ferous* became a living English suffix, capable of combining with any Latin stem, and forms an unlimited number of derivatives'. Modern examples include

> *physaliferous, radiferous, uraniferous* (Greek *physallis* 'bladder', *radium* based on Latin *radius* 'ray', *uranium* based on *Uranus*).

Another productive stem + suffix combination is *-genic*, as in *cryogenic, iatrogenic, neurogenic* (Greek *cryos* 'frost', *iatros* 'physician', *neuron* 'nerve') and many others. This ending appears also with a few independently-occurring bases in non-technical contexts, formed on the pattern of *photogenic* in the sense 'looking good in photographs', e.g. *radiogenic, telegenic, videogenic*.

Many nouns formed in modern times with *-ism* and *-ist* have stem bases, e.g. *ebullism, heurism, holism, phobism, tactism, tectonism, vicinism, vorticism, Hispanist, eugenist*.

-itis, a Greek adjective suffix indicating the nature of a pathological condition, figures in nouns denoting such conditions, specifically involving inflammation, as in *arthritis* from *arthros* 'joint'. OED records around 200 since 1800, the great majority with stem bases, e.g. *adenitis, chondritis, encephalitis, myelitis*. As with *-genic*, the productivity of *-itis* has extended to non-specialized items with word bases, like *fiscalitis, electionitis, telephonitis*: 'Ted has telephonitis and he's on the phone every night' (OED: 1979), *Wagneritis*.[5]

Among other stem-based nouns are names of chemical or biological entities, many of which are complex only to the scientifically well-informed. Some suffixes occurring in these are classical Greek or Latin in origin but put to wholly modern uses, like *-ate, -ine* and *-yl* in *acetate, xanthate, flavine, scopine, acetyl, lactyl* or adapted, like the *-in* of *acetin, dioxin, fibrin* or the *-ium* of *iridium, radium, uranium*. Others are wholly modern. They can often be identified with part of a word, like the *-ase* of *diastase* in names of enzymes, e.g. *coagulase, lactase*, the *-ol* of *alcohol* in *glycol*, or of *phenol* in *thymol*, or of *oleum* in *indol*, the *-ide* of *oxide* in *chloride*, the *-ose* of *glucose* in *cellulose* and *ribose*. These elements may have begun productive life in blends (11.4), but the numbers of words formed with them in recent times are evidence that they can be regarded as suffixes.

9.4.3   Stem compounds

A non-final lexical element in a Greek or Latin compound is a stem, a 'combining form' in OED's terminology, linked to the lexical element which follows it by a 'combining vowel'. The vowel is usually -*o* (in Greek compounds, e.g. *heterodoxia* 'other, different opinion') or -*i* (in Latin compounds, e.g. *aurifer* 'gold-bearing'). If the following element begins with a vowel, there is no linking vowel (*philanthropia* 'love of mankind'). (Examples of non-final stems in this section are generally given along with their linking vowel.) There are considerable numbers of stem compounds and a great variety of modern stem elements. Some were borrowed as parts of Greek and Latin compounds, like *anthropo-, astro-, biblio-, hetero-, philo-* but many, like *pulso-, tecto-, turbo-* (from Latin *pulsus* 'pulse', *tectum* 'roof', *turbo* 'whirlwind'), are modern combining forms. Sometimes such post-classical compound elements can be seen as closer to current English words than to their Latin or Greek relatives. Examples are *immuno-*, which OED describes as the combining form of *immune, immunity, immunology* and related words, *acousto-* (*acoustic*), *adreno-* (*adrenal*), *carbo-* (*carbon*), *monarcho-* (*monarch, monarchic*), *dosi-* (*dose*), *hallucino-* (*hallucination*). *Vibra-, vibro-* is derived from *vibration*, *oxo-* from *oxygen*. *Euro-, galvano-* and *sado-* are based on proper names. A few combinations, in which the native–foreign contrast is foregrounded, have obviously non-classical first elements: those of *swingometer* and *weedicide* are Germanic, that of *jazzophile* is of unknown origin. Inevitably, many stems attain independent word status, often as abbreviated forms of compounds, e.g. *hetero, hypo, logo, macro, physio, schizo, techno, typo*.

Final compound elements which can be modified by stems are words with no independent currency in English, as in *cyanogen, herbivore, leucocyte, ribosome, oscilloscope, thermostat*, or stems with Greek or Latin suffixes, as in *oviraptor, photography, plasmolysis, hydrophobia*, or they may be current English words, usually of Greek or Latin origin: *astro-geology, cytoskeleton, xenotransplant*.

Stem compounds are nouns and adjectives. Final elements may denote entities related to events, as in *bacteriophage* 'bacteria-eater' (Greek *phagos* 'eating'), *plasmolysis* 'plasma-releasing' (Greek *lysis* 'loosening'), but stem compound verbs are predictably rare: two examples are *to biodegrade* and *to photoconvert*, which are based on *biodegradable* and *photoconversion*; *immunodepleting* is a participial adjective. As with word compounds, some modifying or head elements can be found in series of formations, some apparently modelled on others. *Bio-* (Greek *bios* 'life') occurs in a number of words, e.g. *bioengineering, biorhythm, biotope* (see Bauer 1983, 276–8), as does *eco-* in words definable in relation to *ecology* like *ecocide, ecosphere, eco-radical, eco-tourist, 'eco-certified* timber'. Final stem-elements appearing in series of items include:

-*cide* 'killer' or 'killing', as in e.g. *genocide, molluscicide, rodenticide, silvicide*;
-*cracy* 'group' or 'government' (Chapter 4 note 14); -*phone* 'sound' as in

allophone, 'instrument' as in *vibraphone* or 'speaking' as in *francophone*; *-scope*: *kaleidoscope*, *laryngoscope*, *oscilloscope*; *-naut* (Greek *nautes* 'sailor' as in *Argonaut* 'sailor in the Argo'): *astronaut*, *cosmonaut*, *hydronaut*.

Like many productive foreign suffixes, such elements tend to combine with words as well as stems: *pesticide*, *weedicide*, *answerphone*, *headphone*, *radarscope*, *sniperscope*, *chimponaut*.

Not surprisingly, in view of the ubiquity of stem compounds in all kinds of context, there are sometimes variations in the shapes of combining forms, non-final elements. The combining vowel may vary. *Strati-* 'stratum' and *strato-* 'stratus' relate to rock and cloud respectively, as in *stratigraphy* and *stratocirrus*, but in other cases, variation appears unsystematic, as in *spermaduct* and *spermicide*, *toxidermic* and *toxoprotein*, *pulsimeter* and *pulsometer*, *technicolor* and *technophobia*. There may be a shorter and a longer form, e.g. *dermo-* and *dermato-* (Greek *derma*, *dermat-* 'skin'), *pancreato-* and *pancreatico-*. Combining forms may represent Greek or Latin (or English) adjectives as well as nouns, hence *Sino-* and *Sinico-*, *techno-* and *technico-*.

The examples of compounds given so far make sense as modifier–head combinations. Contrasting with these, there is a distinct group of adjectival stem compounds with non-final elements based on adjectives, e.g. 'a *mechanico-acoustic* set-up', 'a *serio-comic* drama', 'a *Sinico-Japanese* agreement', 'technico-economic problems'. These appear to embody something like a relationship of coordination. Compounds like these are not found in classical Greek or Latin texts. Hatcher (1951) identifies the earliest recorded example as *comico-tragical* (OED: 1598), and suggests that this is an Anglicization of a Latin adjective, *comico-tragicus* (1540), itself inspired by a non-serious nominal coinage of Plautus, *tragicomoedia* 'tragicomedy'. In later formations, the first element's stem may represent a noun: *naso-gastric*, *sphero-cylindrical*, *spatio-temporal*. Hatcher finds precursors for compounds of names with nominal combining forms like *Austro-Hungarian*, *Indo-Chinese* in a third-century noun *Gallo-Graeci* 'Gaul Greeks', 'Gauls living in Greece', and in the Latin titles of Renaissance bilingual dictionaries like *Gallo-Belgicus* (1588) 'pertaining to both France and Belgium'.

Nouns corresponding to such adjective compounds, like *chemico-biology*, *lexico-grammar*, are usually best understood as modifier–head. *Anglo-Latin* means 'Anglicized Latin'. An *Anglo-Indian* is an Indian with some English forebears or an English person resident in India. Attributive *Anglo-Saxon* may be comparable to *Anglo-Russian* (War), but *Anglo-Saxons* are 'English Saxons'.

Further adjective + adjective compounds from twentieth-century texts are 'a *clerico-fascist* regime', '*erotico-religious* visions', 'the most extraordinary politico-spiritual outpouring' (Guardian: 1997), 'Anglo-Saxon magico-religious arts' (OED: 1967). As Hatcher notes (1951, 148–9) compounds with first elements adjectival in form are sometimes associated with a satirical tone. She cites a possible early example 'politico-scientific ladies of France' (OED: 1798) beside more recent ones like 'an agglutination of *socio-politico-academic* clichés'. Nouns like *poetico-rhetoric* and *politico-businessmen* can be seen as the results of backformation (11.3).

Notes

1. Accounts of morphology which make reference to strata, or levels to use the more common term, embrace inflection, 'zero' derivation and compounding as well as derivational affixation, and there has been much discussion of the number of levels needed. The 'extended level ordering hypothesis' has compounding at a third level and regular inflection at a fourth. Irregular inflection is at level 1. 'Zero' derivation is divided between levels 1 and 2, verb-to-noun at level 1 and noun-to-verb at level 2. See especially Carstairs-McCarthy (1992, ch. 3), Spencer (1991, ch. 3), Katamba (1993, chs 5, 6 and 7) and Giegerich (1999, ch. 2) for summaries of such generative accounts, and evaluations of them.

2. Giegerich, reserving the term 'stem' for bound forms with word-class membership (cf. Chapter 1, note 2), refers to 'roots'. All stratum 1 combinations as well as their bases are roots, unspecified as to category. A root-to-word conversion rule allows them to figure on stratum 2.

3. The deleted part must be a genuine 'formative' according to Aronoff (1976, 91), not merely a sequence: there is no truncation in *dilatable, frustratable* or *inflatable*. Anderson (1992, 280) points out that formative status need not be relevant if we assume simply that deletable instances of *-ate* must not bear the main stress.

4. The label ISV, 'International Scientific Vocabulary', adopted in Webster (1961), alongside NL, 'New Latin', 'recognizes that the word as such is a product of the modern world and gets only its raw materials, so to speak, from antiquity' (Webster 1961, 7a). Many such words of course are not confined to English, and some may be loans from modern European languages.

5. Giegerich (1999) assumes that affixes which attach to stem bases become productive when they attach also to word bases. *-genic* and *-itis*, by contrast are far more productive in combination with stems than with words.

10

Phonaesthemes

10.1 Scope

The term 'phonaestheme' was first used by J.R. Firth (1930, 184) for sequences like the *sl-* of *slack, slouch, slush* and the *-ump* of *slump, bump, dump.* Firth describes these elements as affective and notes that they have become identifiable after repeated appearances in particular kinds of context. 'It is all a matter of habit' (187). But establishing the nature of phonaesthemes and deciding which parts of words can plausibly be regarded as phonaesthetic (or phonaesthemic) elements is not at all straightforward. In 1.6 phonaestheme formations were collectively described as 'expressive', but at the heart of this area of the vocabulary are words intended to name and represent sounds. We can begin then by looking at some examples of formations which might be called 'imitative' of sound.[1]

Though of course no word can be purely imitative – a copy – of the noise it names, certain consonant and vowel sounds can be more or less non-arbitrarily associated with certain kinds of noise. There is obviously something non-arbitrary in the following examples of sound-denoting words syntactically detached from their surroundings:

Check for gas leaks. Light a match and – whoomph. (OED: 1983)

Thwack! Boston's Jim Rice sends the first pitch sailing over the left-field wall. (OED: 1976)

A typical context for such words is as complement of *go*, with or without a locative adverbial (cf. Rhodes 1994, 281), or as complement of a verb of uttering:

A bullet went 'splat' against a rock. (OED: 1897)

The door said thunk in a well-bred whisper. (OED: 1968)

They may follow an intransitive verb of movement, or a transitive verb and its object:

> Mr London and Mr Featherstonehaugh dived splack into the water lilies. (OED: 1960)
>
> He . . . pitched him swosh into the mud. (OED: 1927)

Nouns denoting sounds often appear as heads of indefinite noun phrases following *with*: 'Our gear came down with a whang as the ship forged ahead' (OED: 1891), or as heads of definite noun phrases of the form *the* (MODIFIER) – of *a/the* NOUN, like *scraw* and *thuck* in:

> the rhythmic scraw of a saw (OED: 1936)
>
> The whine of the rifle bullet and the thuck of its striking home (OED: 1979).

Whine in this last example, though parallel with *thuck*, is much less certainly imitative. Interestingly, verbs appear to be as numerous as nouns in this area of the vocabulary. We can see function as a verb as marking a further stage in conventionalization, though, in contrast to the 'zero'-derived examples of 2.3 and 2.4, it is rarely possible to identify a direction of derivation between noun and verb.

> . . . as her needle plocked in and out of her embroidery (OED: 1931)
>
> A gang of youths sitting astride motor cycles vroomed their engines. (OED: 1976)

Many words synaesthetically suggest movement rather than (or as well as) sound:

> Then whoomff! land on it with all fours. (OED: 1958)
>
> Peeling off the kilometers to the tune of 'Blue Skies', sizzling down the long black liquid reaches of Nationale Sept . . . (Cyril Connolly, *Palinurus*, 1944, Penguin 1967, 110)

Besides sound or movement, *chumps*, *shumbling* and *squirls* in the following evoke other words of similar form and meaning:

> Sir Brian reads his letters and chumps his dry toast. (OED: 1855)
>
> The click-click of the wind in the Indian corn, plucking at the coarse leaves, shumbling them (L. Durrell, *Clea* 1960, Faber 1961, 46)

'What a squiggly handwriting,' she said. . . . 'They would not let us write that way at school. But when I am grown up I shall make lots of squirls.' (OED: 1922)

The initial consonant in *chump* evokes that of *chew*, *champ*, *chomp*; the remainder is found in a group of words less easily related to the meaning of *chump* in this example, such as *bump*, *stump*, *clump*, *flump*, *crump*, only the last of which is clearly imitative of sound, cf. 'The heavy shell . . . ending in a loud "crump" as it bursts on the ground' (OED: 1968); 'Shells began to whizz over and crump in the ravine behind' (OED: 1968).

The context of *shumbling* suggests a meaning akin to that of *shuffling*. It also suggests that noise is involved, as in *shushing*: 'the sound of a gourd rattle to make a "shushing" sound' (OED: 1972). *-umble* occurs in words like *mumble*, *rumble*, *grumble* and *strumble*: 'the strumble of the hungry river of death' (OED: 1938), which in this context is suggestive of a low irregular noise. In the third example, *squirl*, we can identify elements in *squiggle* (cf. *wriggle*) and *squirm*, and the ending of *swirl* is seen also in *twirl* and *whirl*.

Ch-, *sh-*, *squ-*, *-ump*, *-umble* and *-irl*, whether imitative or not, are phonaesthemes in Firth's sense. Phonaestheme words occur usually in informal speech or writing, and they are members of series. The formation of such series of words is what Firth sees as proof of 'habit'.

A third characteristic of words containing phonaesthemes is that, when not indicative simply of sound or movement, they generally imply a non-neutral, affective, attitude, as with *blab*, *bleat*, *frump*, *gripe*, *skulk*, *smarmy*, *whopping* (as in, for example, 'it cost a whopping £10'). *Twitter* suggests 'unwarranted fuss', rather than sound, in:

The much bigger twitter has been caused by the reclusive Thomas Pynchon's peeping from purdah to bestow his fulsome blessing. (Guardian: 1998)

As we see below, groups of phonaestheme words can be characterized by a range of notions, typically negatively valued, including 'awkward', 'bent', 'cheating', 'lazy', 'trivial'. Sometimes a historical development can be traced. Samuels (1972, 46–7) notes, for example, that the association between *gr-* and 'unpleasantness', discernible in the Old English phrase *grim and grædig* 'fierce and greedy', has since widened in scope to include 'seizing' (*grip*, *grope*) and 'abrasive' (*grind*, *grate*, *grit*, *grasp*). Käsmann (1992) traces the development of pejorative senses in words beginning with *sl-* back to Old English (cf. *slaw* 'slow', *slidan* 'to slide)'.

Bolinger's (1950) very useful terms for initial consonant or consonant sequence, and remainder – vowel + final consonant(s) – of words like *chump* are respectively **assonance** and **rime**. We can provisionally define phonaesthemes then as initial assonances like *ch-*, *gr-*, *str-*, and rimes like *-ump*,

-umble and *-irl*, leaving open the question of whether a phonaestheme can take the form of a single consonant, for example the *d-* of *dull, dense, dopey, dud, duff* (Reay 1994) or the *-d* of *plod* and *thud*, and the question of how many words containing a particular sequence constitute a series in which we can recognize a phonaestheme. In 10.5 we shall look at other elements which we might call phonaesthemes.

The term 'sound symbolism' is often used in the discussion of words like these. 'Symbolism', as Reay (1994) points out, is generally used in connection with the arbitrary nature of language, but 'sound symbolism' is regularly understood as referring to 'a direct association between the form and the meaning of language' (Crystal 1997). However since the notion of phonaestheme includes a range of more, and less, and non-onomatopoeic elements, 'sound symbolism' is an apt term to characterize the whole area. Degrees of arbitrariness are to be expected since symbols become more arbitrary with time and new, less arbitrary ones appear. Wescott (1971a, 426) gives two examples of non-imitative words of probably imitative origin: *laugh*, from a root **hlah-*, earlier **klak-*, described by OED as 'probably echoic', and *knock*, Old English *cnocian*, with initial [kn]. Oswalt (1994, 300– 10) suggests that two recent comic-strip words, *shwack* and *fwack* may have appeared because *whack* is now generally pronounced with [w] rather than [ʌ] or [hw], and is thus less imitative than it once was.

10.2   Some assonances[2]

Bl- occurs in a number of words for speech: *to blab, blabber, blaze* (abroad), *blurt* (out), *blat* 'to broadcast, tell tales'; *blat* also means 'to talk noisily or impulsively' (OED), cf. *blare, blast* 'reprimand', *bluster*. *Blather* and *blah* suggest 'nonsense'; *blarney, bluff* and *blague, blagueur* have to do with flattery and deception, evoking a connection with *blurb* and *blandish*. *Bleat* 'complain' is not far from *blub* and *blubber* 'weep' and an older meaning of *blare* is 'to cry noisily'. A group of words for swearing (*bl*aspheming) includes *blessed, blazes, blithering, blooming, blimey* and *bloody*.

A series of words in which 'vehemence' can be perceived (Samuels 1972, 54–5) begins with *br-*: *brabble, brag, brandish, brash, bravado, bray, bristle, bruise, brunt*.

Cl- appears in some 'sound' words, like *clang, clash, clamour, clatter*, but is associated with 'clinging' and 'coagulation' (Samuels 1972, 54) respectively in *clam, clamp, clasp, claw, cleave, clench, cling, clutch* and *clag, clay, clew, clod, clog, clot, clump, cluster*.

Some *cr-* words denote sounds: *creak, crash, crump, crunch, cronk, croak, (corn)crake, crawk, crepitate, crunkle*: 'The crabs . . . crunkled loud and long' (OED: 1900). Some of these forms can be prefixed by *s-* and placed in the *scr-* group below, like *screak, scrumple, scrunch*. *Croon, croodle*: 'She made a queer little croodling sound of comfort' (OED: 1890) and *crool*: 'The monotonous crool of a dove' (OED: 1938) have something in common. *Croodle* can also mean 'to cower or crouch down, snuggle' (OED) and thus has affinities with *cramp, crawl, crick, creep, cringe, crouch, cribbed*, cf. 'cabin'd, cribb'd, confin'd, bound in' (*Macbeth*, III.iv). These share a suggestion of 'bent' (Bolinger 1950, 120), as do *crisp, crimp, crook, crumple, crease*. A *crank* is a handle, a piece of bent metal, and also 'a person with a mental twist' (OED); compare *crackpot, crabbed, crotchety*.

A group of words beginning with **gl-** evokes 'light' (Bolinger 1950): *glare, glaze, gleam, glimmer, glisten, glitter, glitz, gloss, glow*.

Gr- words for harsh sounds include *grate, grunt, growl, grind, gride*: 'The wood which grides and clangs Its leafless ribs and iron horns Together' (Tennyson, *In Memoriam*, cvii), *graunch*: 'They said they could hear the ship "graunching" on the rock' (OED: 1968) and *grinch*: 'It's woe to bend the stubborn back Above the grinching quern' (OED: 1892). Samuels (1972, 47) sees the common denominator 'abrasive' in *grind, grate, gravel, graze, grit*. Words associated with the human production of harsh sounds, and hence with 'complaint', are *grizzle, grouch, grouse, gruff, grumble grumpy, groan, grangle*: 'My mother, the ladies, such talk, every afternoon you'd hear great wrankles and grangles over . . . sewing cloth' (Jack Kerouac, *Doctor Sax*, 1959, 14). *Gripe*, since Old English a member of the *grip, grasp, grope, grab, grapple* set, now also means 'complaint', perhaps by way of a metaphorical extension of the 'grip' sense, cf. 'Grief gryped me so . . .' (OED: 1559) and so joins the *grumble* group. *Grotty* (a shortened form of *grotesque*) and *grunge, grungy* are fairly recent members of a group of generally 'disagreeable' words including *grim, grime, grisly, grubby, gruelling, gross*.

Pl- words often suggest the sound of impact, further specified by the rime: *plock* (10.1), *plod, plop, plonk, plosh, plung* 'the plung of the racket' (OED: 1952), *plunk*. A prefixed *s-* adds, or reinforces, the suggestion of 'liquid' in *splash, splunge, splotch, splodge, splutter* and sometimes *splat*: 'the basket of eggs falls with a "Splatt"!' (OED: 1974). A metaphorical extension of meaning is seen in *splash* 'prominent display' and *splurge*.

'Fast movement' is implied in some **sc-** or **sk-** words: *scurry, scoot, skip, skid, scuttle*, and 'fast movement away from one's responsibilities and duties' (Reay 1994) in *skip, skive, skulk, scab, scrimshank, scarper* – probably from Italian *scappare* 'to escape': OED), *scam* 'swindle', 'racket' and *scuzzy*: 'perhaps Mr Vander Kalm has good intentions about evicting scuzzy malingerers from the dole' (OED: 1976).

Scratch is a typical member of a **scr-** group, cf.

So he scraped and scratched and scrabbled and scrooged, and then he scrooged again and scrabbled and scratched and scraped, working busily with his little paws. (OED: 1908)

'Eke out' (Reay 1994) informs *scratch* (together), *scrimp, scrape, scrounge*.

Many *sl*- words³ have to do with 'sliding': *slip, slither, slope, sled, sleigh, slalom*, with 'slippery substances': *slick, slip, slop, slurry, slather, slime, slush*, and with 'moral flaw', chiefly 'sloth': *slouch, slovenly, slump, slumber, slack, slut, slag, sleaze, sloppy, slush* (fund). A contrasting group suggests 'attack': *slap, slash, slay, slam, slate, slug, slag* (off).

Sn- begins words with referents related to the nose: *snuff, snout, snozzle, snot*, and words involving mainly human noises: *sneeze, sniff(le), snuffle, snore, snort, snarl, snicker, snigger*. *Snaffle, snake, snatch, snig, sneak, snitch* are all verbs meaning 'cheat' or 'steal'.

'Sound' words beginning with (*s*)*qu*- include *quawk* and *squawk, squeak, squelch, squish, squeelch*: 'The *squeelch* and buzz of the windscreen wipers' (Len Deighton, *The Ipcress File*, 1962, Panther 1964, 184). Further pairs are *quash* and *squash, quelch* and *squelch* 'subdue' in 'That'll squelch him, I assure you, and he'll be as quiet as a mouse' (OED: 1978), *quench* and *squench*. *Squiggle, squirm, squirl* 'a flourish or twirl' and *squirt* imply movement.

A group of of *st*- words 'clusters about the meaning of "arrest"' (Bolinger 1950, 134): *staunch, stall, stick, stout, stodgy, stolid, sturdy, stubborn, stable, stymied*. Another suggests 'attack' (Reay 1994): *stab, stamp(ede), strafe, strike, sting, stun*. *Str*- 'stretch out, scatter' (Reay) subsumes *straddle, straggle, stray, strew, string* (out), *stride*.

Sw- words involving 'movement through air or water' (Reay) include *swarm, sway, swerve, swim, swing, swish, swirl, swiggle*: 'To think of you swaying and swiggling at the end of a rope' (OED: 1907), *swipe* 'to draw a card through a machine'. A few share an element of 'dishonesty': *sweedle*: 'Dolly is a "sweedling" extravagant little vixen' (OED: 1908), *swindle, swipe*.

A *tr*- group of which *tread* is typical (Marchand 1969) includes *tramp(le), trek, trail, traipse, trot, trip, trog, troll*: 'I trolled off quite happily and entered the house' (OED: 1981); *tromp*: 'tromping about the living room' (OED: 1974), *trot, trudge*.

10.3   Some rimes

Plosive consonants can suggest contact with a hard surface (Reay), as with -*ack*, -*ap* and -*at* in:

crack, smack, splack (illustrated above in 10.1), *thwack, whack*; *clap, rap, tap, zap*; *bat, pat, rat-tat, splat*.

-*ash* evokes 'contact accompanied by violence and noise' in *bash, clash, crash, dash* (against), *gnash, smash, thrash*.

-umble also links words having to do with noise: *grumble, rumble, shumble, stumble,* but *fumble, mumble, stumble* and *tumble* suggest 'repeated awkward movements' (Reay).

There is something 'awkward' (Reay 1994; Bolinger 1950, 135) too about *-ump* in *bump, chump* 'fool', *dump, frump, gump* 'fool', *grump, lump, slump, stump.*

The series *budge, drudge, grudge, sludge, trudge* suggests 'heaviness'; the notion of 'incompetence' links *fudge, kludge* 'a hastily improvised and poorly thought-out solution to a [computing] fault or bug' (OED) and *smudge.*

Marchand (1969, 419) identifies an element of 'unsteady movement' in *amble, ramble, scramble, shamble, wamble.*

Nasals suggest resonance in *-ang, -ing, -ink, -ong, -oom* and *-um*:

bang, clang, prang, twang, whang; ping, ring, whing, zing; clink, chink; bong, ding-dong, gong; boom, vroom, zoom; drum, hum, strum, thrum.

Other clusters of riming words include *cuddle* and *huddle, growl, howl* and *yowl, prattle* and *tattle, cheep* and *peep, blotch* and *splotch, squirl, twirl* and *whirl, bounce, flounce* and *jounce, flurry, hurry* and *scurry, titter, twitter* and *witter, footle, pootle* and *tootle. Chatter, natter, patter* and *yatter* all mean 'talk'. *Fleer* 'to scoff at', *jeer, leer, sneer* are semantically akin. Dialectal *sleer* means 'to look askance'.

Dust shares *-ust* with other 'surface formation' words: *crust, must, rust. Dusty* consists of noun + adjective suffix, but, dissected into *d-* and *-usty*, it can be linked with 'old' words like *crusty, musty, fusty* and *rusty* (Bolinger 1950, 120f).

10.4 Reduplication

Compound phonaestheme formations, reduplicative sequences, sometimes have more than two members: 'the plane trees going sha-sha-sha through the open window' (Cyril Connolly, *Palinurus*, 1944, Penguin 1967, 110); 'The familar "thunk, zing, ding" of a pinball machine' (OED: 1979). Generally, compounds have two members, sometimes with full repetition: 'The click-click of the wind . . .' (10.1), *cheapo-cheapo* 'very cheap', *yum-yum*. Otherwise, the elements of a reduplicative compound may differ in one of two ways. They may alliterate, as in 'a lazy twing-twang of sound' (OED: 1953). Alternatively, the elements may rime, as in *helter-skelter* or *humdrum*. Jespersen (1942, 10.41) and Marchand (1969, 437) think that riming compounds have a 'less serious character' than alliterative compounds. This is because, as Jespersen puts it, 'many of them distinctly belong to the nursery' (e.g. *Georgy Porgy, piggie wiggie*). These aside, however, there seem to be no marked semantic or pragmatic differences between alliterative and riming compounds. In either kind there may be an intervening syllable (*bric-a-brac, razzmatazz, la-di-da*) or a suffix (*clippety-clop, honky-tonk*), between the members. A miscellaneous handful of forms do not fit these three patterns – repeating, riming, alliterating – but are obviously similar in nature, e.g. *plug-ugly, slap-happy, touchy-feely, bamboozle, wheewhock*: 'the boat . . . wheewhocked on the steep drink' (Saul Bellow, *The Adventures of Augie March*, 1953, Penguin 1967, 578).

In some compounds one element can be identified as the 'kernel' (Jespersen), 'basis' (Marchand 1969) or 'nucleus' (Malkiel 1977), on the ground that it has an independent existence, e.g. the second element of *tittle-tattle* or the first of *easy-peasy*. In others, like *knick-knack* or *fuddy-duddy* there is no independently appearing part. Again, the distinction is of little significance. Crucially, all reduplicative compounds differ from the compounds of Chapters 6–8 in that their elements cannot be perceived as modifier and head. Thus we can exclude from this chapter such riming or alliterating noun compounds as *dream team, fat cat, jet set, prime time, hot-head, sad sack*.

Like one-word phonaestheme formations, compounds can represent sound, e.g. the nouns *twing-twang, chack-chack*: 'the hoarse chack-chack of the field-fare' (OED: 1906), or movement, e.g. *see-saw, zigzag*, or something associated with an affective attitude. Compare the two uses of *chitter-chatter*, 'sound' and 'trivial conversation', and the two uses of *hoo-ha*, primarily 'sound' and primarily 'fuss' respectively in the following:

> Mowgli . . . imitated perfectly the sharp chitter-chatter of Chikai, the leaping rat of the Dekkan. (OED: 1895)

> 'We exhaust you with our chitter-chatter,' they say politely. (OED: 1940)

> He came up under cover of all the hoo-hah on the stage sometime after the event. (OED: 1937)

> Remember the hoo-ha when David Hare on the Late Show dared to suggest that Keats might actually be a better poet than Bob Dylan. (Guardian: 1999)

Further examples of nouns are *argy-bargy* (or *argle-bargle*), *boogie-woogie, clap-trap, creepy-crawly, ding-dong*: 'the ding-dong of public argument' (OED: 1935), *flim-flam, gang-bang, hanky-panky, hocus-pocus, hotch-potch, mish-mash, mumbo-jumbo, rag-bag, riffraff, titbit, wheeler-dealer*. Concrete entities can be named for noises associated with them: *chiff-chaff, hubble-bubble* 'hookah', *tom-tom*.

Affective meaning rather than sound or movement is usually prominent in adjectives, e.g. *chi-chi* 'pretentious', *happy-clappy*: 'That need is not being met by organized religion, in its bells and smells and happy-clappy manifestations'

(Guardian: 1997), *fuddy-duddy*, *goody-goody*, *harum-scarum*, *hoity-toity*, *hotsy-totsy*: 'What the law allows me, is mine . . . So that's all hotsy-totsy' (OED: 1973), *huggy-wuggy*, *itsy-bitsy*, *namby-pamby*, *pally-wally*: 'If you're going to go namby-pamby and pally-wally on me, I'll go find someone else' (OED: 1954), *raggle-taggle*. Reduplication in adjectives sometimes makes for an intensifying effect, as in *cheapo-cheapo*, *lovey-dovey*, *super-duper*, *teeny-weeny*, *tip-top*.

Verbs are less common. Examples include *chack-chack*: 'Stonechats "chack-chack" from the top of a spray' (OED: 1930), *dilly-dally*, *flimflam*: 'Market practices that smacked of flimflamming the public' (OED: 1963), *razzle-dazzle*: 'that Texan smile that razzle-dazzles 'em' (OED: 1976), *hobnob*, *pooh-pooh*, *shilly-shally*.

Compounds can be syntactically detached, as interjections (*yum-yum*) or have quasi-adverbial function: 'So our lives go on, rumble-jumble, like a carrier's cart over ruts and stones' (OED: 1887), 'The shears were going snickersnack' (OED: 1979).

10.5   Problems with phonaesthemes[4]

Reduplicative formations have at least a formal resemblance to the compounds of Chapters 6, 7 and 8. By contrast, assonance + rime combinations cannot easily be compared with the complex words of other chapters, though it has been suggested, rather controversially, that assonance–rime analysis is 'really just a special case of derivational morphology' (Rhodes 1994, 290). In this view, rimes are heads, assonances are modifiers – adverbial/adjectival, e.g. *cl-* 'together' in *clamp*, *clasp*, or classifiers, e.g. *dr-* and *tr-* 'liquid' in *drink*, *drain*, *trickle*, *trough*. Many of the words in 10.2 and 10.3, however, cannot be exhaustively analysed as assonance and rime. *Trail*, for example, has a place in a group of *tr-* words linked by the notion of 'treading', but there is no obvious link with other words containing *-ail*. The *sl-* of *slovenly* aligns it with a group for which 'sloth' can serve as a label, but *-ovenly* has no separate identity.

Besides assonances and rimes, there are various other elements and features of words which might be distinguished as phonaesthemes, for example the prefix-like **ka-** or **ker-** of *kerfuffle*, *ker-plonk*, *ker-splash*: 'Butcher said he didn't know what all the kerfuffle was about' (OED: 1960), 'The boot . . . kerplonked to the carpet as straight and true as Newton's apple' (OED: 1963), 'The boat hit the surface with a solid ker-splash' (OED: 1959).[5] Other affix-like elements are the **sha-** or **she-** of *shazam*, *shebang*, *shemozzle*, *shenanigans*, and the *-eroo* of *boozeroo* 'a drinking spree', cf. 'It's going to be a real *boozeroo* (OED: 1972) and *flopperoo* 'a flop, failure' (OED).

Some endings are more frequent in occurrence than these and more like conventional suffixes. *-le* and *-el* in verbs, and the nouns related to them, are traceable to diminutive or frequentative nominal and verbal suffixes in various languages. Old English has *nist(i)an* 'to nest' and *nistlian* 'nestle'; it has *wadan* 'to go' ('wade') and *dwinan* 'to waste away'; *waddle* and *dwindle* are recorded much later. *Scrabble* and obsolete *scrab* 'to scratch' are from Dutch, and *scribble* is from a diminutive form *scribellare* of Latin *scribere* 'to write'. *Guzzle* is doubtfully derived from Old French *gosiller*, connected with *gosier* 'throat'. In many cases, OED pronounces the history of words in *-le* 'obscure' or 'imitative'. To some modern *-le* words, a 'simple' form recognizably corresponds, though the semantic relation between the two is not always predictable. *Chumble* in 'I can hear the sound of moths chumbling the clothes in that chest' (OED: 1941) is a plausible frequentative, or diminutive, of *chump* as illustrated in 10.1; other possible pairs are *crumb* and *crumble*, *snug* and *snuggle*, *daze* and *dazzle*, *sniff* and *sniffle*, *snivel*, *toot* and *tootle*. More often, as with *fumble*, *guzzle*, *muddle*, *sizzle*, *straggle*, *twinkle* and *whistle* there is no discoverable 'simple' form.

Samuels (1972) identifies *-le* as a kind of phonaestheme distinct from assonances and rimes. He also identifies the *-er* of verbs like *bluster*, *chunter*, *glitter*, *putter*, *spatter* as a phonaestheme. OED describes it as a suffix forming frequentative verbs (*-er suffix* 5). Old English has *scimerian* 'to shimmer' beside *scimian* 'to shine' and *floterian* 'to flutter' beside *flotian* 'to float'. Jespersen (1942, 15.31) compares *quaver*, *sputter*, *stutter* with older unsuffixed forms (Middle English *quaven*, *spouten*, *stutten*) and *waver* with *wave*, noting (15.32) 'Often there is an etymological relationship between a monosyllable and the *-er*-form', as with *beat* and *batter*, *sway* and *swagger*, *wend* and *wander*.' But, as with words in *-le*, such words in OED are very often labelled 'imitative' or 'of obscure origin'. Stems containing [l] are suffixed by *-er*; those with [r] have *-le*, cf. *blabber* and *prattle* (Marchand 1969, 273). Otherwise pairs of alternants like *scutter* and *scuttle* appear to be rare.

In reduplicative adjectives like *itsy-bitsy* and *teensy-weensy*, the *-sy* suffix of affective diminutives like *cutesy* (4.3) is identifiable. An adjective suffix *-y*, recognizable as that of deverbal adjectives like *jumpy* or denominal adjectives like *woolly* (2.5.1, 2), combines with many bases which are phonaesthemic in character:

> *dinky, goofy, grotty, grungy, gungy, kooky, scatty, smoochy, snazzy, stroppy, wacky, yucky, zappy, zingy, zizzy.*

Reduplicative adjectives also often end in *-y*: *airy-fairy, happy-clappy, easy-peasy, fuddy-duddy*. *-y* attaches also to nominal reduplicative formations, in which it has a variant *-ie*: *boogie-woogie, hanky-panky, hurly-burly, walkie-talkie*. As we saw in 4.3, *-ie/-y* also forms affective diminutive nouns like *doggie* and *fatty* (4.3). Nominal and adjectival *-y*, adjectival *-sy* and nominal *-ie*, we might say, have some claim in formations like these to the title of phonaestheme.

The tendency in alliterative formations such as *chiff-chaff*, *see-saw* for a high front vowel to precede [æ] or a low back vowel has been much commented on (see, for instance, Jespersen 1942, ch. 10; Marchand 1969, 431). Samuels (1972, 47) suggests that such gradational variation, evident also in the relation of single words like *tip* and *drip* to *top* and *drop*, is a kind of phonaestheme.

Alternant forms in fact abound in this area of the vocabulary. Compare also *beep* and *bleep*, *spatter* and *splatter*, *plash* and *splash*, *putter* and *splutter*, *quelch* and *squelch*, *blotch* and *blodge*, *chatter* and *chunter*, *champ*, *chomp* and *chump*. We might, with Wescott (1977, 202) distinguish an abstract element {KAK} representing words for 'strident sound' such as *cackle*, *cuckoo*, *quack*, *cluck*, *croak*, or discontinuous sequences like [kl–k] subsuming *click*, *clack*, *clank*, *clunk*, [sp–t] 'rush of liquid' in *spit*, *spate*, *spurt*, *spout* (Bolinger 1950, 135) or [sw–p] in *sweep*, *swipe*, *swoop*. Rimes might sometimes be better represented more abstractly as, for instance, -V*d* in *pad*, *plod*, *thud*, or -V*ddle* in *coddle*, *muddle* and *twiddle*, or -V*ggle* and -V*mp* to include *waggle*, *wriggle*, *struggle*, and *champ*, *stamp*, *tramp*, *chomp*, *stomp*, *clump*, *stump*. And, as Bolinger (1950) demonstrates with various extended examples, phonaestheme words can easily be shown to constitute loose networks or 'constellations' like

		crawl	scrawl	
flump	slump	crump	scrump	clump
flash	slash	crash		clash
	slush	crush		

See also Reay (1994) for a more extensive example. These multiple correspondences underline the fact that words containing phonaesthemes are, paradoxically, at once analysable and unitary (cf. Bolinger 1950, 136; Marchand 1969, 403).

Apart from 'sound' or 'movement', the meanings of phonaestheme formations appear too various to be characterized by any semantic label less general than 'affective'. There is more often than not uncertainty about their semantics. Is the assonance of *slam* more responsible for the word's effect (cf. *slash*, *slay*), or the rime (cf. *bam*, *ram*, *wham*)? *Sl-* 'sliding' and 'sloth' (10.2) are obviously semantically related (Käsmann 1992), but is there more than an accidental connection between the senses of these words and the sense of 'attack' in other *sl-* words, despite the possibility of including *slag* and *slug* in both the 'sloth' and 'attack' groups?

Semantic common denominators are often elusive. Is [sk] 'fast movement' (10.3) identifiable in both the assonance of *skip* and the rime of *whisk*? If there is a common element in *bag*, *drag*, *fag*, *flag*, *hag*, *lag*, *quag*, *rag*, *sag*, *scrag*, *tag*, what is it? An assonance in *spring*, *spry*, *sprint*, *sprout* can perhaps be identified and labelled 'energetic' (Reay 1994). The riming part of *crawl*, *drawl*, *scrawl* and *sprawl* might be labelled 'protracted' and/or 'spread out'.

But are *gobble*, *hobble* and *wobble* linked? Does *rabble* belong in any way with *babble* and *gabble*? *Muddle* and *meddle* go together, and so do *coddle* and *huddle*, and *fiddle*, *piddle* and *twiddle*. Can we merge these groups, relax the riming requirement, add *addle* and still have a series? Bolinger (1950, 125) suggests that *tamp*, *stamp* and *tramp* are 'earth-striking', and that a more general label 'having to do with the earth' would admit *damp*, *clamp* and *ramp*. Reay distinguishes two groups of *st-* words with the common denominator of 'arrest' (10.3): 'reliable, steadfast', including *stable* and *staunch*, and 'implacable, rigid', including *stern* and *strict*. Such fine discriminations take us into the broader area of what Bolinger terms 'word affinities'. He identifies for example (1940, 71) initial *v-* and *vi-* with 'ill-temper' in words like *vituperative*, *vitriolic*, *vindictive*, *vengeful*, *vicious*, *vixenish*, *violent*, *vehement*, *virulent*, *vile* and *-oo-* with 'foolishness' in *boob*, *galoot*, *loon*, *moon* and other words. Wescott (1971b) assembles numerous examples in support of an association of velar and labial sounds with derogation.

Phonaestheme formations are characterized generally by elusiveness of meaning, and subjectivity in judgments about it, by proliferation and volatility of form, and even sometimes by variation in spelling. But they are used and on occasion 'created' by all speakers, and they are certainly frequent enough, and analysable enough, to claim attention in an account of word formation.

Notes

1. Rhodes (1994) places sound-imitative words on a scale, the ends of which he calls 'wild' and 'tame'. Sequences at the 'wild' end, like *bzz*, *hmm*, *meow*, contrast with 'tame' words like *chatter* or *smack*, which can denote something other than sounds. Among 'semi-wild' words are some which contain non-English sequences, like *boing*, *pting*, *thwack*, *vroom*.
2. For copious similar examples, see Marchand (1969, 405–19).
3. See Käsmann's thorough study of *sl-* (1992) for many examples.
4. See Plank's (1981, 220–5 and 230–46) observations on phonaestheme formations, illustrated by German and English examples, in the context of a discussion of the nature of rules in word formation.
5. OED explains the *cur* of the verb *curfuffle* (1583) as 'perh. Gaelic *car* twist, bend, turn about'. Cassidy (1983) relates the currency in American English from the mid-nineteenth century of 'echoisms' prefixed by *ker-*, *ca-*, *che-*, *ka-* and other variant forms to the arrival in the USA of Ulster Scots in the eighteenth century.

11

Reanalysis

Scope

When a complex word whose structure is perceived in a certain way is compared to other words to which it can be seen as somehow similar, it may be reanalysed, and perceived as having a different structure, thus paving the way for an abductive change. Abduction 'proceeds from an observed result, invokes a law, and infers that something may be the case' (Andersen 1973, 775).[1]

In previous chapters, examples of reanalysis of various kinds have been noted in passing, and many more could have been mentioned. Some suffixes, like *-dom*, *-hood* and *-less*, were once also words, cf. Old English *on dryhtlicestum dome* 'in most noble state', *papan had* 'papal dignity', *firena leas* 'free from crimes'. The prefixation of suffixed verbs like *decolonize* can suggest, in cases like *demagnetize*, in which the base can easily be seen as nominal, a 'partnership' of prefix and suffix involved in noun-to-verb transposition (1.2.2, 3.2). The *-ery* of *pottery* (4.4) might be seen as two suffixes, the *-er* of *potter* and *-y* as in *photography*, but *-ery* can only be one suffix in *piggery*. *Allocable*, containing the stem of *allocate*, conforms to a pattern established by loan words like *imitable*, many of which also have corresponding verbs in *-ate*. The pairing of adjectives or nouns in *-ate* and nouns in *-acy* in e.g. *adequate* and *adequacy*, *advocate* and *advocacy*, *pirate* and *piracy* is behind such occasional formations as *complicacy* or *invertebracy*. A fairly recent series of adjective-based nominalizations relating to 'communication' includes *articulacy*, *computeracy*, corresponding to *computerate* 'computer-literate' (OED: 1981), *literacy* and *numeracy*. *Oracy* 'ability in the oral skills' (OED: 1965) has as yet no corresponding adjective.

We can see *non-participation* as prefix + nominal base, but the appearance of *to non-cooperate* (3.4) suggests that *non-cooperation* is analysed as verb base + suffix. *Co-executor* is superficially like *co-driver*, but only the second has a corresponding verb, *to co-drive*. The noun *sit-in* is transpositionally related to a verb + particle collocation, but *think-in* is formed on the pattern of other nouns ending in *-in* (5.4). According to whether its second word is seen as based on a verb or not, *oak-panelled* (7.3.3) is paraphraseable as 'panelled in oak', comparable with *fear-fuelled*, or as 'having oak panels', like *pigeon-toed*. All the verb compounds of Chapter 8 which are not transpositional presuppose the reanalysis of a nominal or adjectival expression. Many of the assonance + rime combinations of 10.2 and 10.3 are likely to evoke one another as units.

Reanalysis implies change. It may involve the activation of possibilities that were there all along, as with the formation of some verbs on the basis of their nominalized forms, or it may result in the emergence of new formative units. In the next section we look at some ways in which reanalysis can affect affixes. Section 11.3 looks at reanalysis and backformation. The topics of 11.4 and 11.5 are respectively blends and shortened forms, both often the results of the reanalysis in rather unexpected ways of simple forms as complex.

11.2   Affixes[2]

A foreign affix becomes a formative element in its new language once it can be recognized in a series of borrowed words: affixes are not generally 'borrowed' as such (1.5). The prefix *de-*, once it had become identifiable in a series of loan words like *deprive* and *deface*, began to appear in new English words like *debowel* and *deforest*. The formation of *onement* 'union' (MED: *c.* 1395) presupposes an acquaintance with pairs like *achieve* and *achievement*. *Beautify* appeared only after a number of earlier loans from French and Latin like *purify* and *glorify* had become current. Thirteenth-century *hermitage* and fourteenth-century *parsonage* are recorded in French as well as in English, but *vicarage* (OED: 1425) is English. Jespersen's term (1922, 384) for this kind of development is **secretion**. *-nik* (4.2) – helped by a couple of leader words – is a recent case of secretion. Other modern 'secreted' suffixes may well be the products of more deliberate naming processes. Examples are *-ase*, *-ide*, *-ol*, *-ose* (9.4.2) and the two suffixes discernible in *electron*. The constituents of this word are identified by OED as the stem of *electric* and *-on*, secreted from *ion* 'electrically charged atom or molecule'. (Greek *electron*, Latin *electrum*, means 'amber'.) *-on* subsequently appeared in names of subatomic particles (*meson*) and other entities (*graviton*, *muton*), and *-tron* in the names of many stem-based nouns like *kenotron*, an electron tube, *cosmotron*, a particle accelerator, *mesotron*, a subatomic particle, *phytotron*, a plant laboratory, and numbers of trade names.

Two other kinds of development, which we can refer to as **extension** and **combination**, are worth noting as affecting English suffixes.[3] In extension (Jespersen 1922, 384), an already existing affix incorporates part of an element which is often found adjacent to it. *-let* and *-ling*, as we noted in 4.3, have been extended. *-an*, often attached to names ending in *-ia*, has an extended variant in *Canadian* and *Baconian* (Marchand 1969, 245). The *-pl-* of the stem of *haploid* 'having a single set of chromosomes' appears in words like *hexaploid* 'containing six sets of chromosomes'. The *-n-* in the stems of *botanist* and *Platonist* appears unhistorically in *tobacconist*.

The suffix **-ation** (as in *taxation*) is historically a combination of *-at-* in Latin stems (as in *demonstration*) and *-ion*. Similarly, the suffix *-ive* has an extended form **-ative**, as in *calmative, exploitative* (beside *exploitive*), *reportative, segmentative, supportative* (beside *supportive*), which in some words can be seen to preserve the pattern of bases ending in [t] (2.5.1): *affirmative, performative, rebukative*: 'No Janet, I'm not backbiting, so don't be so rebukative' (OED: 1950). *Magnitude* and *solitude* correspond to Latin and French nominalized forms ending in *-tudo, -tude*; *adaptitude* and *correctitude* have word bases + *-itude*. Words with bases corresponding to Latin adjectives in *-ax, -acis* end in *-acious*: *capacious, loquacious, veracious*. By contrast, *-ac-* is an unetymological extension in *scribacious* 'given to writing': 'Popes were not then very scribacious' (OED: 1677) and *verbacious* 'good with words' (John Bratby, *Breakfast and Elevenses*, 1961, 30); *vitreous* and *herbaceous* correspond to Latin adjectives in *-eus*, but in *courteous* and *carbonaceous*, *-ous* is extended.

Combining suffixes is also a way of extending them. *-al* attaches to bases also suffixed by *-ic*. Some of these may have both *-ic* and **-ical**, usually with some difference of use or meaning: *historic, historical, economic, economical* (2.5.2) but a few items, like *common-sensical, farcical, nonsensical* and *parsonical*, are simply base + *-ical*. In words like *mathematician, statistician*, **-ician** is a suffix sequence; attached to word bases as in *dietician, paradoxician* (OED: 1909), *stylistician*, and bases which cannot be suffixed by *-ic*, it can be seen as a fixed combination.

Some adjectives ending in **-istic** have no plausible base in *-ist*: *anachronistic, cannibalistic, criminalistic, simplistic, vandalistic, voyeuristic*.[4] Others, like *impressionistic, naturalistic, tokenistic*, may not be understood as based on an *-ist* noun, or the *-ist* noun may be rather rare, cf. *animalistic, annalistic, energistic, euphemistic, jingoistic, legalistic, mediumistic, ritualistic*.

-ary and **-an**, in adjectives and nouns, have functioned as a single suffix from the early modern English period. Latin adjectives ending in *-arius* might have two forms in English, e.g. sixteenth-century *disciplinary* and *disciplinarian*, both adjective and noun. *-ary* forms could be augmented by *-an*, and bases not corresponding to Latin adjectives in *-arius* could take *-ary* (*budgetary*) and *-arian* (*libertarian*). As a result, both adjective and noun may end in *-arian* (*humanitarian*) or *-ary* (*missionary*), or *-ary* may mark an adjective and *-arian* a noun (*parliamentary, parliamentarian*). In combination, the suffixes have come to be associated with particular semantic areas. Many words containing them have meanings related to matters of conviction or political affiliation, often carrying an implication of rigour, explicit in *strictarian*.

Besides *disciplinarian*, other early words were *sacramentarian* 'denier of the doctrine of the real presence', *sectarian* 'member of a sect' and *trinitarian* 'believer in the Trinity'. Milton comments on his coinage *antiquitarian*: 'for so I had rather call them then Antiquaries, whose labours are usefull and laudable' (OED: 1641). Later formations include *latitudinarian*, *libertarian* 'believer in free will', *predestinarian*, *pulpitarian* 'preacher', and *Tractarian*: 'Lawless in formation, certainly, is *Tractarian*; and yet it will live in history, to the exclusion of *Tractite*, *Tractuist* and *Tractator*, all of which have been proposed in its stead' (OED: 1892). Bases ending in [t] are favoured: OED evidence suggests that *necessitarian* 'a believer in necessity', *sabbatarian*, and *ubiquitarian* 'a believer in the doctrine that Christ is present everywhere' are favoured at the expense of *necessarian*, *sabbatharian* and *ubiquarian*.

The earlier area relating to religious conviction is widened to include politics: *communitarian* 'a member of a community formed to put into practice communistic or socialistic theories' (OED: 1841), *egalitarian*, *establishmentarian*, nineteenth-century and later uses of *libertarian*, *majoritarian* 'one who believes in government by the majority' (Webster 1961), *proprietarian* 'an advocate or supporter of proprietary government in the N. American colonies' (OED: 1776), *totalitarian*, explained in Webster (1961) as 'from *total* and *-tarian* (as in *authoritarian*)', and more general moral concerns: *humanitarian*, *charitarian*, *hereditarian*, *perfectibilitarian*. *Animalitarianism* is 'the view that animals are more natural, happier and admirable than human beings' (Webster 1961). A group for which *vegetarian* looks like a leader-word includes *dietarian*, *fruitarian*, *meatarian*, *nutarian* and *breatharian*: 'Fresh air could replace fresh vegetables as the source of health if claims by a group of people calling themselves "breatharians" are to be believed' (Guardian: 1998).

All these cases, in which suffixes combine to form, in some words at least, a new unit, can be distinguished from others in which two productive suffixes are simply found together very often. Thus, adjectives in *-able* regularly nominalize with *-ity* and verbs in *-ize* and *-ify* with *-ation*. Words like *roadability*, *coniferization* and *yuppification* might thus be seen as base + *-ability*, *-ization*, *-ification*, as OED in fact suggests, but corresponding adjectives and verbs (*roadable*, *coniferize*, *yuppify*) are always possible.[5]

11.3   Backformation

Many complex words in which more than two elements are discernible are subject to reanalysis. Examples are the prefixed nominalized formations *non-cooperation* and *co-driver* mentioned in 11.1, and noun and adjective compounds with nominalized and participial heads like *telephone tapping*, *self-locking* and *gift-wrapped*. The derivation of verbs, *telephone-tap*, *self-lock*, *gift-wrap* presupposes reanalysis as complex base and suffix, and the subtraction of the suffix.

In these examples, internal relationships – verb and negative element, verb and object – are 're-affirmed' in the shorter forms; in other cases the longer form is more coherent semantically, e.g. *guest editor* 'editor who is a guest', yielding a verb *to guest-edit*, or *electrical engineering*, from which another noun *electrical engineer* can be seen as derived. Prefixed parasynthetic adjectives like *poly-angular* and *multi-hulled* can also yield nouns: *poly-angle*, *multi-hull* (3.4).[6]

In other cases of backformation, a base in a word hitherto seen as only partially analysable becomes independent, e.g. the adjective *tatty* (probably related to Old English *tættec* 'a rag'), assumed to have a nominal base, yields the noun *tat* 'worthless goods'. *To laze* is similarly related to *lazy*, and the noun and verb *peeve* 'complaint' and 'to complain' to *peevish*. The verb *hawk*, 'to practise the trade of a hawker', was assumed to be the base of a German or Dutch loan word of uncertain derivation. The sources of the verbs *darkle* 'to grow dark', *grovel* and *sidle* are adverbial or adjectival *darkling*, *grovelling* and *sidling*, which exemplify an Old English way of forming adverbs, cf. *bæcling* 'backwards, behind'. OED derives *gangling* from a putative form **gangle*, explained as formed with frequentative *-le* (10.5), which actually occurs in 'Ronald Pickup gangles his way suspendingly through this lark' (Evening Standard: 1968). Verbs that were once only stems within loan words include *emote, intuit, liaise, obsess, opt, psych, repercuss*.

It is not always clear in particular cases whether or not backformation should be recognized. The rare adjectives *kempt* and *sipid*: 'The flesh of the Crocodile . . . was wholesome, white, and sipid' (OED: 1660) look as if they are – and on occasion no doubt have been – backformed from *unkempt* and *insipid*. In fact, OED dates *kempt* in the late fourteenth century and *unkempt* in the late sixteenth. *Sipid* and *insipid* are both early seventeenth century: *sipid* is listed in Cockeram's *English Dictionarie* (1923). OED assumes that the source of *to co-drive* is *co-driver*. It derives *casualize* from the related noun in *-ation*. Dates are supportive in this case – 1920 for the nominalized form and 1950 for the verb – but only just, and it would be reasonable to say that with the formation of the noun, the verb could be assumed to exist as well. *Orate* (1600) from fourteenth-century *oration* might seem a clearer example of backformation. Meaning is often felt to be a more relevant criterion than date: the verbs can be defined as 'act as a co-driver', 'subject to casualization', 'deliver an oration'. But it is worth asking why the perception of backderivation should be stronger in some cases than in others. *Co-exist*, *vandalize* 'act like a vandal', or *appreciate* (all recorded later than the nominalized forms) are probably not felt to be backformed despite the reasonable glosses 'enjoy co-existence', 'subject to vandalism', 'show appreciation'.

The most important factor is frequency. If one member of a pair of derivationally related words is much less frequent or usual than the other, it is less likely to be recognized and therefore more likely to be perceived as derived (Bybee 1988, 132ff). If there are at the same time formal grounds, such as the absence of an affix, for taking the less frequent word as basic, it will be seen as backderived, and in a good definition, a less familiar word is best explained in terms of a more familiar one.

Words perceived as backformed, whether accompanied by formal reanalysis or not, are overwhelmingly verbs – compound verbs, prefixed verbs and verbs like *orate*, *commentate*, *curate*, 'act as a curator', *formate* 'fly in formation', *predate* 'be a predator, seek and eat prey', *spectate*. Pennanen (1966, 90) notes peaks in recorded backformations in the middle of the seventeenth century and in the nineteenth, and links them with rates of lexical borrowing. Where the need for new learned and technical terms is the impetus for borrowing, loan words are most likely to be nouns. Since there were already many suffixed French and Latin nouns in Middle English, these newer loans would look to English speakers like derived words, and if corresponding verbs were felt to be needed, their obvious route into English was by backformation. Many verbs related to Latin and Greek participles and nouns, like *effervesce*, *fluoresce*, *luminesce*, *phosphoresce*, *diagnose*, *metempsychose*, *necrose*, *catalyse*, for example, are later than the corresponding nouns. Adjective-to-verb transposition in fact also accounted for many new verbs derived from anglicized participial forms, e.g. *to tribulate* (1637), from sixteenth-century participial *tribulate* as well as fourteenth-century *tribulation*. Such participial forms were later regularly suffixed by *-ed*, and the related verb could then appear backformed in any case. *Separate* has had a similar history but, having become familiar, is not seen as a backformation.

Verbs do not predominate in the vocabulary, conceived of as the body of words in current general use. According to figures given by Miller and Fellbaum (1992, 214), the percentages of different nouns and verbs recorded in Collins English Dictionary are 75 and 25 respectively. Similar proportions of nouns to verbs derived from the CELEX Lexical Data Base are noted by Baayen and Lieber (1991, 829). New verbs may, more often than nouns or adjectives, be not often needed or much used; hence we have numbers of verbs related to apparently derived members of other classes, but with few citations recorded in dictionaries, and the appearance of having been backderived.[7]

In general though, backformation accounts for rather few words compared with transposition, prefixing, suffixing and compounding. It is doubtful whether it is properly a derivational process at all,[8] since abduction is involved, and circumstances like frequency and familiarity largely govern whether words are perceived as backformed or not.

11.4   Blending

Blending, like backformation, involves the analysis of words in new ways. A blend is made up of two contributory words, one or both of which may be only partially present in the new word. The parts may overlap, as in *selectorate* 'section of a political party with power to choose a representative', or may not, as in *breathalyser*. Blends can be formed unintentionally, as speech errors, slips of the tongue,[9] or slips of the pen in hasty writing, such as *distruption* (*destruction* and *disruption*), *fixidity* (*fixity* and *rigidity*) and *sombriety* (*sombreness* and *sobriety*), attested in student examination papers. Such formations are usually combinations of near-synonyms. The blends we are concerned with in this section are deliberate formations like *selectorate* and *breathalyser*, *glitterati* 'celebrities' (cf. *literati*), or *fakesimile*: 'Old maps, old countries, genuine fakesimiles' (D.J. Enright, 'Empire Games').

Unintentional and deliberate blends might seem to have little in common, but Kubozono (1990) shows that lexical blends of all kinds are subject to similar constraints on their shapes. Typically, a blend conforms, or approximates, to the shape of one of the source words, almost always the final one, as in *camelcade* 'camel cavalcade', 'a train of people on camels' (OED: 1886). Intentional blends thus have, more or less obviously, the character of puns. In a not uncommon pattern, an initial monosyllabic word replaces the first syllable of a longer final element: *blaxploitation*, *guestimate*, *keytainer*, *mockumentary*, *seavacuation* (the name of a World War II scheme for evacuating children), *shamateur*. Examples given in other chapters which could be called blends include compounds formed on the pattern of specific other compounds, like *whitelist* or *greenwash* (6.2), and suffixed words and stem compounds which in form as well as meaning evoke leader-words, such as *peacenik* (4.2), *cookdom* (4.4), *dietarian* (11.2), *chimponaut* and *telegenic* (9.4.3).

A reanalysed element may appear in a series of new formations. *Resistor* 'device which impedes the flow of an electric current' is represented in names for semi-conductor devices like *neuristor*, *spacistor*, *transistor* and *thermistor*. Further examples are the *-(o)tel* of *hotel* in *motel*, *boatel* and *lorrytel*: 'Opening Soon – the Dockside Lorry-Tel' (Evening Standard: 1964), the *-cade* of *cavalcade* in *aerocade*, *aquacade*, *autocade*, *motorcade* and *Beatlecade*: 'Paul and George arrived in their blue Bentley at the head of the "Beatlecade"' (Evening Standard: 1965), the *-ar* of *star* in *pulsar* 'pulsating star', *spinnar* 'spinning star', and *collapsar* 'collapsing star', the ending of *escapade* in *icecapade* 'ice show' and *sexcapade*, the ending of *Sandinista* in *Camcordista* 'protester with a video-camera' (Guardian: 1996) and *feminista*: 'old-school feministas' (Guardian: 1997), the stem of *utopia* in *motopia*, *queuetopia* and *subtopia* (cf. *suburbia*), the ending of *Marathon* (a Greek place name) in names for competitive, fund-raising or just lengthy events like *cyclethon*, *talkathon*, *swimathon*, *telethon*, and the ending of *alcoholic* in a larger group of words such as *computerholic*, *spendaholic*, *workaholic*. Later additions to such groups may conform less closely to the shape of the source word (Beard 1998, 57). In such cases, the distinction between blending and secretion is not sharp.

Occupying an uncertain area between spontaneous errors and deliberate inventions are some phonaestheme formations of 10.2, like *splunge* (*splash* and *plunge*?) or *squench* (*squash* and *quench*?), and words like those in the following observation: 'How often our writers have used the phrase "to banish the mists" – because it suggests *vanish*! *Pendulous*, for all its Latin origin, is a more vivid word in some contexts than *dangle*, probably because it has been enriched by *tremulous*. . . . *Ravage* is more devastating than *raze* or *despoil* because of the overtone *savage*' (Bolinger 1940, 72).

Most blends formed with any degree of intentionality are nouns. A few verbs, which look as though they might have originated as errors, are combinations of synonyms: *baffound* (*baffle* and *confound*) (EDD), meld (*melt* and *weld*?) (OED: 1939), smothercate (*smother* and *suffocate*) (EDD). Adjectives are also likely to be combinations of synonyms, cf. *aggranoying, irregardless, solemncholy*. Synonymous adjectives can be combined for emphasis, as in 'Robert Benchley's new mirthquake, colossapendous, stupeficent, magnossal' (New York Times, quoted in *American Speech* 13, 1938, 239); 'FANTABULOUS is the only word' (Gavin Lambert, *Inside Daisy Clover*, 1963, Penguin 1966, 38).

Nominal blends show greater variety. They may be names which express iconically the notion 'hybrid', cf. 'Is it a horse? Is it a zebra? No it's a zorse' (Guardian: 1996). Other examples are *catalo* (*cattle* and *buffalo*), *celtuce* (*celery* and *lettuce*), *liger*, offspring of a male lion and a female tiger), *plumcot* (*plum* and *apricot*), *zebrule* (*zebra* and *mule*). Blends may be coined as appropriate names for new artefacts: *ballute* (Science News: 1966), *compander* (*compressor* and *expander*), *elevon* (*elevator* and *aileron*), *passenveyor* ('passenger conveyor'), *Posturepedic* (mattress), *submarisle*: 'an undersea island which could house a base for submarines' (Daily Telegraph: 1972), *transceiver* ('transmitter-receiver'). *-ator* represents *elevator* in *ruddervator*, *generator* in *stellarator* 'device for generating power by reactions similar to those in stars', *cultivator* in *rotavator*, *indicator* in *trafficator*, and *modulator* in *wobbulator* 'device for producing a signal of varying frequency'. Hybrid concepts can also find appropriate expression in blends, as in *infotainment*: 'Editors . . . began to understand that their readership was insatiable in its demands for gossip "infotainment", which was rapidly displacing news' (Guardian: 1997), and the coinage in: '"Education or Creation" as a title for the book . . . seemed clumsy. That is how the word EDUCREATION was born: to fill a need. The need for one word to signify a new growth-oriented concept of education' (Paul Rutter, *Educreation*, 1966, xiv). Blends are likely to occur in trade names and advertisements: 'COMPUCESSORIES . . . a new word? Yes! . . . We've just coined it to describe those Data processing Accessories *we* at PCA delight in designing'; 'with added catisfaction (from an advertisement for cat food); 'Stimulotions for refreshing and stimulating'.

Blends are useful where words are required to draw attention to themselves – in newspaper headlines for example: 'Scrollduggery' (Observer: 1966, accompanying an account of fortunes made by dealers in Dead Sea scrolls); 'Deep Blue's victory proves giant step for computerkind' (Guardian: 1997, over an account of a chess contest between a computer and a grand master).

Other examples not meant to be more than transient, and elucidated by their contexts are: 'We are concerned with people who suffer from "affluenza" – a condition induced by guilt at having too much money' (Guardian: 1997); 'Aerobics teachers are, apparently, being asked to advise on car-seat work-out tips for those stuck in traffic jams. A typical "car-obics" routine might involve buttock clenching and steering wheel grips' (Cycle Touring and Campaigning: 1996); 'Genetic engineering has raised consumer fears of mutant "Frankenfoods"' (Guardian); 'It is a shabby thought, Cuba reverting to type, selling its children to become a "sextination" again, a playground for the rich and foreign' (Guardian: 1995); 'he's a ward in Chancery, my dear. . . . the whole thing will be vastly ceremonious, wordy, unsatisfactory, and expensive, and I call it, in general, Wiglomeration' (Dickens, *Bleak House*, 1858, Penguin, 148).

In blends, motivation is impeded in a variety of ways. In addition to potential difficulties of interpretation,[10] blends are subject to uncertainties of spelling: *botel* and *boatel*, *guestimate* and *guesstimate*, *swelegant* and *swellegant*. There may also be difficulties in pronunciation, where compression results in a stress clash: *anecdotage* (*ánecdote* and *dótage*), *ballute* (*ballóon* and *párachute*), *thermistor* ('thérmal resístor').[11] A few blends from earlier centuries have been preserved, among them *blatterature*: 'That Fylthiness and all such abusion which the later blynde worlde brought in, whiche more rather may be called "Blatterature" than literature'; (Colet, *Statutes for St Paul's School, c.* 1512), *foolosopher* (OED: 1549), *foolosophy* (OED: 1592), *niniversity* (OED: *c.* 1590); *knavigation*: 'the knavigations of false discouerers' (OED: 1613). The scarcity of recorded earlier examples can probably be put down to the characteristic transience of blends. Only in modern times have they been recorded in appreciable numbers but despite this, blending inevitably remains a marginal process, its products ephemeral and restricted in use.

11.5 Shortening

Under this head we can include any form derived in some way from a longer form and synonymous with it. Excluded are forms resulting from the phono-logical loss of initial or final elements like *'cos* or *an'*; adjectives and nouns in noun phrases with 'elliptical' heads, like 'the *preliminaries*', 'a *return* (ticket)', and abbreviations of phrases other than noun phrases which do not yield nominal expressions, like *c.o.d.*, *m.p.h.*, *a.k.a.*, *O.T.T.*, *AWOL*.

Acronyms (not strictly a matter of reanalysis) consist of the initial letters, not usually more than five (Kreidler 1979, 25), of longer, usually nominal expressions. They may be pronounced as a series of letters: TV, RSPCA. As words: *NASA*, ['næsə], *UFO*, ['juːfəʊ], sometimes containing sequences of letters not found elsewhere: *ASCII*, ['æskɪ], *NAAFI*, ['næfi], they may include other than initial letters to make them more word-like: *radar* 'radio detecting and ranging'. They may be devised to be semantically indicative of the referent of the longer form: ASH 'Action on Smoking and Health'. Like other words, they can be affixed and compounded: *Natoism, ufo-ish, ufologist, vatable, vatman*.

In shortened forms, sometimes the initial part of a source word is omitted, as in *cello, chute, copter*. In rare cases, both initial and final parts are missing: *flu, fridge, script* '(doctor's) prescription'. In the majority of cases, the final part is omitted. Shortened forms are generally of one syllable, e.g. *ad*(vertisement), *ex*(-spouse), *con*(vict), *ref*(eree), *op*(eration), *veg*(etable), or two, e.g. *advert, admin, decaff, prefab, refurb*, and occasionally three: *intercom*. Shortened forms may disregard syllable division as with *cuc*(umber): they usually end in a single consonant, or *r* and another consonant: *porn, perm* (Kreidler 1979, 31–2). They are usually nominal, though expressive adjectives are occasionally shortened: *brill, fab, glam*. They are subject to derivational processes like transposition: *to lube, perm, rev* (up), *recap*, and compounding with unshortened words: *op art, con trick* or with other shortened forms: *biopic, cyborg*, from *cybernetic* and *organism*, 'an integrated man-machine system' (OED), *hi-fi, sci-fi, sitcom*.

Both acronyms and shortened forms are likely to be restricted to particular registers and speech communities. Both can serve as proper names. As alternative expressions for synonymous forms, they can be compared with the 'situational' diminutive expressions discussed in 4.3. Acronymic names, as convenient short forms, are typically not hypocoristic in nature, but Malkiel (1968, 382) interestingly notes the common practice of addressing and referring to office superiors by their initials at a level of formality intermediate between familiar and formal.

Like the 'situational' diminutives of 4.3, shortened names and other words in informal use often have the endings *-ie*, *-y*, *-o* and *-s*. Some examples are:

alkie, Aussie, bicky, Bolshie (or Bolshy), cardy, ciggy, commie, cozzie, hanky, loony, prezzie, techie, tranny, veggie

Afro, aggro, ammo, combo, journo, limo, provo

Babs, civvies, maths, specs, turps.

Further examples, in which the ending is also part of the longer form are *deli, divvy, Indie* and *telly*; *Expo, intro, repro, physio, psycho* and *speedo*.

Words like these can also be compared with some 'expressive' examples in Chapter 10. As we saw in 10.5, reduplicative formations are not infrequently suffixed by *-ie, -y* or *-sy*, and Malkiel (1968, 382) points out that pet-name status can be conferred by reduplication (*Fifi, Jojo, Zizi*). Another ending found with shortened and sometimes otherwise modified forms in restricted and very informal situations is the 'public school' *-er* or *-ers*, as in *brekker, footer, rugger, soccer; Divvers* 'Divinity Moderations', *Jaggers* 'Jesus College', *Quaggers* 'Queens College'.

Notes

1. Andersen (1973, 775) contrasts abduction with induction and deduction: 'While inductive inference proceeds from observed cases and results to establish a law, deduction applies a law to a case and predicts a result.'
2. See Malkiel (1966) and Haspelmath (1994) for detailed discussion and classifications of developments involving affixes from various languages. Haspelmath includes under 'secretion' some kinds of reanalysis which I term 'extension'. See also Marchand's discussion of 'the origin of suffixes' (1969, 210ff).
3. Haspelmath (1994) sees the growth of affixes as compensating for the effects of phonological reduction, and points out that the reanalysis of affixes often brings about, or preserves, preferred syllable structures.
4. There is often a corresponding noun in *-ism*; Aronoff (1976, 120–1) accordingly suggests that such nouns are the bases of adjectives in *-istic*.
5. See Raffelsiefen (1992) for a discussion of such partnerships between productive processes, which, however, she sees as evidence of a rule of historical reanalysis.
6. 'Mismatches' of form and meaning occur in a range of expressions not involved in backformation. Nominal expressions like *flat earth, particle physics, criminal law, four legs* can be suffixed to form *flat earther, particle physicist, criminal lawyer, four-legged*. In each of these cases, the obvious bipartite division, *flat + earther* etc., is at odds with the meaning. For extended discussion of such 'bracketing paradoxes', see especially Spencer (1991, ch. 10) and Beard (1991).
7. Plag, Dalton-Puffer and Baayen (1999, 222), comparing the productivity of various affixes, find that derived nouns make a much larger contribution to the size of the vocabulary than other patterns.
8. Opinion is divided on this. Marchand (1969) sees backformation as having 'diachronic relevance only' (391) and Aronoff (1976, 27) agrees. Pennanen (1966) cautiously disagrees. Bauer's (1983) view is that it 'must be allowed for in a synchronic grammar' (65), and Becker (1993, 6) supports him, pointing out that it makes available new models for future formations.
9. On blends as errors, see Aitchison (1994), especially 20–1, 139–40, 198–9 and references.
10. See Lehrer (1996a) for a detailed examination of factors involved in the perception, interpretation and evaluation of blends.
11. Praninskas (1968) in an examination of trade names, notes: 'More than one informant has refused to try to pronounce CALEMONA, CIRCOLAIR, FEATHAIRE, HAP-P-NUT (when peanuts were in evidence), NYLONGE (a nylon sponge) and SERV-ICE' (35).

12

Overview

12.1 Patterns

Some of the patterns we have looked at in earlier chapters can be described in terms of a word formation rule of the kind outlined by Aronoff, in which both the base of a complex word and the complex word itself are specified in terms of their category and meaning. With prefixation by *pre-*, *mis-* and (generally) *re-* (3.2) for example, it is necessary to specify only that the bases are verbs, and that prefixed verbs are 'accomplishments'. *-en* attaches exclusively to monosyllabic adjective bases to form verbs (*sweeten*), and *-ive* to verb bases ending in [s] or [t] to form 'subjective' adjectives (*replacive, pollutive*). According to the 'unitary base hypothesis', a word formation rule 'will never operate on either this or that'[1] (Aronoff 1976, 48), and its output is predictable. But rules, or patterns, are not always so concisely definable, and the forms they are perceived to take will depend on the relative importance we may attach to phonology, to the syntactic relationship between base and complex word, and to meaning.

Where there are differences in the category of complex words formed with the 'same' affix, I have generally recognized distinct patterns, as with deverbal nouns and adjectives in *-ant* (*dispersant* 2.4.1, *repentant* 2.5.1), adjective-forming *un-* as distinct from verb-forming *un-*, and noun-to-adjective *-ly* (*painterly*) as distinct from adjective-to-adverb *-ly*.[2] By contrast, adjectival and adverbial items in de-adjectival *-ish* (4.1) and denominal *-wise* (2.6) have not been treated separately.

The 'same' affix sometimes figures in words of one category which have bases of more than one category. In some cases of this kind I have recognized more than one pattern. In the case of suffixation by *-ed*, the meaning of the suffixed word can be predictably related to the category of its base. *Alarmed*, perceived as noun-based, means 'equipped with an alarm' (1.2.3), whereas in *John was alarmed* it is seen as verb-based. Accordingly, in Chapter 2 two adjective-forming *-ed* suffixes were recognized. *Un-* in combination with noun bases yields verbs with privative meaning (*unsaddle*), and with verb bases it yields reversative verbs (*unwind*). Again, two patterns were assumed, transpositional in 2.3.1 and non-transpositional in 3.2, though we might have recognized only one, of prefixed verbs with either noun or verb bases meaning roughly 'to restore (some entity) to an earlier state' (Plank 1981, 55–7).[3] The adjective and noun bases of adjectives in *-ish* regularly correspond with the meanings 'somewhat ADJECTIVE' and 'like NOUN' respectively. In this case too, non-transpositional and transpositional formations were treated separately (*trueish* 4.1, *pantherish* 2.5.2), though as we noted in connection with the noun formations of 4.3, the senses 'approximation' and 'resemblance' both figure in a group of patterns which can be treated under the heading of 'diminutive'.

Nouns suffixed by *-er* with verbal bases (*writer, computer*) were noted among the transpositional patterns of Chapter 2, and those with nominal and other kinds of base (*roofer, foreigner*) in Chapter 4. Nouns in *-er* too might be seen as the products of a single pattern. In a cognitive approach, Ryder (1999) suggests that since *-er* in a noun signals only that the noun is countable, the best kind of base is one which contributes most to ease of interpretation. Verbs, as generally referring to simple events, are the most suitable bases from this point of view. Nouns, referring to participants in events, admit of greater ambiguity and are thus less favoured as bases: *garager* might mean 'garage man', 'car', 'event associated with a garage', etc. (278). OED documents various uses of *beacher* in the senses 'person playing on a beach', 'worker on a beach', 'a trip ashore', and, in relation to surf-riding, the sense illustrated in 'It needs practice if you want to show off . . . shooting a "beacher" on your back' (1956).

In other cases where complex words of the same form and category reflect more than one kind of internal relationship, I have not recognized more than one pattern. Nouns in *-ee* (2.4.1) and adjectives in *-able* (2.5.1), in general verb-based, occasionally have noun bases referring to a participant in an event (*suicidee, roadable*). Verb-based *-ee* nouns reflect various relationships between verb base and referent (*blackmailee, borrowee, collapsee, amputee*). Verb-based *-able* and *-ed* adjectives can occasionally be subjective (*corrodable, collapsed*) as well as objective (*contactable, chewed*).

Derivational patterns fall fairly easily into groups within which they can be usefully compared – adjectives, primarily verb-based and suffixed by *-ing*, *-ive, -y, -able* and *-ed* for example, or prefixed verbs, or words formed with the prefix-like particles *out, over* and *under* (5.3), or primarily verb-based nouns denoting individuals and suffixed by *-ant, -ee* and *-er*. Some groups are semantically interrelated in complex ways – the diminutives of 4.3 for example and the suffixes of 4.4, which share a range of senses. Each suffix in 4.4 was seen to have its own 'profile', but the partial overlapping of meaning in words with different suffixes, and the relatedness of senses makes it reasonable to consider these suffixes together. Denominal verbs (2.3) comprise a number of patterns best treated together, with examples falling into one or more of a few semantic groups according to the relation between the meaning of the noun base and that of the verb. In this case too the several patterns, *de-*, *dis-*, *un-*, *-ize*, *-ify*, *-ate* and 'zero', overlap to varying extents but retain their separate identities. (See Plag 1999 for a comparison of 'zero' and the suffixes.)

Interconnections of different kinds can be seen to link the various patterns of adjectives suffixed by *-y* and nouns suffixed by *-y* and *-ie*. A suffix *-y* (2.5.2) forms noun-based adjectives generally meaning 'resembling NOUN' (*hostessy*) and 'having NOUN' (*pot-holey*). It might be identified with the *-y* of subjective deverbal adjectives (2.5.1), which have monosyllabic bases (*bouncy*, *jumpy*, *yappy*). Monosyllabic bases which however are not easily categorizable also characterize another group of *-y* adjectives such as *goofy*, *grungy*, *scatty*, *smoochy*, *snazzy*, *stroppy*. These were noted among the phonaestheme formations of Chapter 10. Adjectives suffixed by *-y* occur too among reduplicative compounds (*fuddy-duddy*), and shortened forms (*sarky*). Reduplicative and shortened-base nouns may be suffixed by *-y*, or *-ie* which in these words can be seen as an alternant form of *-y* (*hanky-panky*, *boogie-woogie* 10.4, *hanky*, *veggie* 11.5). All these formations of Chapters 10 and 11 have informal, affective uses comparable with those of 'situational' diminutive nouns in *-y* or *-ie* (*cabby*, *bookie* 4.3).

12.2 Productivity

The factors which may limit – or promote – the productivity of word-forming processes are many and diverse. The term 'productivity' in fact is best regarded as no more than a useful heading under which we can review an array of conditions and circumstances which may affect the ease or frequency with which words are formed on particular patterns.

Some affixes combine only with bases conforming to certain shapes. Verb-to-adjective *-y* and noun-forming *-ster* have monosyllabic bases; the monosyllabic bases of de-adjectival *-en* verbs never end in vowels or in certain consonants. Deverbal nouns in *-al* invariably have two-syllable bases with the stressed syllable next to the suffix (*dispersal*, *renewal*). *-ify* must always attach to a stressed syllable (*pulpify*, *humidify*), and *-eer* to an unstressed syllable (*leafleteer*, *sloganeer*). In many other cases, requirements are less strict. The bases of nouns in *-ism* and verbs in *-ize* usually but not invariably end in an unstressed syllable; those of almost all nouns in *-let* are monosyllabic. By contrast, no base is prevented by its formal characteristics from forming part of an adjective in *-able* or a noun in *-er*.

Bases as we have seen are more or less restricted as to class-membership. Uncompounded participial adjectives in *-ing* are necessarily based only on intransitive verbs. Nouns in *-al, -ment* and *-ation* are always deverbal, but many more bases are available to *-ation* since it is the favoured nominal ending for verbs in *-ize* and *-ify*. *-able* adjectives and *-ee* nouns are generally deverbal but noun bases are also possible. Nouns in *-let* always have noun bases, but nouns in *-er* and *-ist*, though chiefly deverbal and denominal respectively, can have bases of any class.

Bases can be more or less restricted as to meaning. Denominal *-ly*, for example, attaches mainly to nouns with human referents of a certain kind (*writerly*), *-esque* only to proper names. The bases of *-ful* adjectives are typically nouns of abstract meaning (*characterful*), and those of *-let* nouns are more often than not nouns with concrete inanimate referents (*booklet, streamlet*). Nouns in *-ant* have bases denoting either a human referent engaged in particular kinds of activity (*discussant, retreatant*) or a substance (*dispersant*). Verb-forming *un-, de-* and *dis-* attach to bases denoting actions of reversing or taking away.

It is obvious that a complex word will be more readily understood if its structure is clearly perceivable. The changes in the form of bases associated with certain suffixes (9.1) may thus have an effect on productivity. This is one reason why nouns in *-ity* are said to be less productive than those in *-ness*. Phonological transparency is relative: the bases of *domesticity* and *fatality*, with shift of main stress and change of vowel quality in their initial syllables, are potentially less recognizable than those of *similarity* or *suppressibility* (Cutler 1981). But given the choice between *-ity* and *-ness*, some speakers might well choose the form they felt surest of being able to pronounce (Romaine 1983, 189). It is certainly not hard to think of unlikely or unacceptable-looking forms in *-ity*, such as *genuinity, horribility, magicality, querulosity, saccharinity* (all of which, however, can be found in OED). Raffelsiefen (1992) relates the productivity of the suffix sequences *-ization* and *-ability* (11.2) to the fact that, unlike *-ation* and *-ity* alone, they are never associated with altered stress placement in their bases.

The semantic transparency of complex words is clearly important if a process is to be productive. Nouns suffixed by productive *-ness* can generally be depended on to mean just the quality indicated in the base.[4] In *-er* nouns, verb bases may be favoured over noun bases for reasons of interpretability, as Ryder suggests. *-ist*, by contrast, more informative than *-er* since it reliably signals a human referent, can attach much more readily to noun bases. The meanings of nouns in *-let* with diminutive referents or of denominal adjectives in *-ish* are generally clear out of context. The interpretability of items *in* context, however, may well be more relevant for productivity than the transparency of words considered in isolation. Nouns in *-ation* are usually associated with process or result readings only in context. Denominal verbs like *ghost* or *Hansardize* for example may be opaque in isolation but clear in use. 'State', 'realm' or 'collectivity' meanings cannot generally be ascribed to *-dom* words in isolation, but new words with this suffix are rarely obscure in use.

In earlier chapters we have noted some pairs or groups of patterns on which complex words with similar meanings are formed. The notion of 'rivalry' between comparable processes and the effect this might have on their productivity has been much discussed. *De-* and *un-* might be seen as competing for bases to form reversative verbs, though to the extent that these prefixes attach to different kinds of base, and form words likely to appear in different kinds of discourse, they are not in competition, and moreover there are often alternatives which can also be considered 'rivals': *exhume* instead of *unearth*, for example, *spread out* for *unfold*, *sever* for *disconnect*. *-ness* and *-ity* generally 'prefer' different kinds of base. Plag (1999, 228–30) shows that there is almost no overlap between the sets of bases which combine with *-ify* and *-ize*. With formations on 'rival' patterns, it is hardly ever the case that the resulting words are true competitors, substitutable for one another in any context. However, in 4.4. we saw that apparently genuine alternatives do sometimes occur – *outsiderdom* and *outsiderism* meaning 'belief', for example, or *citydom* and *cityship* in the 'territory' sense, or *tadpolehood* and *tadpoledom* (OED: 1863) in the sense of 'state'. As we saw especially in 4.4, the formation of a new complex word is only likely to be pre-empted by a synonym if the synonym is well-enough established to be readily accessible. Coinages like the examples just mentioned, being rare or once-only events, can often co-exist in a very limited kind of rivalry which does not provoke blocking.

It seems self-evident that a process will be productive if it is useful, providing means for speakers to make words for the kinds of entities, properties and situations they often need to mention. Since nouns in *-ee* name only sentient beings, this pattern may well be less productive than that of nouns in *-er*, which are not restricted in this way (Barker 1998, 701). If verb-forming reversative *un-* is not very productive it is because occasions for referring to reversible actions do not arise very often. If nouns in *-er* most often denote people or instruments, it is because these are most often talked about. Established noun compounds are likely to name entities in culturally useful ways (6.2). Any combination of two nouns is serviceable as a noun compound as long as it makes sense in use.

Changes in productivity can sometimes be linked – at least in part – to specific cultural factors, for example the increase in numbers since the late medieval period of nouns in *-age*, once chiefly limited to words for payments (see Chapter 4 note 10), and that of nouns in *-ist* since the early modern period to name 'experts' and 'professionals' in various areas of knowledge and art. Other patterns have had brief bursts of what looks like productivity in response to transient circumstances, e.g. twentieth-century nouns in *-nik*, or nouns and adjectives formed with elements of certain compounds. Examples of probably very transient productivity include nouns in *in* (5.4), adjectives in *happy* (7.4.1), the *speak* of *Newspeak* in items like *computer-speak*, *newspaper-speak*, *therapy-speak*, and the *ware* of *software* (after *hardware*) in *censorware, familyware, groupware, netware, shareware, webware*. Stems like *eco-* and *bio-*, *-cide* and *-naut* (9.3.3), and parts of blends such as *-cade*, *-holic*, *-topia* (11.4), have also appeared in series of words. These elements are all rather specific in meaning, and hence rather limited in the bases with which they are compatible and the occasions on which their use is appropriate. Some elements, such as nominal *monger* have remained minimally productive over long periods, cf. sixteenth century *fashion-monger* and *news-monger*, *punctilio-monger* (1761), *verbal-inspiration-monger* (1863) and modern items like *doom-monger, opinion-monger, panic-monger, trivia-monger*. Another example is adjectival *ridden*, with examples from the seventeeth century (*hag-ridden, priest-ridden*) to the twentieth, cf. '*asbestos-ridden* tower-blocks', '*faction-ridden* campaigns'. But none of these elements seems likely to develop any greater degree of productivity, as has happened in the past with a few compound constituents which have lost or are losing their semantic autonomy to become suffixes, such as *-dom, -hood, -less* and *-like*.[5]

Productivity has often been assumed to be a property of particular rules or patterns (cf. Aronoff 1976, ch. 3). But patterns may be more productive in some registers and types of discourse than in others. 'Situational' diminutive forms like *doggie* and *weirdo* are obviously confined to very informal registers. In Chapter 9 we noted some formatives, like *epi-* and *para-*, *-form* and *-ferous*, which were peculiar to, or frequently encountered only in, specialized scientific registers. Noun-forming *-ee* was once restricted to legal contexts. Its greater present productivity is a consequence of its extension to words in everyday use (Barker 1998, 699). Romaine (1985) links changes in the productivity of *-ness* and *-ity* with the rise of genres in which abstract nouns are likely to be prominent. In a detailed investigation, Cowie (1999) finds that sermons and fiction are favourable environments for names of qualities in *-ness*, whereas nouns in *-ity*, often more specific in meaning, are more likely to be encountered in scientific and medical texts. There is clearly a great deal to be discovered along these lines about many other patterns.

Complex words are formed in response to more than one kind of need. They may of course have the lexical function of labelling a concept that is felt, temporarily or permanently, to need a name. Typically, complex words encapsulate material otherwise expressible at greater length, in paraphrases, and they may thus also have a textual function – that of 'condensing' material within a discourse to constitute a kind of proform (Kastovsky 1982, 1986a, 1986b). In Chapters 6 and 8 we noted a number of noun and verb compounds which in their contexts could be seen to have this cohesive role. A further example of a noun compound which obviously has this function is *fax dumping* in the following. The 'new' information in the finite clause reappears as 'known' in the nominalized subject of the second sentence. In its third appearance, the now familiar information in *by fax* is defocused in the modifying element of the compound.

> Until recently I subscribed to the Luddite point of view that technology is a heinous blight upon our enforced urban consciousness – until I dumped my inconstant girlfriend by fax. . . . Dumping by fax is sweeping the nation. . . . Fax dumping is swift, effective, cuts out unnecessary emotional turmoil . . . (Guardian: 1993)

Compare also the adjective compound *gravity-defying* in 'The trail ascends . . . through spruce woods where trees nearly 30 m tall seem to defy gravity, growing on the steepest slopes with the thinnest soil. Also gravity-defying are the cows . . .' (Guardian: 1998), and the noun *drop-by* in: 'President Clinton will "drop by" the office of the vice-president today . . . Mr Clinton staged a similar "drop-by" last week' (Guardian: 1997). In the following, *outblowing*, its form dictated by its premodifying function, points back to the preceding verb + preposition collocations: 'Blowing towards and in upon the polar regions to make good the drain caused by the surface outblowing south-easterly winds' (OED: 1900). The new formations *relampshaded* and *directee* take up the notions already introduced by the familiar nouns *lampshade* and *director* in: 'The lampshade craze increasing in virulence, they had between them re-lampshaded the entire house' (OED: 1918; cf. 3.2); 'By paying the director more than the directee it creates a difference of class between them' (OED: 1928).

A third kind of condition favouring the formation of complex words is not clearly distinguishable from the two just mentioned. A new name for an entity, quality or situation may owe its – usually fleeting – existence to the exigencies of a particular circumstance and a particular linguistic context. We have seen many such occasional formations in the preceding chapters, cf. those in 'She's kangarooing up the road' (1.5), 'Have a listen to this' (2.4.1), 'I felt tired and out-gambited' (5.3.2). A much-cited example of a complex word formed for one occasion only is Downing's noun compound *apple-juice seat*, 'the seat in front of which a glass of apple-juice had been placed' (1977, 818).

To the extent that these three functions can be considered separately, the first, the making of new names which are likely subsequently to appear in new contexts, may well have less to do with productivity than the other two. Baayen and Renouf (1996) report that though 'productive word formation is not exceptional in written English' (73), their corpus studies showed the filling of lexical gaps to be a comparatively rare phenomenon (79). Ryder (1999), discussing the formation of nouns in -*er*, thinks that 'much more could be learned about the likelihood of various -*er* formation patterns in connection with different contexts if they were to be studied in naturally occurring language' (292). Reversative *un*- occurred in Baayen and Renouf's corpus in a number of occasional formations such as *unspread, unmuck, uncaress* (1996, 85), and OED's records suggest that this prefix is more productive than might appear from the scarcity of potential bases denoting actions readily thought of as reversible, cf. 'These mad attempts to untheologize (if I may coin a word) the language of theology' (OED: 1873), 'if you have once thoroughly bored somebody it is next to impossible to unbore him' (OED: 1922), 'It is not in him to unhate his hates' (OED: 1896), 'It may not be possible to un-invent the motor car' (OED: 1962). (See also Jespersen 1942, 26.4.)

Following Baayen and Renouf, it is useful to distinguish – very roughly – three degrees of productivity. The patterns represented by, for example, adjectival *beechen*, verbal *crispen*, adjectival *inviscid* and *goodly* can safely be said to be nearly or quite unproductive. At the other end of the scale, the formation of words on obviously productive patterns, like adjective-to-noun *-ness*, or adjective-to-adverb *-ly*, or the compounding of nouns with process nominalizations or with participial adjectives in *-ing* and *-ed*, often yields 'spontaneous, unintentional and ephemeral' coinages (Baayen and Renouf 1996, 78), and may thus be compared with the formation of phrases. Between these two extremes come a variety of patterns which we can say are productive in principle, but less often, or in some cases quite seldom, resorted to.

Barker (1998) judges *-ee* to be 'robustly semi-productive' (704), comparing the productivity of this suffix with that of *-er* in a large corpus. He shows that when the number of once-only items with each suffix is divided by the total number of tokens with each suffix (cf. 1.3), the results suggest, counterintuitively, that *-ee* is more productive than *-er*. However, another calculation, that of dividing the number of once-only examples of a pattern with the total number of once-only formations on any pattern in a corpus yields an indication of 'global productivity' (Baayen 1993; Baayen and Renouf 1996). This procedure allows a comparison of patterns with respect to their productivity. By this measure, *-er*, more often resorted to than *-ee*, is the more productive suffix. Barker notes (704) 'native speakers often report that an unfamiliar word in *-ee* seems weird or nonstandard in a way that a never-before-encountered word in *-er* does not'.

'Productive in principle but not often resorted to' (and thus in many cases not easily studied by quantitative methods) is a description which fits a good many, perhaps the majority, of the patterns described in previous chapters. Many of the formations on those patterns may as a consequence seem to some extent 'weird'. Yet such words are often the transient creatures of linguistic context or extra-linguistic circumstance, and in this they are comparable with many nouns in *-ness* and *-ity*, or adverbs in *-ly*, generally agreed to represent truly productive processes. Speakers or writers can readily form new nouns in *-dom*, *-hood*, *-ee* or *-ery*, new *out-* verbs meaning 'surpass in VERBing', or new denominal adverbs in *-wise* even though they might do so only on rare occasions.

A final factor with some relevance to productivity is that of word class. The classes constitute varying proportions of the vocabulary. Working with a corpus of eighteen million words (the CELEX database) Baayen and

Lieber (1991) found that verbs, simple and complex, made up only 19 per cent (4,964) of the total number of verbs, adjectives and nouns (25,591); there were 5,428 adjectives and 15,199 nouns. The classes also vary according to the proportion of complex to simple words in each class. The great majority of adverbs are derived words. Less than half the verbs in the corpus investigated by Baayen and Lieber were derived. Derived adjectives appear to be very much more numerous in English than simple adjectives, an impression supported by Baayen and Lieber's figures: 69.4 per cent of adjectives were found to be derived. Of the nouns, 56.6 per cent were derived.

In 11.3 we noted the predominance of verbs among backformed items in relation to the fact that verbs constitute a relatively small proportion of the vocabulary. This fact is also relevant when we look at complex words which serve a textual function. Kastovsky and Kryk-Kastovsky (1997), discussing the role of complex words in the cohesion of texts, find that nominalized forms, encoding known information, are most frequently the recapitulatory items in texts. Verbs, syntactically less independent, are usually the items referred back to. The greater syntactic integration of verbs in sentences may well have a general restraining effect on the productivity of verb-forming patterns (cf. Baayen and Renouf 1996, 85). In 8.6 we noted that the scarcity and typical conspicuousness in context of compound verbs can be related to the contrast between the role of verbs within verb phrases and that of verbal elements within compounds.

Complex verbs of other kinds are also likely to attract notice as innovations. In their paper on 'zero' denominal verbs, a pattern generally agreed to represent the most productive transpositional verb-forming process, Clark and Clark (1979, 801) ask 'Why invent denominal verbs?' Their answer is for 'economy of expression', with its advantages of precision, vividness and surprise. The following passage, part of a longer piece, is parodic, but it underlines the vulnerability of complex verbs, 'zero'-derived, affixed, compounded and backformed, to prescriptive attack:

Edgewaying another word

As some commentator on the Yugoslav crisis observed on the Today programme this week, it is always hard to crystal ball-gaze. Still, as Nye Bevan would no doubt have put it had he been speaking today, why bother to crystal ball-gaze when you can so easily book-read? The practice of which we complained in these columns a few months ago of pressing defenceless nouns, and occasionally adjectives, into service as verbs has pejorated since. You don't need to be able to soothsay to suspect it is going to nadir any day now.... for a news bulletin, even at 11 o'clock at night, to refer to Lech Walesa 'tea-ing' with the Queen, as one of our monitors insists occurred in late April, suggests it is time for BBC chiefs to revigilantise themselves. (Guardian: 1991)

The processes of word formation and their products can be described in terms of rules (or regularities) of various kinds relating to phonology, syntax and semantics, and in terms of specific analogies. Regularities of semantic relationship and semantic extension may also be involved. The relation between form and meaning in complex words is often not straightforward, and simply formulated rules rarely account for every possible case. In response to the demands of linguistic context and extralinguistic circumstance, established and familiar patterns can easily seem to be 'stretched' or extended, as for example in verbs like *Handsardize, suave, unspread, relampshade* or *spectate*, adjectives like *unfurtive, roadable, computerate* or *exploitative*, and nouns like *suicidee, differentness, islandhood, eco-tourist, strumble* or *pulsar*. Not surprisingly, it is sometimes hard to make a distinction in principle between what is regular and what is exceptional. In an observation which has often been quoted because it seems to point to an essential quality of complex words, Bolinger describes the word-coiner as 'looking for the best way to express [a new meaning] without going to too much trouble' (Bolinger and Sears 1981, 60) . The making of new complex words in appropriate contexts both depends on and guarantees the flexibility and indeterminacy typical of their patterns.

Notes

1. In fact Aronoff allows bases to be either noun or adjective.
2. Historically *-ly* is one suffix: Old English noun-to-adjective *-lic*, as in *cynelic* 'kingly', and adjective-to-adverb *-lice* (*-lic* + adverbial *-e*) as in *swetelice* 'sweetly', developed from a nominal element, represented in Old English by *lic* 'body'.
3. Plank's more precise formulation is: 'jemand/etwas auf geeignete Art und Weise aus einem Zustand in den Komplementärzustand (zuruck-)versetzen (wobei dieser Zweit-Zustand als unmarkiertes Glied einer konzeptuell privativen Opposition aufgefasst werden kann)' (1981, 56). 'To transfer or restore someone or something in the appropriate way from a state to a complementary state understood as the unmarked member of a conceptually privative opposition.'
4. Romaine (1985) observes: 'The fact that the semantics of *-ity* formations is less predictable and less regular than that associated with *-ness* formations is implicated in productivity since people will tend not to use words whose meaning is unclear to them' (456). However, in a historical study, Cowie (1999) finds that the vigour of deverbal nominalization in *-ation* and deadjectival nominalization in *-ity* does not appear to have been diminished by the numbers of lexicalized items with these suffixes.
5. It is usually assumed that meanings expressible in derived words must be rather general – 'instrumental', 'resultative', 'similarity', 'state', 'collectivity', etc. Beard (1995, 1998) proposes that derivational meanings are essentially

those of grammatical case systems. Malkiel (1978), on the other hand, notes some affixes in rather specific sets of words, e.g. Sardinian *-ile* in words for animal enclosures. In 9.4.2 we noted some noun-forming suffixes in groups of nouns such as 'enzymes' (*-ase*) or 'alcohols' (*-ol*). Notions of 'derivational meaning' will of course vary according to what is counted as an affix.

References

Abney, S. 1987 *The English Noun Phrase in its Sentential Aspect*. Dissertation, M.I.T.

Adamson, Sylvia 1990 'The What of the language?' in Christopher Ricks and Leonard Michaels eds *The State of the Language*. London: Faber and Faber, 503–514

Aitchison, Jean 1994 *Words in the Mind: an introduction to the mental lexicon* 2nd edition. Oxford: Blackwell

Andersen, Henning 1973 'Abductive and deductive change', *Language* 49: 4, 765–793

Anderson, Stephen R.1992 *A-Morphous Morphology*. Cambridge: Cambridge University Press

Anshen, Frank and Mark Aronoff 1981 'Morphological productivity and phonological transparency', *Canadian Journal of Linguistics* 26: 1, 63–72

Anshen, Frank and Mark Aronoff 1988 'Producing morphologically complex words', *Linguistics* 26, 641–56

Aronoff, Mark 1976 *Word Formation in Generative Grammar*. Cambridge MA: The MIT Press

Aronoff, Mark 1980 'The relevance of productivity in a synchronic description of word formation' in Jacek Fisiak ed *Historical Morphology*. The Hague: Mouton, 71–82

Asher, R.E. and J.M.Y. Simpson eds 1994 *The Encyclopedia of Language and Linguistics*. Oxford and New York: Pergamon Press

Baayen, R. Harald 1993 'On frequency, transparency and productivity' in Booij and van Marle eds, 181–208

Baayen, R. Harald and Rochelle Lieber 1991 'Productivity and English derivation: a corpus-based study', *Linguistics* 29, 801–43

Baayen, R. Harald and Antoinette Renouf 1996 'Chronicling the *Times*; productive lexical innovations in an English newspaper', *Language* 72: 1, 69–96

Barker, Chris 1998 'Episodic -*ee* in English: a thematic role constraint on new word formation', *Language* 74: 4, 695–727

Bauer, Laurie 1983 *English Word-formation*. Cambridge: Cambridge University Press

Bauer, Laurie 1998 'When is a sequence of two nouns a compound in English?', *English Language and Linguistics* 2: 1, 65–86

Beard, Robert 1991 'Decompositional composition: the semantics of scope ambiguities and "bracketing paradoxes"', *Natural Language and Linguistic Theory* 9, 195–229

Beard, Robert 1995 *Lexeme-Morpheme Base Morphology*. Albany NY: State University of New York Press

Beard, Robert 1998 'Derivation' in Andrew Spencer and Arnold M. Zwicky eds, 44–65

Becker, Thomas 1993 'Back-formation, cross-formation, and "bracketing paradoxes"' in Booij and van Marle eds, 1–25

Berg, Thomas 1998 'The (in)compatibility of morpheme orders and lexical categories and its historical implications', *English Language and Linguistics* 2: 2, 245–62

Biber, Douglas 1988 *Variation across Speech and Writing*. Cambridge: Cambridge University Press

Bloomfield, Leonard 1933 *Language*. New York: Holt

Bolinger, D.L. 1940 'Word affinities', *American Speech* 15, 62–73

Bolinger, D.L. 1944 'Among the new words', *American Speech* 19, 60–61

Bolinger, D.L. 1950 'Rime, assonance and morpheme analysis', *Word* 6, 117–36

Bolinger, D.L. 1961 'Ambiguities in pitch accent', *Word* 17, 309–17

Bolinger, D.L. 1967 'Adjectives in English: attribution and predication', *Lingua* 18, 1–34

Bolinger, D.L. 1985 'Defining the indefinable' in Robert Ilson ed *Dictionaries, Lexicography and Language Learning*. Oxford: Pergamon Press in association with the British Council, 69–73

Bolinger, D.L. and D.A. Sears 1981 *Aspects of Language* 3rd edition. New York: Harcourt Brace Jovanovich, Inc.

Booij, Geert and Jaap van Marle eds 1988– *Yearbook of Morphology*. Dordrecht: Kluwer

Borer, Hagit 1990 'V+*ing*: It walks like an adjective, it talks like an adjective', *Linguistic Inquiry* 21: 1, 95–103

Brinton, Laurel J. 1988 *The Development of English Aspectual Systems*. Cambridge: Cambridge University Press

Brömser, B. 1985 'On the derivation in English verbal compounds' in W. Kürschner and R. Vogt eds *Akten des 19 Linguistischen Kolloquiums Vechta* 1984 Bd I *Grammatik, Semantik, Textlinguistik*. Linguistische Arbeiten 156. Tübingen: Niemeyer, 99–113

Buck, R.A. 1997 'Words that are their opposites: noun to verb conversion in English', *Word* 48: 1, 1–14

Bybee, Joan 1988 'Morphology as lexical organization' in Michael Hammond and Michael Noonan eds *Theoretical Morphology: approaches in modern linguistics*. San Diego: Academic Press, 119–41

Bybee, Joan 1995 'Regular morphology and the lexicon', *Language and Cognitive Processes* 10: 5, 425–45

Carroll, John M. and Michael K. Tanenhaus 1975 'Prolegomena to a functional theory of word formation' in *Papers from the 11th Regional Meeting of the Chicago Linguistic Society: Papers from the Parasession on Functions*, 47–62

Carstairs-McCarthy, Andrew 1992 *Current Morphology*. London and New York: Routledge

Cassidy, Frederic G. 1983 'The intensive prefix KER-', *American Speech* 58: 4, 291–302

Chomsky, Noam 1970 'Remarks on nominalization' in R.A. Jacobs and P.S. Rosenbaum eds *Readings in English Transformational Grammar*. Waltham MA: Ginn and Co, 184–221

Clark, E.V. 1993 *The Lexicon in Acquisition*. Cambridge: Cambridge University Press

Clark, E.V. and H.H. Clark 1979 'When nouns surface as verbs', *Language* 55: 4, 767–811

Cowie, Claire 1999 *Diachronic Word-Formation: a corpus-based study of derived nominalizations in the history of English*. PhD dissertation, University of Cambridge

Cruse, D. Alan 2000 *Meaning in Language: an introduction to semantics and pragmatics*. Oxford: Oxford University Press

Crystal, David 1997 *Dictionary of Linguistics and Phonetics* 4th edition. Oxford: Blackwell

Cutler, Anne 1981 'Degrees of transparency in word formation', *Canadian Journal of Linguistics* 26: 1, 73–7

Dalton-Puffer, Christiane 1999 'Screenfuls of classifier-type things: noun classes and derivation in English', *Vienna English Working Papers* 8: 1, June, 7–21

de la Cruz, Juan M. 1975 'Old English pure prefixes: structure and function', *Linguistics* 145, 47–81

Dixon, R.M.W. 1982 *Where Have All the Adjectives Gone? And Other Essays in Semantics and Syntax*. Berlin: Mouton

Dixon, R.M.W. 1991 *A New Approach to English Grammar on Semantic Principles*. Oxford: The Clarendon Press

Downing, Pamela 1977 'On the creation and use of English compound nouns', *Language* 53: 4, 810–42

Dressler, W.U. and L. Merlini-Barbaresi 1994 *Morphopragmatics: diminutives and intensifiers in Italian, German, and other languages*. Trends in Linguistics Studies and Monographs 76. Berlin and New York: Mouton de Gruyter.

Farrell, Patrick 1998 'Comments on the paper by Lieber' in Steven G. Lapointe, Diane K. Brentari and Patrick M. Farrell eds, *Morphology and its Relation to Phonology and Syntax*. Stanford: CSLI Publications, 130–81

Firth, J.R. 1930 *Speech*. Oxford: Oxford University Press 1964

Fleischman, S. 1977 *Cultural and Linguistic Factors in Word Formation: an integrated approach to the development of the suffix -age* University of California Publications in Linguistics 86. Berkeley and Los Angeles: University of California Press

Fowler, H.W. 1925 'Broadcast(ed): a compromise', *Society for Pure English Tracts*, 32–4

Fowler, H.W. 1965 *A Dictionary of Modern English Usage* 2nd edition, revised by Sir Ernest Gowers. Oxford: Oxford University Press

Funk, Wolf-Peter 1971 'Adjectives with negative affixes in modern English and the problem of synonymy', *Zeitschrift für Anglistik und Amerikanistik* 19, 364–386

Gerdts, Donna B. 1998 'Incorporation' in Andrew Spencer and Arnold M. Zwicky eds, 84–100

Giegerich, Heinz J. 1999 *Lexical Strata in English: morphological causes, phonological effects*. Cambridge Studies in Linguistics 89. Cambridge: Cambridge University Press

Givón, Talmy 1967 'Some noun-to-noun derivational affixes'. MS System Development Corporation, SP 2893

Goldberg, Adele 1995 *A Construction Grammar Approach to Argument Structure*. Chicago: University of Chicago Press

Grimshaw, Joan 1990 *Argument Structure*. Cambridge MA: The MIT Press

Hall, R.A. Jr 1956 'How we noun-incorporate in English', *American Speech* 31, 83–8.

Halle, Morris 1973 'Prolegomena to a theory of word-formation', *Linguistic Inquiry* 4: 1, 3–16

Harder, Kelsie B. 1968 'Coinages of the type of "sit-in"', *American Speech* 43, 58–64.

Harris, Catherine L.1993 'Using old words in new ways: the effect of argument structure, form class and affixation', in *Papers from the 29th Regional Meeting of the Chicago Linguistic Society: Papers from the Parasession on the Correspondence of Conceptual, Semantic and Grammatical Representations*, 139–53

Haspelmath, Martin 1994 'The growth of affixes in morphological reanalysis' in Booij and van Marle eds, 1–29

Hatcher, Anna G. 1951 *Modern English Word-Formation and Neo-Latin: a study of the origins of English (French, Italian, German) copulative compounds*. Baltimore: The Johns Hopkins Press

Hinton, Leanne, Johanna Nichols and John J. Ohala eds 1994 *Sound Symbolism*. Cambridge: Cambridge University Press

Houghton, Donald E. 1968 'The suffix *-wise*', *American Speech* 43: 3, 209–15

Huddleston, R.D. 1984 *Introduction to the Grammar of English*. Cambridge: Cambridge University Press

Hudson, R.A. 1987 'Zwicky on heads', *Journal of Linguistics* 23, 109–132

Jespersen, Otto 1905 *Growth and Structure of the English Language* 9th edition 1954. Oxford: Basil Blackwell

Jespersen, Otto 1914 *A Modern English Grammar on Historical Principles* Part II: *Syntax* (1st volume). Copenhagen: Ejnar Munksgaard.

Jespersen, Otto 1917 *Negation in English and other Languages*. Copenhagen: Kgl. Danske Videnskabernes Selskab: Historisk-Filologiske Meddelelser Vol 1, No 5

Jespersen, Otto 1922 *Language: its Nature, Development and Origin*. London: George Allen and Unwin

Jespersen, Otto 1927 'The ending "-ster"', *Modern Language Review* 22: 2, 129–36

Jespersen, Otto 1939 'The history of a suffix', *Acta Linguistica* 1. In *Selected Writings of Otto Jespersen*. London: George Allen and Unwin 1962, 361–9

Jespersen, Otto 1942 *A Modern English Grammar on Historical Principles* Part VI: *Morphology*. Copenhagen: Ejnar Munksgaard

Jurafsky, Daniel 1993 'Universals in the semantics of the diminutive', *Proceedings of the 19th Annual Meeting of the Berkeley Linguistic Society: Parasession on Semantic Typology and Semantic Universals*, 423–36

Jurafsky, Daniel 1996 'Universal tendencies in the semantics of the diminutive', *Language* 72: 3, 533–78

Karius, Ilse 1985 *Die Ableitung der denominalen Verben mit Nullsuffigierung im Englischen*. Linguistische Arbeiten 159. Tübingen: Max Niemeyer Verlag

Käsmann, Hans 1992 'Das englische Phonästhem *sl-*', *Anglia* 110: 3/4, 307–46

Kastovsky, Dieter 1982 'Word-formation: a functional view', *Folia Linguistica* 16, 181–98

Kastovsky, Dieter 1986a 'Diachronic word-formation in a functional perspective' in Dieter Kastovsky and Aleksander Szwedek eds *Linguistics across Historical and Geographical Boundaries* Volume I. Berlin, New York and Amsterdam: Mouton de Gruyter, 409–21

Kastovsky, Dieter 1986b 'The problem of productivity in word formation', *Linguistics* 24, 585–600

Kastovsky, Dieter 1992 'Semantics and vocabulary' in Richard M. Hogg ed *The Cambridge History of the English Language* Volume I *The Beginnings to 1066*. Cambridge: Cambridge University Press, 290–408

Kastovsky, Dieter and Barbara Kryk-Kastovsky 1997 'Morpholexical and pragmatic factors in text cohesion' in Heinrich Ramisch and Kenneth Wynne eds *Language in Time and Space: studies in honour of Wolfgang Viereck. Zeitschrift für Dialectologie und Linguistik* Neue Folge 97. Stuttgart: F. Steiner, 462–75

Katamba, Francis 1993 *Morphology*. London: Macmillan Press

Kay, Paul and Karl Zimmer 1990 'On the semantics of compounds and genitives in English' in S.L. Tsohatzidis ed *Meanings and Prototypes: studies in linguistic categorization*. London and New York: Routledge, 239–46

Kim, John J., Steven Pinker, Alan Prince and Sandeep Prasada 1991 'Why no mere mortal has ever flown out to center field', *Cognitive Science* 15, 173–218

Kiparsky, Paul 1997 'Remarks on denominal verbs' in A. Alsina, J. Bresnan and P. Sells eds *Complex Predicates*. Stanford CA: CSLI Publications, 473–99

Kreidler, C.W. 1979 'Creating new words by shortening', *Journal of English Linguistics* 13, 24–36

Kubozono, Haruo 1990 'Phonological constraints on blending in English as a case for phonology-morphology interface' in Booij and van Marle eds, 1–20

Langacker, R.W. 1987 *Foundations of Cognitive Grammar* Volume I *Theoretical Prerequisites*. Stanford: Stanford University Press

Lehrer, Adrienne, 1996a 'Identifying and interpreting blends: an experimental approach', *Cognitive Linguistics* 7: 4, 359–90

Lehrer, Adrienne 1996b 'Why neologisms are important to study', *Lexicology* 2: 1, 63–73

Levi, Judith N. 1978 *The Syntax and Semantics of Complex Nominals*. New York: Academic Press

Levin, Beth and Malka Rappaport 1986 'The formation of adjectival passives', *Linguistic Inquiry* 17: 4, 623–61

Levin, Beth and Malka Rappaport-Hovav 1995 *Unaccusativity*. Cambridge MA: The MIT Press

Lieber, Rochelle 1998 'The suffix *-ize* in English: implications for morphology' in Steven G. Lapointe, Diane K. Brentari and Patrick M. Farrell eds *Morphology and its relation to Phonology and Syntax*. Stanford: CSLI Publications, 12–33

Liberman, Mark and Richard Sproat 1992 'The stress and structure of modified noun phrases in English' in Ivan A. Sag and Anna Szabolcs eds *Lexical Matters*. Stanford: CSLI Publications, 130–81

Ljung, Magnus 1970 *English Denominal Adjectives*. Gothenburg Studies in English 21

Lubbers, K. 1965 'The development of "-ster" in modern British and American English', *English Studies* 46, 449–70

Mackenzie, Ian B.G. and Igor A. Mel'čuk 1986 'English constructions of the type *French-built [widgets]*', *American Speech* 61: 2, 99–120

Malkiel, Yakov 1966 'Genetic analysis of word formation' in Thomas A. Sebeok ed *Current Trends in Linguistics* Volume III *Theoretical Foundations*. The Hague: Mouton, 305–64

Malkiel, Yakov 1968 'Secondary uses of letters in language', *Essays on Linguistic Themes*. Oxford: Basil Blackwell, 359–73.

Malkiel, Yakov 1977 'Why ap-*ish* but wormy?' in Paul J. Hopper ed *Studies in Descriptive and Historical Linguistics*. Festschrift for W.P. Lehmann. Amsterdam: John Benjamins, 341–64

Malkiel, Yakov 1978 'Derivational categories' in Joseph Greenberg ed *Universals of Human Language* Volume 3 *Word Structure*. Stanford: Stanford University Press, 125–49

Marchand, Hans 1964 'A set of criteria for the establishing of derivational relationship between words unmarked by derivational morphemes', *Indogermanische Forschungen* 69, 10–19

Marchand, Hans 1969 *The Categories and Types of Present-day English Word-formation* 2nd edition. München: Oscar Beck

Marcus, Gary F., Ursula Brinkmann, Harald Clahsen, Richard Wiese and Steven Pinker 1995 'German inflection: the exception that proves the rule', *Cognitive Psychology* 29, 189–256

Meijs W.J. 1975 *Compound Adjectives in English and the Ideal Speaker-Listener: a study of compounding in a transformational-generative framework*. Amsterdam: North-Holland

Miller, George A. and Christiane Fellbaum 1992 'Semantic networks of English' in Beth Levin and Steven Pinker eds *Lexical and Conceptual Semantics*. Oxford: Basil Blackwell, 197–229

Mithun, Marianne 1984 'The evolution of noun incorporation', *Language* 60: 4, 847–94

Mithun, Marianne 1994 'Word-formation: incorporation' in Asher and Simpson eds, 5024–6

Murray, K.M. Elisabeth 1979 *Caught in the Web of Words: James A.H. Murray and the Oxford English Dictionary*. New Haven and London: Yale University Press

Mühlhäusler, Peter 1983 'Stinkiepoos, cuddles and related matters', *Australian Journal of Linguistics* 3, 75–91

Oswalt, Robert L. 1994 'Inanimate imitatives in English' in Hinton *et al*. eds, 293–306

Oshita, H. 1994 'Compounds: a view from suffixation and A-structure alteration' in Booij and van Marle eds, 179–205

Pennanen, Esko V. 1966 *Contributions to the Study of Back-formation in English*. Acta Academiae Socialis Series A Volume 4. Tampere: Publications of the School of Social Studies

Pinker, Steven 1999 *Words and Rules*. London: Weidenfeld and Nicolson

Plag, Ingo 1999 *Morphological Productivity: structural constraints in English derivation*. Berlin and New York: Mouton de Gruyter

Plag, Ingo, Christiane Dalton-Puffer and Harald Baayen 1999 'Morphological productivity across speech and writing', *English Language and Linguistics* 3: 2, 209–28

Plank, Frans 1981 *Morphologische (Ir-)Regularitäten*. Tübingen: Gunter Narr

Plank, Frans 1994 'Inflection and derivation' in Asher and Simpson eds, 1671–8

Praninskas, J. 1968 *Trade Name Creation: processes and patterns*. The Hague: Mouton

Pulgram, Ernst 1968 'A socio-linguistic view of innovation: *-ly* and *-wise*', *Word* 24, 380–91

Raffelsiefen, Renate 1992 'A nonconfigurational approach to morphology' in Mark Aronoff ed *Morphology Now*. Albany NY: State University of New York Press, 133–62

Raffelsiefen, Renate 1996 'Gaps in word formation' in Ursula Kleinhenz ed *Interfaces in Phonology*. Studia Grammatice 41. Berlin: Akademie Verlag, 194–209

Raffelsiefen, Renate 1998 'Phonological constraints on English word formation' in Booij and van Marle eds, 225–87

Rainer, Franz 1988 'Towards a theory of blocking: the case of Italian and German quality nouns' in Booij and van Marle eds, 155–85

Rappaport-Hovav, Malka and Beth Levin 1988 '-*er* nominals: implications for the theory of argument structure' in E. Wehrli and T. Stowell eds *Syntax and the Lexicon*. Syntax and Semantics 26. New York: Academic Press *c.* 1992, 127–53

Reay, I.E. 1994 'Sound symbolism' in Asher and Simpson eds, 4064–70

Rhodes, Richard A. 1994 'Aural images' in Hinton *et al.* eds, 276–92

Roeper, Tom and Muffy E.A. Siegel 1978 'A lexical transformation for verbal compounds', *Linguistic Inquiry* 9: 2, 199–260

Romaine, Suzanne 1983 'On the productivity of word formation rules and limits of variability in the lexicon', *Australian Journal of Linguistics* 3, 177–200

Romaine, Suzanne 1985 'Variability in word formation patterns and productivity in the history of English' in Jacek Fisiak ed *Papers from the Sixth International Conference on the History of Linguistics*. Amsterdam: John Benjamins, 451–65

Rosen, Sara Thomas 1989 'Two types of noun incorporation: a lexical analysis', *Language* 65: 2, 294–317

Russell, I. Willis 1947 'Among the new words', *American Speech* 22, 226–31

Ryder, M.E. 1994 *Ordered Chaos: the interpretation of English noun-noun compounds*. Berkeley and Los Angeles: University of California Press

Ryder, M.E. 1999 'Bankers and blue-chippers: an account of -*er* formation in present day English', *English Language and Linguistics* 3: 2, 269–97

Sadler, Louisa and Douglas J. Arnold 1994 'Prenominal adjectives and the phrasal/lexical distinction', *Journal of Linguistics* 30, 187–226

Samuels, M.L. 1972 *Linguistic Evolution with special reference to English*. Cambridge Studies in Linguistics 5. Cambridge: Cambridge University Press

Scalise, Sergio 1986 *Generative Morphology* 2nd edition. Dordrecht: Foris Publications

Shimamura, R. 1983 'Backformation of English compound verbs', *Papers from the 19th Regional Meeting of the Chicago Linguistic Society: Papers from the Parasession on the Interplay of Phonology, Morphology and Syntax*, 271–82

Sifianou, Maria 1992 'The use of diminutives in expressing politeness: Modern Greek versus English', *Journal of Pragmatics* 17, 155–73

Spencer, Andrew 1991 *Morphological Theory*. Oxford: Basil Blackwell

Spencer, Andrew and Arnold M. Zwicky eds 1998 *The Handbook of Morphology*. Oxford and Malden MA: Blackwell Publishers

Sprengel, Konrad 1977 *A Study in Word-Formation: the English verbal prefixes fore- and pre- and their German counterparts*. Tübingen: Gunter Narr

Sweet, Henry 1891 *A New English Grammar, Logical and Historical* Part I. Oxford: The Clarendon Press

Taylor, John R. 1996 *Possessives in English: an exploration in cognitive grammar*. Oxford: The Clarendon Press

Traugott, E.C. 1989 'On the rise of epistemic meanings in English: a case-study in the regularity of semantic change', *Language* 65: 1, 31–55

von Lindheim, Bogislav 1958 'Die weiblichen Genussuffixe im Altenglischen', *Anglia* 76: 4, 479–504

Warren, Beatrice 1978 *Semantic Patterns of Noun–Noun Compounds*. Gothenburg Studies in English 41

Wescott, Roger W. 1971a 'Linguistic iconism', *Language* 47: 2, 416–28

Wescott, Roger W. 1971b 'Labiovelarity and derogation in English: a study in phonosemic correlation', *American Speech* 46: 1–2, 123–37

Wescott, Roger W. 1977 'Ideophones in Bini and English', *Forum Linguisticum* 2: 1, 1–13

Wierzbicka, Anna 1982 'Why can you *have a drink* when you can't **have an eat?*' *Language* 58: 4, 753–99

Wierzbicka, Anna 1984 'Diminutives and depreciatives: semantic representation for derivational categories', *Quaderni di Semantica* 5: 1, 123–30

Wierzbicka, Anna 1988 'Oats and wheat: mass nouns, iconicity, and human categorization' in *The Semantics of Grammar*. Amsterdam: John Benjamins, 499–561

Williams, Edwin O. 1981 'On the notions "lexically related" and "head of a word"', *Linguistic Inquiry* 12: 2, 245–74

Zimmer, Karl E. 1964 *Affixal Negation in English and other Languages: an investigation of restricted productivity*. Supplement to *Word* 20: 2

Dictionaries

| Cobuild | *Collins Cobuild English Language Dictionary*. London: HarperCollins 1987 |
| COD | *Concise Oxford Dictionary* 10th edition. Oxford: Oxford University Press 1999 |

Collins	*Collins Dictionary of the English Language*. London and Glasgow: Collins 1979
EDD	*The English Dialect Dictionary* ed Joseph Wright. London: Henry Frowde 1898
LDOCE	*Longman Dictionary of Contemporary English*. London: Longman 1978
MED	*Middle English Dictionary* ed H. Kurath *et al*. Ann Arbor: University of Michigan Press 1952–
OED	*The Oxford English Dictionary*: being a corrected re-issue with an introduction, supplement, and bibliography, of *A New English Dictionary on historical principles*, ed James A.H. Murray. Oxford: Clarendon Press 1933
	The Oxford English Dictionary Second Edition on Compact Disc. Oxford: Oxford University Press 1994
OEDS	*A Supplement to the Oxford English Dictionary* I–IV 1987
Webster 1961	*Webster's Third New International Dictionary*. London and Springfield MA

General index

Plank, F., 5, 40n4, 113, 132n4, 145,
153n3
polysemy of derived words, 13–14,
25–6, 59, 66–9, 70n14
of particles, 71, 74
of prefixes, 41–2, 116
Praninskas, J., 143n11
prefix, 2, 4, 41–3, 71
prefixation, 2, 4, 11, 15, 16, 19, 23–4,
26, 38, **41–51**, 110, **115–16**,
144, 145, 146, 147, 148, 149,
150–1
productivity, **7–8**, 9, 14–15, 17,
146–53
proper name, 26, 58, 80, 95, 142, 143,
147
Pulgram, E., 39

Raffelsiefen, R., 21, 22, 112–13, 114,
143n5, 147
Rainer, F., 67
Rappaport-Hovav, M. and B. Levin,
40n7, 79, 88n2
reanalysis, 16, 17, 56, 81, 101, 105,
133–43
Reay, I.E., 124, 125, 126, 127, 131, 132
reduplication, **127–9**, 130, 142, 146
Rhodes, R.A., 121, 129, 132n1
right hand head rule, **3**, 109
rime, **123–7**, 129, 131, 134
'rivalry' of affixes, 32, 40n8, 148
Roeper, T. and M.E.A. Siegel, 90, 93,
99n3, 105
Romaine, S., 40n8, 147, 149, 153n4
root, 17n2, 120n2
Rosen, S.T., 109
rule, 8–10, 111, 112, 144, 153
Russell, I.W., 96, 97
Ryder, M.E., 40n7, 69n2, 84, 85, 89n8,
145, 147, 150

Sadler, D.J. and L. Arnold, 81
Samuels, M.L., 123, 124, 125, 130,
131
Scalise, S., 18n7, 69n7, 105, 114
secretion, 134, 139, 143n2
shortened form, 16, 17, 58, 134, **141–3**,
146

Sifianou, M., 69n7
sound symbolism, 124
Spencer, A., 17, 82, 88n1, 94, 102,
120n1, 143n6
Sprengel, K., 45
stem, 2, 10, 12, 13, 16, 17n2, 29, 41,
42, 46, 57, **110–20**, 149
See also compound, stem; adjective,
stem-based; noun, stem-based;
verb, stem-based
prefixed, 41, 46, 110, **115–16**
suffixed, 57, 110, 114, 115, **116–17**
stratum, 110–13, 120n1, n2
suffix, 2, 4, 17n1
suffixation, 2, 9, 11, 12, 13, 15, 16,
18n7, **19–40**, **52–70**, 110, 115,
116–17, 139, 144–54
Sweet, H., 84
synonymy of derived words, 14, 47, 59,
67–8, 148
of base + particle and particle + base
verbs, 73

Taylor, J.R., 80
transposition, 15, 16, 18n6, **19–40**, 41,
43, 44, 52, 74, 100, 101, 102,
103, 138, 142, 144, 145, 146,
147, 148, 149, 150, 151, 152
Traugott, E.C., 40n12
truncation, 113, 114

unitary base hypothesis, 144

verb, compound
de-adjectival, 10, 11, 19, **26–7**, 138,
144, 146
denominal, 4, 19, **22–6**, 43, 102,
120n1, 145–6
deverbal, 4, 9, **43–5**, 145
'emotional event', 6–7, 33, 34, 45,
92, 94
particle + base, 4, 9, 11, 71, **72–3**,
74–5, 77n1, 102, 103, 109
phrasal, 3, 4, 11, 35, 71, 72, 73, 76,
109
stem-based, 116
see also compound, verb
von Lindheim, B., 69n5

Index of word-elements